# Angel
# Financing

## Other books in the *Wiley Investment* series

# Angel Financing

## How to Find and Invest in Private Equity

Gerald A. Benjamin
and
Joel Margulis

JOHN WILEY & SONS

New York • Chichester • Weinheim • Brisbane • Singapore • Toronto

*For my Father*

G.A.B.

*To Dinah*
*"Created of every creature's best,"*
*With Love and Affection*

J.M.

This publication is designed to provide accurate and authoritative information in regard to the subject matter covered. It is sold with the understanding that the publisher is not engaged in rendering professional services. If professional advice or other expert assistance is required, the services of a competent professional person should be sought.

*Library of Congress Cataloging-in-Publication Data:*

Benjamin, Gerald A.
   Angel financing : how to find and invest in private equity / Gerald
A. Benjamin and Joel Margulis.
     p.  cm.—(The Wiley investment series)
   Includes bibliographical references and index.
   ISBN 0-471-35085-0 (cloth : alk. paper)
   1. Angels (Investors)  2. Venture capital.  I. Margulis, Joel,
1937– .  II. Title.  III. Series.
  HG4751.B46  2000
  658.15'224—dc21                         99-33743

Printed in the United States of America

10  9  8  7  6  5  4  3  2  1

# Contents

*Preface      ix*
*Acknowledgments      xix*
*Introduction      xxi*


PART 1    THE CHALLENGE AND THE SOLUTION                                 1

*Chapter 1    The Challenge*                                             3
   Introduction                                                         3
   The Challenge                                                        3
   The Direct, Private Investor                                         5
   Structure of the Private Investor Market                            7
   Investor Activity in Early-Stage Deals                             10
   Angels, a Golden Capital Source                                    10
   Investors Worth Accessing                                         11

*Chapter 2    The Private Placement Investment*                        13
   The Private Placement Investment                                   13
   Selecting the Right Capital Source                                 15
   Is Your Deal Financeable?                                          15
   Are *You* Financeable?                                             21
   Is Your Risk Financeable?                                          24
   The Benefits and Disadvantages of Equity                          25
   Making Your Search for Investors More Efficient                   28
   The Problems with Conventional Wisdom                             29

*Chapter 3    A Strategy That Works*                                   31
   An "Inefficient" Market Defined                                    31
   A Strategy That Works                                              32
   Dreamers and Dream-Makers                                         55

PART 2    THE ANGEL INVESTOR                                          57

*Chapter 4    Alternative Sources of Capital*                         59
   The Impact of Political and Economic Trends on the Accessibility
      of Capital                                                      61
   Alternative Sources of Capital and How They Affect Early-Stage
      Investment                                                      69
   Business Angels as the Best Sources of Capital, Especially
      for Early-Stage Investment                                      69
   The Appropriateness of Your Venture for a Direct, Private Investment  69
   Professional Venture Capital as a Funding Resource for Early-Stage
      Companies                                                       75
   Comparison of Angel Investors with Professional Venture Capitalists  77
   Professional Venture Capital: Help or Hindrance to Your
      Funding Success?                                                79

*Chapter 5    What Do Private Investors Look for in a Deal?*          81
   The High-Net-Worth Investor Market                                 81
   The Informal, High-Risk, Investor Profile                         83
   Advantages of Direct Venture Investing                            85
   The Private Investor's Criteria                                    86
   Common Reasons Why Angels Reject an Investment                    90
   Variations in Preferred Level of Involvement after Investment     91
   How Angel Investors Can Help—Beyond Capital                       92
   Private Investor Motivation                                        93
   The Allocation Decision                                            96
   Principles of Direct Venture Investing                            98

*Chapter 6    Types of Private Investors*                            101
   Introduction                                                      101
   The Value-Added Investor                                          103
   The Deep-Pocket Investor                                          109
   The Consortium of Individual Investors                            120
   The Partner Investor                                              123
   The Family of Investors                                           125
   The Barter Investor                                               126
   The Socially Responsible Private Investor                         129
   The Unaccredited Private Investor                                 131

*Chapter 7    The Newest Breed of Angel: The Manager-Investor*       133
   The Manager-Investor                                              133

PART 3    RESOURCES: FINDING ANGEL INVESTORS                        139

*Chapter 8    Alternative Funding Resources in Accessing Angel Capital*  141
   History of the Development of Alternative Funding Resources        141
   Overview of Alternative Funding Resources                         144

Performance of the Top 20 Formal Investor Networks | 152
Directory of Alternative Funding Sources | 153

*Chapter 9    Building Your Own Database of Angel Investors* | 163
Introduction | 163
Hurdles | 164
Data Entry | 167
Backup | 168
Cost | 168

*Chapter 10    The Role of the Placement Agent in Raising Capital:*
*A Marketing Partner for Your Deal* | 170
Introduction | 170
The Placement Agent: A Marketing Partner | 170

PART 4    THE INVESTOR PERSPECTIVE | 175

*Chapter 11    The Venture Process* | 177
Introduction | 177
Driving Forces Creating Direct Investment Opportunities | 177
History of Early-Stage Investing | 178
Overview of the Omnibus Budget Reconciliation Act of 1993
    and Its Implications for Private Investing in High-Risk Deals | 179
Disadvantages of High-Risk Investing | 179
Risk Characteristics | 180
Hedging Strategies—How Angels Manage Risk in Direct Investing | 182
The Syndication Bias | 183
How Investors Generate Deal Flow | 184
Financial and Nonfinancial Return on Investment: Angels'
    Expectations | 185
Elements in Structuring the Private Placement | 186
Approaches Angels Use to Monitor Investments | 187
Harvesting Returns: Realistic Exit Strategies | 188

*Chapter 12    The Valuation Process in Private Transactions* | 189
Introduction | 189
Sweat Equity | 190
The "Living Dead" | 190
Risk | 192
Negotiating Valuation | 194
Valuation and Stage of Development | 195
Truisms in the Valuation Process | 197
Caveats—For Entrepreneur and Investor Alike | 199

*Chapter 13    Due Diligence* | 202
Introduction | 202
Due Diligence Questionnaire | 205

*Chapter 14    On-Line Options: Entrepreneurs, Investors, and Web Sites*    *219*
   On-Line Links    220
   Promises and Pitfalls    225

*Chapter 15    Answers to Common Business Angel Investor Questions*    *229*

*Conclusion*    *244*

*Appendix A    Legal Primer on Securities Law Issues for Nonlawyers*    *246*
   1. Overview    249
   2. Private Offerings—The First Step    255
   3. Public Offerings    257
   4. Disclosure Documents    260
   5. Integration Rules: Timing    260
   6. Restricted Securities and Trading    261
   7. The Internet    263
   8. Federal/State    264
   9. The '40 Act    265
   10. The Usual    266
   11. Sales—"Agents" (California)    266

*Appendix B    Preparing an Investor-Oriented Business Plan*    *267*
   Introduction to the Business Plan    267
   What Does Your Business Plan Need to Contain?    267
   Creating a Business Plan    268
      I. Executive Summary    268
      II. Mission or Charter    268
      III. Description of the Business    269
      IV. Ownership Structure and Equity    270
      V. Description of Product/Service    271
      VI. The Market    272
      VII. Description of Industry and Trends    275
      VIII. Marketing Strategy    276
      IX. Marketing Plan    278
      X. Sales Plan    280
      XI. Operations, Research and Development Strategies, and Plans    282
      XII. Management, Organization, Personnel, and Information Systems    284
      XIII. Objectives and Milestones    287
      XIV. Financial Projections    289
      XV. Supporting Documents    292

*Suggested Reading List*    *300*
*Index*    *303*

# Preface

*If we could first know* where *we are, and whither we are tending,*
*we could then better judge what to do, and* how *to do it.*

Abraham Lincoln

*Angel Financing: How to Raise and Invest in Private Equity* is about the manner in which successful entrepreneurs, private investors, and intermediaries must go about the business of doing business, the efficient manner of knowing where they are, where they are going, what they are doing, and how they are doing it.

This book describes a model of the funding process uniquely suited to the private placement transaction. A model of this process is the only way to consciously manage the increasingly demanding, exhausting process of efficiently and effectively raising money.

*Angel Financing* is about the careful planning entrepreneurs and intermediaries must do in order to ensure the success of the capitalization and financial transaction process. This book offers the expertise of the people who have created the largest network database of private investors in the country and by the firm that is recognized as the leading expert on accessing and cultivating relationships with angel investors.

In addition, the book is about the secretive, highly specialized segment of the investor market that is a major source of funding for entrepreneurial ventures. It provides intelligence on a segment of high-net-worth investors specially interested in financing earlier-stage, developmental-stage, and expansion-stage ventures.

*Angel Financing* covers a lot of ground. Part 1, "The Challenge and the Solution," focuses on how entrepreneurs are creatively addressing the challenge of practicing capitalism without the capital. We suggest how they should structure their search for capital as they confront an "inefficient" market.

Part 2, "The Angel Investor," explores angel investors—who they are and where they can be found. In addition, we present alternative sources of capital. A comparison is made between angel investors and the institutional investor community, correcting the misconception that the institutional community is the primary source of funding for early-stage deals. Then, from scores of presentations and interviews, we turn to what private investors look for in a deal—*their* criteria and *their* expectations. We explain who the private investors are and how they relate to others in the capital market, including a new breed of investor—the manager-investor. Investors share their wisdom about the venture process and, in particular, about valuation and due diligence.

Part 3, "Resources: Finding Angel Investors," deals with the search. Since angel investors prize their privacy, finding them poses a formidable task. While some entrepreneurs attempt to raise money on their own, many turn to alternative funding sources for assistance and support. In addition, the role of the placement agent is explored— though entrepreneurs may decide to go it alone. If they do, however, they will need to master the skills presented here to build their own databases. Part 3 also contains a directory of funding resources.

In Part 4, "The Investor Perspective," entrepreneurs will gain an enriched perspective of the importance of both valuation and due diligence in the investor's decision to commit to a transaction. A great many investors, as well as entrepreneurs, are hungry for information about how deals are generated and completed. So we must not only help entrepreneurs understand where they are in the venture process but aid investors in their quest to enter this arena with a portion of their private equity portfolio. Investors need information on how to get started in their own search for investments. Finally, some basic investor questions are answered.

The entrepreneur, private investor, and intermediary will each benefit from reading *Angel Financing*.

## THE ENTREPRENEUR

Entrepreneurs in need of capital need this book. This book is about initiating the process of raising capital for companies at earlier stages of development and for whom traditional financing resources are not available. For the entrepreneur who has failed at these traditional sources of financing, *Angel Financing* offers a step-by-step formula for reaching the highly secretive and selective market of the private investor, a segment of the investor market that has become a major source of funding for entrepreneurial ventures.

Entrepreneurs include those people raising capital on their own, CEOs of ongoing businesses looking for nontraditional financing, and owners of small businesses failing to qualify for loans from traditional sources and seeking expansion capital to grow their businesses. This category also includes owners of financially troubled companies who seek capital to reorganize and inventors who desire capital to commercialize their technologies. Further, the entrepreneurial group encompasses people who have acquired technologies through various research centers and defense conversion centers that look for financing to commercialize those technologies. Finally, this group includes company employees who dream about starting their own business.

We present guidelines not only for making a deal financeable—enabling entrepreneurs to evaluate the workability of their transaction—but also for developing a capitalization strategy for the funding process uniquely suited to the private-placement transaction. Entrepreneurs must learn to efficiently and conscientiously manage the increasingly demanding, exhausting process of raising money. We have tried to define the problem and offer nontraditional resources for those companies that merit funding. If entrepreneurs don't know where they're going in trying to raise alternative forms of capital for their venture and have no clear road map to point the way, they will likely end up in a place they did not expect to be and do not recognize. *Angel Financing* provides a road map to financing on a path that otherwise would remain tortuous.

*Angel Financing* is not a dry compendium of alternative forms of financing nor a public domain directory of out-of-date funding sources available in any library. It is, instead, a set of tools that enables entrepreneurs to (1) determine whether private investors are a workable and appropriate source of capital for their deal, (2) increase their awareness of the private investor perspective so they can frame an investment proposal with the greatest chance for success, and (3) develop a winning strategy to locate, contact, and establish relationships with angel investors.

Few entrepreneurs relish raising capital. Not having been trained for the task, they view it as an onerous activity. Still, it is an activity inextricably woven into their chances for success. The troublesome task of raising capital is simply inescapable. *Angel Financing* analyzes the problem, then presents strategies for addressing it. But more important, the book provides entrepreneurs with tools for articulating their vision, enabling them to move forward in the private market, furnishing contacts with which to begin their search for capital. However, too often the entrepreneurs are ill-prepared, not having built their management team, prepared for valuation and due diligence, or written their business plan. In a word, they have not developed a capitalization strategy. This book presents a workable capitalization strategy.

For entrepreneurs, *Angel Financing* also provides protocol on how to cost-effectively begin developing their own proprietary infobase of high-net-worth individuals. The book contains a directory to the major networks that resulted in substantial investments in 1993, 1994, and 1995, plus a complete state-of-the-art workbook on writing a business plan. In addition, the book contains exhibits that entrepreneurs can use in educating the rest of the players in their company.

Entrepreneurs must understand how different the process is for approaching the private investor. They must know where they are in the process—whether prospecting or screening investors, getting ready for a first presentation, or doing due diligence on the investors' ability to invest. They must know where they are in the process—whether going through the negotiation process and structuring the transaction, completing the transaction with attorneys and accountants and other financial and legal advisers, or managing the relationship with investors *after* they have invested of money. In the maze of emotion, complexity, and hard work, they can get lost.

Finally, this book will help the entrepreneur become a more informed consumer of financial intermediary services. Once entrepreneurs have exhausted their personal network, reaching out to the private market can be time-consuming and expensive. People starting start-ups haven't the luxury of time, especially when they are without proprietary protection, patents, or other types of intellectual property protection. Nor do those engaged in early-stage ventures possess the requisite collateral, cash flow, or assets, a circumstance that renders banks and other forms of loans impracticable as a source of funding.

What's more, today anyone with a telephone, a business card, and a computer can become a financial intermediary or a "finder." Despite the SEC's recent concern, this area of funding process remains unregulated, leaving the unsuspecting entrepreneur vulnerable to placing trust in an unscrupulous intermediary, paying hefty up-front fees, or advancing other expenses. The unsuspecting entrepreneur finds out after three or six or nine wasted months that the finder's efforts have generated few results. Too often we have heard the woeful tale from the entrepreneur who unfortunately placed faith in an individual who was unable to deliver on the infamous "best effort" basis.

Finding private investors is all about building relationships with self-made millionaires, 90 percent of whom are worth between one and ten million dollars, people who have owned their own businesses, and are successful because they know what to invest in and wish to broaden their investments. This book provides resources and contact information so people can get started in the process of financing their ventures on their own, bestowing on them some of the most powerful tools they will need, while saving them thousands of dollars in consulting fees.

Because private investors prize their privacy and because they do not *have* to invest—as do professional investors, fund managers, or bankers—the traditional models and methods of searching for financing simply will not work in penetrating this market. Books presently flooding the mass market and business literature advocate models for accessing venture professional capitalists, venture leasing, or SBA loans, but these approaches will not help in accessing the private investor. So the entrepreneur has to understand the private financing process, a process completely different from that of applying for a loan, or seeking out professional venture capital or funds from professional money managers, who are paid a fee to manage the institutional money. *Angel Financing* gives valuable insight into the investor's motivation, investor preference, and investor expectation. In their own words, these investors provide a set of guidelines on how to approach them in ways that won't run afoul of what is legitimate and appropriate.

This personal testimony by the investors themselves regarding what the active private investor looks for in a deal allows the entrepreneur to know—without wasting time pursuing the wrong investors—whether his or her venture meets investment criteria. If the venture does meet the criteria of particular investors, this book becomes a valuable resource as the entrepreneur proceeds to search for them, stimulate their interest, and establish contact and build relationships with them.

The capital-raising process cannot be successfully navigated in ignorance. This book offers the entrepreneur an efficient means for tapping into capital and doing so quickly. There is the need for tools—understandable, realistic tools—that will help the entrepreneur, particularly in early-stage ventures, to embark on fund-raising, capital-finding tasks. The defining factor of the entrepreneur is the ability to raise money. When entrepreneurs can raise money, they become credible.

## THE PRIVATE INVESTOR

This book is also about investing in higher-risk transactions, a form of investing that allows the investor to influence the outcome of the investment. This highly selective segment of the investor market that *Angel Financing* addresses has become a major source of capital for these particular types of transactions.

However, this is not a market tracked by economists or written about in the *Wall Street Journal, Fortune,* or *Forbes.* It is, nonetheless, a huge market by any standard: more than 700,000 transactions, amounting to $56 billion a year. Even when corrected for high-risk venture investing, experts agree that at least $2 to $4 billion had been invested directly into seed and start-up financing. International Capital Resources estimates that at any given time there exists a market in the United States of between 100,000 and 140,000 high-net-worth, high-risk private investors who make decisions on their own. This private investor market is, in fact, a principal source of capital, contributing to the financial stability of smaller companies that make up a sizable source of jobs in the United States. Successful investors deliver insight directly into the process of high-risk, high-return investing. Through them, we have captured what constitutes the effective way of embarking on this type of investing. With the $4.5-trillion high-net-worth market growing at a rate of between 14 and 20 percent per year, a sizable percentage of the 2.5 million U.S. households comprising this market are prospective targets for early-stage deals seeking financing.

Included in the private investor category are, first, the high-net-worth private investors who choose a target of interest in companies operating at particular stages of development with which they are familiar. There are also the fund managers and managers of venture capital funds who must screen thousands of deals a year to identify those that the firm will invest in, helping their clients to make better, more informed decisions. Fund-raisers raising their own funds or trying to put together a pool of money to invest would also fall within the category of private investor.

This book can help private investors learn how to avoid the big mistakes and ubiquitous pitfalls inherent in this high-risk investing arena. Private investors must avoid the traps that have ensnared other investors. They need to know what kinds of investments other small, successful investors are making, their investment approaches, and some of the critical aspects that other private investors attend to, particularly valuation and due diligence. Investors also need to know the right questions to ask to bring winning investment opportunities bubbling to the surface.

There are many books on investing in mutual funds, stocks, and bonds, but few aimed toward direct private equity investing into early-stage and expansion-stage ventures. What we have tried to do is to solidify the discussion of the direct equity venture process and explore in greater detail two critical areas: valuation and due diligence, the areas that the investor has to manage to avert financial disaster.

As we have said, little information exists on direct investing, an esoteric, idiosyncratic arena in which high-net-worth private investors choose a target of interest in companies operating at the stages of development with which they are familiar. Moreover, as we have likewise mentioned, private investors prize their privacy—a major reason for their interest in this arena in the first place—so it has taken the authors the past few years to interview hundreds of these investors to plumb their perspectives.

Private investors, after all, are just that—private; by design they are difficult to reach. They safeguard their privacy, expressly avoiding any form of solicitation. Moreover, these private investors do not have to invest. They invest with caution because they are risk-averse. But they also invest with a broader range of criteria beyond internal rate of return and the return on investment normally associated with the institutional or professional investor. These are distinguishing characteristics. Further, investors are, in the words of one of them, "very smart" and appreciate those who deal with them honestly and straightforwardly.

Investors are eager to find out about what other private investors are thinking and doing, and they are likewise interested in increasing their own deal flow—aspects of this area of investing covered in detail in *Angel Financing*. No other resource currently available comprehensively covers what these particular investors look for, nor does any other resource contain critical information dispensed by the investors themselves on what they are looking for in an investment and just how they prefer to be approached.

## THE INTERMEDIARY

In order for intermediaries to be competitive, they must add value. *Angel Financing* will benefit those tens of thousands of people in the consulting business constantly called upon to offer advice on how to find money. The book will quickly become a resource for attorneys and accountants who provide referrals for their clients, certified appraisers who assist companies in establishing their valuation, and finders. For instance, every lawyer operating in the securities industry would benefit from reading this book. With the added value of having investors to introduce their clients to, they enhance their credibility and performance.

This book not only provides important information to intermediaries about their clients and their clients' problems—which helps them become better diagnosticians—but also, as we have indicated, offers new insight into the investor community. Intermediaries will benefit from an accurate picture of the problem faced by investors and entrepreneurs and will be able to position themselves to become more competitive in offering their services and the solutions proposed in this book. Few entrepreneurs and intermediaries understand this particular market, and they probably do not have the time or the money to do the research we have done. Entrepreneurs and intermediaries owe it to themselves to learn to raise money from private investors.

Consultants are too busy to do more than manage their own career development. They haven't the time to return to school. Ten to 20 percent are dedicated to financial-related services for entrepreneurial clients: marketing research, developing cash-flow forecasts, creating business plans, developing financial proposals valuations, analyzing deal structures—many of which will be reviewed by investors. A highly competitive business, to say the least! An added benefit to attorneys, accountants, and appraisers as they are working for their clients is knowledge of the investor's perspective, the ability to tailor their boilerplates to the individual needs of the private investor.

Neither the challenge nor the problem is new. But the formulation of our strategy is. This so-called inefficient private-placement market seems unorganized. International Capital Resources (ICR) and the authors have penetrated this huge but hidden, misunderstood market. The authors have placed on the reader's plate a meaty analysis of angel investors as alternative sources of capital: what they look like and what they look for in a deal. But most important in looking at the private investor is the typology, a review of the different types of private investors. Nothing like it has ever been compiled before.

*Angel Financing* is about our experience in creating one of the largest private investor networks in the country and about what works and doesn't work. This book is about our experience in working with more than 500 companies a year. It's about our experience in building a proprietary database of more than 9,000 private investors, engaging them in conversations, and in arranging their presentations at forums over the past few years. It's about bringing to bear our experience in penetrating this highly lucrative market. More than $550 million has been invested by the top 15 alternative capital resource networks in the United States.

If a venture cannot be categorized as one of the "darling" industries, or a company that will achieve $50 to $100 million in sales within five years, the only resource is the private investor market. Start-ups in just a few industry segments receive the lion's share of invested capital. As VentureOne Corporation reported, of the $515.1 million invested in Bay Area start-ups for the first quarter of 1996, over $419.9 million went into only five industry segments: communication and networking, software and information services, electronic and computer hardware, semiconductors and their components, and medical devices and equipment. Thus, in the first quarter, five industries received 82 percent of the total amount invested in start-ups. Therefore, institutional investors, professional venture capitalists, and banks are not practical financing resources for developing companies that lack assets, fully developed technology, cash flow, and other collateral.

More than 30,000 very early-stage companies rejected by the traditional financing sources in this country receive financing from private capital every year. The total private market investment is estimated to range from $20 to $30 billion a year, depending on the studies used to arrive at that figure. In ICR's experience, through our ten U.S. offices, every month 300 or 400 companies contact ICR because they can't find capital and because they know that these are the investors they need to find.

In addition, with the graduate academic community seemingly without guidance on raising money among private investors, *Angel Financing* offers professors and students alike a practical resource guide for MBA programs that continue pumping out those who are filling the investment banking market.

We have tested all the suggestions, everything that's appeared over the last few years. What works we have integrated into a cohesive strategy; what doesn't we've discarded. We narrowly target those specific individuals looking for higher-risk deals, transactions that typically entail an investor's taking a more active role.

Finally, *Angel Financing* is important for macroeconomic reasons: Larger companies are reducing their workforces, not creating jobs. But successful early-stage companies hold the promise of technological advancement and the increasing competitiveness of American industry. Such companies also possess the potential for jobs in various recessionary economies, both nationally and, particularly, regionally. Where do these companies go when banks have turned them away? Where do these companies go when they don't have collateral and cash flow? The Small Business Administration (SBA) is restrictive, and the venture capital industry has moved out of early-stage investing for economic and demographic reasons.

Private investors have stepped into the breach, attempting to fill the void. Thus, *Angel Financing* debunks the misconception that the venture capital industry is the primary source of capital for these early-stage deals. Because of a shakeout in the industry, large funds have resulted. Large funds must make large investments in order to put their money to work. Their inclination is to make investments based on 1998 statistics, ranging from $3 million to $7 million per transaction. Moreover, the compensation structure in the venture capital industry is such that the companies are rewarded for the money under management: One to 3 percent of the money under management is paid to the general partners. So not a lot of economic incentive exists to raise a small fund, nor is there a lot of time to do so. From the venture capital industry's point of view, it seems better to work with a couple of institutional investors with a couple of large deals than it is to work with scores of smaller investors or scores of much riskier entrepreneurial ventures requiring nurturing to develop the business.

*Angel Financing* is not a dry textbook sporting different financing methods that have no applicability. It offers an inside look at the emergence and making of a capital market that holds the prospect for the financing of people's dreams. This book is not designed as an encyclopedic, shelf-bound dust collector but rather a useful manual, crafted to benefit entrepreneurs, private investors, and intermediaries in planning, managing, organizing, executing, and monitoring the effectiveness of what they are doing and how they are doing it, where they are and whither they are tending, as they attempt to penetrate one of America's largest capital markets.

The entire process of private transactions is covered, from developing the initial deal flow through to the harvesting of returns. As Warren Buffett has declared, what counts is not the size of a motor but its degree of efficiency. This is a book that efficient entrepreneurs, investors, and intermediaries will want nearby for the new millennium.

Gerald A. Benjamin
Joel Margulis

# Acknowledgments

We are deeply grateful to the very best of literary agents, John Willig of Brielle, New Jersey, who connected us to people at John Wiley & Sons, especially Mina Samuels, Jack Gaston, and Michael Detweiler. We also wish to thank William D. Evers of Evers and Hendrickson for his expert and invaluable contribution on securities law issues for small businesses. And we also want to thank E. Jeffrey Lyons of Marquette Consulting Group, Inc., for his professional and insightful contribution on the promises and pitfalls of the Internet for entrepreneurs and investors.

# Introduction

*It is the mark of an educated man to look for precision in each class of things just as far as the nature of things admits.*

Aristotle

A number of trends are setting the stage for increases in business angel financing. These include more ventures, more capital, and improved survival rates for start-ups.

According to the Small Business Administration (SBA), Wells Fargo, and the National Federation of Independent Businesses (NFIB) Educational Foundation Study on Business Start-Ups, in 1997 more than 3.5 million new businesses were started up in the United States. In addition, 900,000 businesses were purchased by owners, and 68,000 were inherited or acquired otherwise. To place this astounding growth in perspective, in 1990 the total of all small businesses in the United States was just 5 million companies.

According to the SBA's Office of Advocacy in its 1997 "Facts About Small Business," "[u]nder a broad definition—a definition that includes not only persons running a business full-time, but also those doing so part-time—about 16 million Americans are engaged in some entrepreneurial activity. These 16 million entrepreneurs represent about 13 percent of all non-agricultural workers in the U.S." What we see here is a major trend in our society toward entrepreneurial behavior. Instead of having a resume handy, everyone seems to have a business plan in his or her top desk drawer, creating a diverse array of investment possibilities. Little wonder that one in three American households includes someone who has started, tried to start, or helped fund a small business. Entrepreneurial behavior is a major trend in our society.

Along with this growth trend in dreaming, potential dream makers are growing in numbers and shifting their investment orientation as well. In 1990 U.S. consumer assets totaled $8.2 trillion with 20 percent held by baby boomers. For the beginning of the new century, the U.S. Bureau of the Census has projected U.S. consumer assets will have increased to $9.8 trillion, of which 39 percent will be held by baby boomers in their 50s, the typical age for private venture investing.

According to the Federal Reserve Survey of Consumer Finances in 1992, households with a net worth of $1 to $10 million placed 66 percent of their discretionary net worth into equity investments and 31 percent into savings deposits. The Federal Reserve projected this amount would increase to 83 percent placed into equity investments by the first year of the new century. Clearly, there is no shortage of risk capital.

According to a Dun and Bradstreet longitudinal study, of all small businesses started in 1985, within ten years—1994—fully 74 percent had survived and were still operating. The failure rates for small, start-up businesses are not what they were in the 1970s and 1980s.

In spite of ample numbers of promising ventures, available equity capital, and higher probability of ventures' success, there still exists a capital gap and corresponding investment opportunity. According to Arthur Andersen's 1995 national study, 36 percent of small, fast-growing companies reported that they were unable to meet their capital needs. Using these data and information on the size of private transactions, Arthur Andersen calculated a $61 billion shortfall nationwide. If slow-growth companies are added in, this shortfall could increase to $100 billion.

Let's take a closer look at the gap between supply and demand for capital. With venture capitalists placing $11.4 billion, angels $30 billion, the Internet via direct public offerings and private placements generating $175 million (only 7 percent of which was received by small companies), and founders—family and friends—committing $10 billion in "love money," according to Forrester Research, current research suggests a minimum capital gap of $10 billion to a potential maximum gap of $50 billion.

Studies from the Center for Venture Research suggests that less than 1 percent of all investable assets are making their way to these hungry, smart, start-up companies.

According to the National Venture Capital Association (NVCA), 640 venture capital firms have more than $45 billion under management. Professional Venture Capital funded approximately 1,800 companies in 1998, placing about $11.4 billion—about $1.1 billion of which went into only 300 early-stage companies, a number of which had already received venture capital investment or represented a limited number of ventures exclusively from the information technology and healthcare industries. Venture capitalists are investing larger amounts per round into fewer deals than individual investors are and are continuing the trend of increasing fund size, which, according to research published in *The Red Herring,* suggested that the average fund manages $80 million, up from $50 million in 1990. And the average amount of capital per partner has increased to the point that many venture capital firms cannot afford the time to consider investments under $2 million.

Venture capitalists also are continuing the trend of increasing fund size because of changes in the law, changes that permit investment of retirement funds into venture capital transactions, increase money management services for larger institutional investors, promise lucrative fees associated with managing larger funds, and cover rising overhead transaction and research costs. These ingredients are contributing to a corresponding increase in the size of the mean investment, according to Coopers & Lybrand and VentureOne to more than $5 million average investment, which, according to the SBA, now reaches approximately $6.5 million per deal.

Furthermore, venture capitalists are not necessarily inclined to court angels, since venture capital follows only 10 percent of angel-invested companies. As Arthur Rock has stated, "VCs are more concerned with creating wealth than creating companies."

The SBA, through 478 banks across the United States, has been helpful by providing long-term credit—not equity—of $15.8 billion to 67,000 operating companies—not start-ups—between 1995 and 1996. Banks provided just $25 million in unsecured debt to start-up businesses, while in 1997, 200 companies in the Small Business Investment Company (SBIC) program invested a mere $100 million, primarily in subordinated debt. For early-stage companies without significant reserves or substantial collateral, such debt capital is simply not an available option.

Initial public offerings (IPOs) helped 590 established companies (firms that met rigorous stock exchange financial criteria) raise $40 billion in needed funds. However, with the cost of raising $5 million averaging $700,000 and involving 900 hours of principals' time to complete an offering, this option served fewer than one-tenth of 1 percent of all companies raising capital.

Although important, these sources and bootstrapping from retained earnings of operating companies provided only a fraction of the capital needed to fuel the growth of this rapidly expanding sector of our economy during a time when society is shifting from a manufacturing, labor-based economy to an entrepreneurial, knowledge-based, technology-driven economy. Also, this capital for the most part does not help to reduce the capital shortfall for very early-stage companies that lack cash flows and that require relatively smaller financing amounts.

The fact is that the majority of all small businesses, start-ups, and expansion ventures in North America and a significant portion in Europe continue to be financed initially by the founders, their family, and their friends. After this initial funding, in the United States 90 percent of all rounds of financing under $1 million and 80 percent of all dollars invested in early-stage companies will continue to be provided by about 250,000 to 300,000 active business angel investors each year.

Business angel investors have been referred to as the "invisible" or "hidden" market. However, for early-stage private companies experiencing sales under $5 million, serving nonglobal markets, seeking smaller rounds (typically $250,000 to $1,500,000), lacking patented technologies, and resting among industries not currently the rage of Wall Street, Sand Hill Road, and Route 128, angel investors remain the primary source of funding for early- and expansion-stage capital.

Amazingly, all this investing occurs regardless of: (1) inadequate capital gains tax incentives, particularly inadequate when compared to similar incentives in other countries; (2) a scarcity of legitimate, well-organized investment networks to facilitate matching of investors and ventures; (3) the downsized lending of banks as a result of stricter enforcement of banking regulations; (4) educational institutions that have failed to provide investors and entrepreneurs with a full understanding of this unique type of investment transaction and what is involved in planning for the capitalization and investment process; and (5) a climate of legal and regulatory constraints that is strangling the free flow of information between ethical, well-intentioned entrepreneurs and sophisticated, self-made, affluent private investors possessing the experience, analytical skills, and understanding of the risks involved when they make their own informed investment decisions.

We are living at a time when macro-socioeconomic forces are converging, making this the most opportune time for starting a business and for direct venture investment.

The economy is booming; wealth is increasing in real dollars. Between 1983 and 1989, the assets of the richest 500 families in the United States rose from $2.5 to $5 trillion; corporations are downsizing, releasing experienced executives with substantial severance and cashouts; the market remains strong; the IPO market, while not sizzling, remains vigorous (524 nationwide in 1998, and climbing); and the society continues its shift, driven by technological development and desire for wealth accumulation.

Investors understand that these new companies are the cornerstone of our economic success, having created, according to the SBA, 67 percent of all jobs, a total 20 million new jobs between 1979 and 1993—and 12 million more than that by 1997. Start-up businesses specifically create 27 percent of new jobs (according to David Birch at MIT) and 91 percent of new jobs in California (according to the Census Bureau). Small companies represent 47 percent of all sales, 51 percent of the private gross domestic product, 52 percent of business net worth, and 99 percent of all companies in the United States. Small business employers increased to more than 5 million in 1994, a 6.5 percent increase from 1988. By 1996 new businesses established another record level. According to the Bureau of Labor Statistics, small firms will contribute about 60 percent of the new jobs between 1994 and 2005. In addition, 55 percent of all innovation comes through these small companies, helping to keep the United States globally competitive—small companies boast twice the number of product innovations per employee as large companies.

In the words of the SBA, "Interest in owning or starting a small business has never been greater." And it is clearer than ever before that small firms are the struts of our economic stability and growth; that is why these small companies need the capital to keep charging the battery of the nation's economic vitality.

The importance and significance of the angel investor contribution can no longer be ignored.

This type of investing is not easy. It requires a high tolerance for risk, necessitating one to live with the unexpected and to understand and live with the anxiety and stress caused by such disadvantages as lack of diversification, lack of liquidity, high mortality rate, and significant dissatisfaction with existing channels of communication with businesses seeking financing.

It is true that the rate of return is very significant on successful ventures. Angels have soared with this past century's technology start-ups. Witness Ciena Corporation. Angel investor Kevin Kimberlin invested $100,000 in the company in 1994. Three years later, having floated an IPO, his investment grew to a value of $285 million. In this example, the IPO became valued at 11,500 percent return over the first-round private equity share price, and that share price quickly rose to more than 200 times the first-round private equity price.

*However,* these investors appreciate that 33 percent of the time, direct investors will experience a complete loss or savings account levels of return for their effort after as much as an eight-year hold. Angel investing requires industry savvy in order to analyze deals and demands the energy and personality to actively attract promising deals from among the many seeking capital. It requires significant time commitments since the investments are more active than passive. Assistance and hand-holding by these sophisticated mentors is often a precondition that goes along with early- and expansion-stage investing, a precondition that becomes a rewarding responsibility and that becomes integral to gaining a knowledge and understanding of the management team as well as to hedge downside risk and avert problems. It requires patience. And it requires long-term horizons.

Part of the problem is the absence of an efficient private venture investor market leading to under investment, because no organized capital provider system targets entrepreneurial companies. Information about sources of funds or venture opportunities is not readily available. No secondary market currently provides small company investors with an exit strategy; restrictive securities regulations limit the flow of information; and many securities industry professionals believe these companies are not investable because of a lack of standard, consistent deal structures, structures that raise transaction costs and create high liability costs per transaction.

However, the rewards include not only return of investment and return on investment with high capital appreciation, but there is no middleman. The investor alone can hit a home run with unlimited upside potential, furnishing the only way private investors can get first crack at the next high-rise stock prior to IPO. It is satisfying and revitalizing indeed to experience being a part of the birth and growth of a new company. Angel investing remains one of the few investment arenas in which the investor can significantly influence the outcome of the investment while earning a range of nonfinancial rewards valued by individuals at their stage of life.

But capital shortage is fatal for small, growing businesses. The future success of those that survive start-up is dependent on availability of additional growth capital as well as the entrepreneur's ability to develop the skills and attitudes to be successful at the money-raising game. Today venture capital firms, lenders, government programs, and other traditional financing sources are rarely willing to take the risk, and when they do, it is with unacceptable valuation concessions and cost to the entrepreneur. On the other hand, early-stage ventures have the best chance for funding, survival, retention of a larger share of venture ownership and control, and long-term success by developing an efficient capitalization strategy to find and approach angel investors.

Ironic, isn't it, that in a time such as this, it is so hard to find capital? And ironic, too, is the fact that capital seems so hard to find at a time when investors want to look at more deals and when entrepreneurs would rather start a company than look for a job. After all, these two groups share much more than at first might appear. In fact, their similarities far exceed their disparities. They need to seek and identify the similarities between these two types of risk-takers. They need to build on this similarity with every contact they make, whether in search of capital or in search of deals.

We are living in a very exciting time, a time when our society is transforming itself from primarily a labor-based manufacturing economy to one that in 1997 saw 3.5 million individuals opt for entrepreneurialism over employment and start their own companies. Fifteen years ago executives kept a resume fresh; today many are polishing business plans. Little wonder that the consistently hottest-selling business books in the United States are about how to write a business plan.

Such entrepreneurial fervor is being matched by a real increase in wealth and income, an increase in discretionary net worth, and a willingness on the part of self-made millionaires to explore investments into early-stage, private-equity transactions. Investors realize that these are the companies that will create tomorrow's jobs and tomorrow's tax base and will develop the technological innovations to keep the United States globally competitive.

Contrary to the popular belief, there is no shortage of pre-IPO risk capital. Based on studies by International Capital Resources, approximately 2 million U.S. investors today have the demographic profile and the financial resources—more specifically, the discretionary net worth—to eliminate the capital gap. However, interestingly enough—and for reasons we will discuss in the book—only about 250,000 to 300,000 of this group are active. And the great challenge for intermediaries and entrepreneurial finance services and introduction networks is to make this market more efficient, allowing more of the qualified 2 million to become active in the market. This, then, is the challenge we address in the book, the challenge of facing the inefficiencies blocking the other 1.75 million from getting actively involved. So the issue centers not only on entrepreneurs who are uneducated about the process of raising capital but also on the millionaires—90 percent of whom are self-made—who know how to grow a company but not necessarily how to invest in early-stage transactions.

Thus, the gap is not the problem but a symptom of the failure of our society and elected representatives to change antiquated securities laws, laws that effectively strangle the free flow of communication between ethical entrepreneurs and sophisticated, well-informed capitalists. This chasm in what we call the "pre-IPO" market will continue to exist only as long as we fail to muster the courage and take responsibility for bridging the gap with pragmatic solutions based on rigorous research.

Do you truly believe that significant differences exist between entrepreneurs and business angel investors? Risking their life savings, homes, and children's education to make their dream a reality, entrepreneurs face a 25 percent failure rate for start-ups. Risking hard-won capital, high-net-worth, self-made entrepreneurial investors face a complete loss 33 percent of the time. These groups of individuals are indeed two sides of the same coin!

The similarities between these two groups of risk-takers far outweigh their differences. But for entrepreneurs and investors to recognize and build on these similarities in their quest for capital or returns, they must do four things:

1. Overcome their insecurities about raising capital and asking for money

2. Reassess their values/attitudes toward asking for money

3. Take time to learn the art of successful private investing from experienced veterans who have made the most and financially survived to tell their stories

4. Determine if they have or know how to get the skills to be effective at the money-raising and investing game

This last challenge is most critical since, in our opinion, the defining factor of successful entrepreneurs is not whether they have created a better mousetrap but whether they can raise the money to bring the better mousetrap to market.

The solution to the capital gap begins with research and understanding of the similarities between entrepreneurs and angels. Understanding the similarities between the dreamers and the dream-makers will provide the foundation for a bridge linking ventures with capital, so that a viable, long-term market for private securities can be created in the United States.

# Part 1

## The Challenge and the Solution

# The Challenge

## INTRODUCTION

The grand impresario Florenz Ziegfeld had a backer—an "angel," in Broadway parlance—named Jim Donahue who at the time of the 1929 stock market crash was disastrously affected financially. Deeply despondent over his losses, Donahue took his own life by throwing himself out of his office window. When Ziegfeld heard the news, he immediately penned a note to Donahue's widow that read, "Just before your husband 'fell,' he promised me $20,000." Needless to say, three days later the money arrived. And that's the kind of chutzpah it took then—and takes now—to raise capital for high-risk deals.

## THE CHALLENGE

Make no mistake: Raising funds for an early-stage venture or a small-growing business is an arduous task.

Where do you turn once you have exhausted the founders' financial resources and those of family and friends, but are not yet able to access venture capital? What if you're worn out from struggling with venture capital firms, banks, factors, leasing companies, and the like? What if you lack the ability to fund growth from cash flow or retained earnings? What if you have not yet achieved financial strength and public reputation sufficient to support a small corporate offering registration (SCOR) or an initial public offering (IPO)? What if your venture is not defined by the venture capital community as a "darling" industry? What if your deal is too small for institutional players—say, in the $100,000 to $300,000 range?

During the formative years of a start-up, entrepreneurs assume the responsibility for, and risk associated with, making their dream become a reality. Typically, a substantial portion of their net worth is committed to the venture. But by the first major round of funding, entrepreneurs often have exhausted their own financial resources and those of family, friends, associates, and business contacts. So entrepreneurs face a daunting challenge.

This challenge so often faced by entrepreneurs reveals only part of the task involved in early-stage capital formation. Even though these entrepreneurs create benefits—jobs, advancement of technology, capital expenditures, asset growth, and contribution to tax revenues—the supply of needed capital for early-stage ventures recently has been dwindling. There are three reasons for this: (1) start-ups need more money than in past years; (2) traditional capital and financing have diminished; and (3) more competition exists for start-up capital.

Taking each of these points in turn, first, a 1986 study by the National Venture Capital Association (NVCA) and Coopers & Lybrand (C&L) revealed that venture-backed companies founded between 1981 and 1985 needed an average of $7 million in capital during those five formative years. By contrast, repetition of this study in 1994 for the period 1988 to 1992 disclosed that required start-up financing—enough to survive and thrive—had increased to an average of more than $19 million in private equity. While it is true that the amount of seed capital required is correlated with the technology (the higher the technology, the higher the seed capital required), the NVCA/C&L studies demonstrate a 173 percent increase in funding needs in only seven years! Moreover, as *Forbes* magazine reminded us at the end of 1998, traditional venture capitalists are agents of other people's money and seldom finance brand-new companies. Small companies are setting their sights well below the mean venture capital deal of between $3 million and $7 million. Small companies simply do not need that level of funding.

Second, while the need for capital has been increasing, the supply of traditional capital has been decreasing. According to statistics taken from *Reviving the American Dream* by Alice Rivlin, net private saving shrank from 8.7 percent of national income in the years 1947 to 1973 to 4.9 percent in the years 1986 to 1990. Since 1980, net domestic investment—private *and* public—has declined from 7 percent of national income to 4.7 percent.

The third reason why it is more challenging today to raise capital among those with impressive personal wealth—especially those interested in investing in higher-risk deals—is that they are the target of everyone from charitable fund-raisers to the most successful money managers. In a word, there is simply more competition for the money that is out there than there was ten years ago.

Ten years ago everyone had a resume tucked neatly away in the desk drawer; today everyone has a business plan. And with the people currently intent on starting their own businesses, cities such as Boulder, Nashville, Tampa, Miami, and San Francisco have become zones of entrepreneurial fervor. A radical new way to wealth can involve coming up with an idea, then raising the money to fund it into a reality. Today, more than ever before, highly successful individuals are attempting to achieve their own success and enhance their personal wealth through entrepreneurial ventures.

Understandably, new money managers, foreign money managers, and other advisers seeking to manage funds aggressively target higher-net-worth individuals. In fact, a survival mentality has gripped those who compete with professional money managers for private capital. Besides, as the flow of deals surges, private investors become more sophisticated in evaluating what constitutes an attractive high-risk/high-reward opportunity.

International Capital Resources of San Francisco (ICR) recently conducted a survey of more than 480 entrepreneurial ventures seeking capital. The entrepreneurs cited an expanding array of financing methods they were relying on to accomplish their financing goals. However, the majority identified one alternative financing resource as a practicable and preferred option: private equity and debt investors.

Exhibit 1.1 presents the primary funding methods mentioned during those interviews (no percentage is given for methods receiving only minimal recognition).

ICR discovered that 61 percent of entrepreneurs who came to its investment banking firm in their search for capital were relying on the direct participatory investment, casting an eye primarily toward informal, high-risk venture investors as their means of raising capital. Eighteen percent anticipated relying on their personal financial resources and those of family, friends, and business contacts. Only 9 percent of these primarily earlier-stage and developmental-stage companies were capable of relying on profits and working capital in order to fund their growth plans. Only 7 percent turned to banks for debt financing, and 3 percent chose joint ventures and alliances. Finally, only 2 percent of the 480 companies queried showed interest in approaching professional venture capital firms to fund their venture.

## THE DIRECT, PRIVATE INVESTOR

The term *angel* was coined by Broadway insiders to describe the well-heeled backers of Broadway shows who made risky investments in order to produce shows. Angels invested in these shows for the privilege of rubbing shoulders with theater personalities they admired. As a review of the biographies of the great impresarios attests, money for those shows was raised as much by attitude, good preparation, and luck, as by the quality of the offerings.

Angels today—numbering about 300,000, according to *Forbes*—are in many ways the same: wealthy individuals and families willing to invest in high-risk deals offered by people they admire and with whom they seek to be associated. Angels are also financially sophisticated private investors willing to provide seed and start-up capital for the higher-risk ventures. In essence, angels are private informal venture capitalists.

Exhibit 1.1  **PRIMARY TARGETED FUNDING SOURCES**

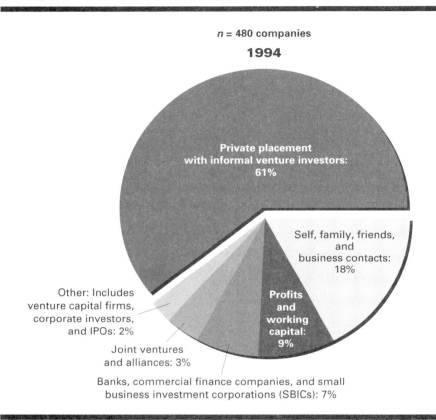

n = 480 companies

**1994**

Private placement with informal venture investors: 61%

Self, family, friends, and business contacts: 18%

Profits and working capital: 9%

Other: Includes venture capital firms, corporate investors, and IPOs: 2%

Joint ventures and alliances: 3%

Banks, commercial finance companies, and small business investment corporations (SBICs): 7%

Source: International Capital Resources

Angel investors possess the discretionary income needed for such risky ventures. In fact, a portion of their private equity portfolio is often set aside for this purpose. This discretionary income sets the angel investor apart—even from the merely affluent. An affluent individual may have an annual income of $100,000 but annual expenses totaling $150,000. Large incomes, we know, can carry even larger debts. For this reason, we distinguish between those who are *affluent* and those who are *wealthy.* In setting standards for targeting investors in these high-risk ventures, many entrepreneurs mistakenly judge investors solely on their income; income alone has little to do with what counts in these types of ventures. What counts are the discretionary funds for early-stage, high-risk transactions, funds possessed, again, only by wealthy angel investors, not by the affluent, whose debts can exceed their considerable annual incomes.

Angel investors—or the *nonpoor*, as we choose to refer to them—also possess a healthy appetite for self-arranged private deals. Such direct investment serves to maintain the self-confidence of these high-net-worth investors and demonstrates their continuing ability to make money. These investors have amassed wealth precisely because they know how to invest. Further, it is reasonable to assume that they will remain active investors. Many want to enjoy the small percentage of their capital allocated for private equity. After all, even the most conservative investment adviser will leave a client some money to play with. It is this "play money" that ought to become the target of entrepreneurs seeking funding for high-risk, relatively illiquid, direct investment securities. These deals, in turn, offer the possibility of capital appreciation.

Angel investors include such high-net-worth individuals as the retired officers of corporations and private companies with $1 million to $5 million in pension assets to invest; the recipients of the estimated $20 billion in windfall transfers projected for the 1990s; the high-net-worth casualties of corporate downsizing; and the thirty-something and forty-something chief executive officers (CEOs) of small capital companies. These investors have saved money, are financially astute, and possess engaging, challenging intellects.

Further, these angel investors are concerned with after-tax returns and return after expenses—the expenses, for example, of due diligence, intermediaries, and investment banking fees. They represent "patient" money, remaining comfortable with a long-term, buy-hold strategy, money not designed, as the Atlanta, Georgia, G&W *Premium Finance Gazette* puts it, "for high current income," but instead money that "often won't be available for some time." (The *Gazette* cites some examples: $25,000 invested in 1956 in Warren Buffett's Berkshire Hathaway has a 1995 estimated value of $90,000,000; the same amount invested in 1989 in Home Depot reached an estimated value of $3,500,000.) Last, angel investors define risk idiosyncratically, for example, the nature of potential loss—irrecoverable or affordable—the need for liquidity, and the need for control.

## STRUCTURE OF THE PRIVATE INVESTOR MARKET

The structure of the high-net-worth private investor market (Exhibit 1.2) can be segmented into four categories: first, investors with a net worth of about a minimum of $500,000, comprising a little more than 1.7 million U.S. households; second, a group of investors with a net worth of $1 million to $5 million (about 672,000 households); a third group worth $5 million to $10 million (about 158,000 households); and last, a segment with a net worth of more than $10 million (roughly 9,000 households).

Exhibit 1.2 **STRUCTURE OF THE HIGH-NET-WORTH
PRIVATE INVESTOR MARKET**

STRUCTURE OF NET WORTH

| Net Worth | U.S. Households |
|---|---|
| $    500,000 | 1,773,593 (1.9%) |
| $ 1,000,000 | 672,098 (.72%) |
| $ 5,000,000 | 158,690 (.17%) |
| $10,000,000+ | 9,334 (.01%) |
| $8.2T market | 2,613,715 |

STRUCTURE OF AFFLUENCE (INCOME)

| Adj. Gross Income* | No. of Returns[†] | %[‡] |
|---|---|---|
| $    100,000–200,000 | 2,597,908 | 2.26% |
| $    200,000–500,000 | 676,038 | .5% |
| $    500,000–1,000,000 | 118,350 | .1% |
| $1,000,000 or Greater | 52,019 | .045% |
| | 3,444,315 | 2.905% |

Source: International Capital Resources
*Total number of returns = 114,700,000.
[†]Includes salary, interest, dividends, stock sales, capital gains.
[‡]Could be individual, joint return, single, or unmarried filing separately.

This market includes the target group that offers the entrepreneur or inventor maximum possibility for finding investors. Growing at an annual rate of 14 to 20 percent, this high-net-worth market compares favorably, for example, with the current 8 percent growth rate in pension funds. Furthermore, each of these segments is adding about 1,000 households a year.

While we deemphasize the use of income as a primary demographic in targeting the high-net-worth group, Exhibit 1.2 shows a similarity between the structure of affluence, or income, and net worth. Notwithstanding our earlier distinction between income and net worth, some correlation naturally exists between net worth and income. But do not be swayed by the numbers.

In the United States, people with incomes between $200,000 and $500,000 a year submitted about 676,000 returns to the Internal Revenue Service (IRS) in 1991, accounting for 0.5 percent of the households. Those with incomes between $500,000 and $1 million submitted about 118,000 returns, or 0.1 percent of the total. While no direct correlation exists, those with higher incomes—say $200,000 to $1 million—overlap with those having a high net worth of $1 million to $10 million. So when we compare the numbers in two sections of Exhibit 1.2 we see similarities.

We see that there are about 672,000 households with a net worth of $1 million to $5 million and 158,000 households worth between $5 million and $10 million. Also note that 0.7 percent have a net worth of $1 million to $5 million. Less than 0.2 percent have a net worth of $5 million to $10 million. So the percentages of households correlate closely to those percentages of returns. Those with incomes of $200,000 to $500,000 equal 0.5 percent of returns; those with incomes of $500,000 to $1 million filed 0.1 percent of the returns. Thus, the numerical similarities point to a similarity between the structure of income and net worth. Still, the fact remains: Discretionary net worth forms the true measure of our target market.

The majority of investors represented in the categories of net worth ranging from $1 million to $10 million are self-made. Most rich Americans have earned their money; theirs is not inherited money, reveals the 1995 RAND study by the Santa Monica nonprofit research group. These individuals have built and own their own companies and have generated their personal fortunes through hard work and through understanding an industry or a business.

However, while these numbers seem large—a $4.5-trillion market and approximately 2.6 million U.S. households that might be appropriately targeted—the market for higher-risk, developmental, or expansion deals is substantially less than that. A portion of these investors is not composed of *accumulators,* or people investing in growth investments with possible capital appreciation; instead, they represent savers and those looking for income from their investments—circumstances incompatible with earlier-stage investments.

Other circumstances also lessen the pool of investment dollars. The dollars diminish when you correct statistics for geographical locale and proximity of the company seeking the direct investment. The dollars also diminish when you scan such items as net worth (exclusive of house and car), previous investment history, current holdings, status and role in the business community, and interests in specific industries.

Considering the circumstances, our own calculations indicate that for higher-risk, early-stage, manufacturing-related deals, the true market contracts to about 300,000 investors. This range exists because investors who engage in direct investing in early-stage deals typically surface only a few times a year, and only when seeking new investments that follow a liquidation or windfall event—or simply when they are in the mood for a change.

## INVESTOR ACTIVITY IN EARLY-STAGE DEALS

While it is true that private investors prize their privacy and that obtaining information about private transactions in this highly secretive market is difficult, International Capital Resources' proprietary research, plus other important studies, can help us understand the extent of the activity of the high-net-worth investor's direct investment in early-stage deals.

In his landmark study funded by the Small Business Administration, Dr. Robert J. Gaston suggests, as we noted in the preface, that approximately $55 to $56 billion a year is being placed into as many as 720,000 companies. Dr. William Wetzel, Jr., at the University of New Hampshire Whittemore School of Business has suggested that approximately $15 billion of this $55 to $56 billion was being placed into approximately 60,000 very-high-risk, early-stage, seed, research and development (R&D), or start-ups per year. And in one of his speeches, Robert Pavey, a general partner at Morganthaler Ventures in Cleveland, also suggested the $55 to $56 billion figure, with as many as 500,000 companies receiving the disbursement of capital from the private investor market per year. Meanwhile, the Small Business Development Center at the University of California, Irvine, has suggested that in California alone approximately $30 billion is being invested in about 240,000 transactions per year.

Although these estimates vary, the amount of capital and number of transactions involved signal a vast market. In contrast, the venture capital industry in 1994 invested a total of $4.9 billion, of which approximately $1.09 billion went into about 314 seed and first-round transactions. By comparison, then, we see that the private investor market fairly glitters as a major source of capital for the higher-risk, early-stage investment.

Simply put, private investors, or business angel investors, are a primary, if not *the* primary, source of capital for early-stage and growing companies.

## ANGELS, A GOLDEN CAPITAL SOURCE

So we see that angels are investors worth accessing. Cass Apple, former president of Sierra Designs and founder of Digital Records Corporation, thinks so. He felt motivated to turn to an angel instead of an institutional investor because of the willingness of angels to commit large stakes in individual companies based on the understanding that angels, in turn, want a voice in management. Speaking to the *San Francisco Business Times,* Apple put it this way: "The typical venture capital firm wants to get involved only when you are further along—and for more money than you need. The primary advantage of going with individuals is that it is much quicker and you can tailor the details of the deal to the individual investor."

Apple also valued early funding from someone who added brain power, plus the perspective of an experienced partner. Such an early investor, he concluded, could help develop a marketing strategy as the company prepared to bring its product to market.

He surmised still another advantage: Despite the healthy return for the angel from a successful start-up, the angel would exercise less control at the beginning than would a venture capitalist. The ability of the investor to deal with the entrepreneur was, for Cass Apple, where "the rubber hit the road"—and with a lot less friction.

## INVESTORS WORTH ACCESSING

So, as Cass Apple found out, these investors are worth accessing.

Still, there exists the old problem of meeting these investors. In his book *Giant in the West,* Julian Dara writes that for *19 years* Joseph Strauss attempted to get funding to build the Golden Gate Bridge! Nineteen years before he found A. P. Giannini, who ultimately financed the $6 million necessary for construction. Although contemporary entrepreneurs have been creative in identifying and accessing alternative sources of capital for their growing ventures, we have to be realistic: How many of us have the patience of a Joseph Strauss?

For many entrepreneurs, finding, attracting, building relationships with, and closing with private business angel investors remains inefficient. The reason is simple: Angels prize their privacy. These individuals are hard to find; moreover, a fair review of the literature will indicate that there is little formal guidance in identifying their whereabouts. Currently, most angel investors are located primarily by word-of-mouth contacts from other investors or by reliance on professional intermediaries with a book of investors in related fields.

Angels are hard to locate for the simple reason that they are secretive about their investment interests, since everyone eagerly solicits them to access their wealth. Is it any wonder they cling to their privacy? Because of these circumstances, you could make hundreds of presentations, spend countless hours, and waste thousands of dollars searching for private investors. Largely, labor lost. Lost, that is, unless you learn to use proven strategies that make the search more efficient. This means not only identifying these people but also establishing contact and managing relationships with them throughout the funding process.

The challenge, then, lies in efficiently accessing these investors. How do you find them? Chapter 3 will tell you how. But before tracing a strategy that works, you need the information in Chapter 2 on direct, private investment to determine whether your deal—and *you*—are, in fact, financeable.

# 2

# The Private Placement Investment

*Pure gold is recognized by testing.*
Leonardo da Vinci

## THE PRIVATE PLACEMENT INVESTMENT

Sixty percent of transactions concluded at the seed, R&D, and start-up stages have fairly fixed financing structures. It is no accident that the transaction structure most commonly used by angels is the private placement investment. The formal definition of a private placement investment is the issuance of treasury securities of a company to a small number of private investors in the form of senior debt, subordinated debt, convertible debt, common stock, preferred stock, warrants, or various combinations of these securities. While the vast majority of these investments to institutional investors involves debt securities, exempt offerings are common, involving direct, equity and/or debt investing by private investors.

With private placement investments, private investors often require direct participation in a venture in order to limit the downside risk associated with relatively illiquid investments. These direct participatory investments begin with transactions for a smaller amount and generally are more quickly arranged than public offerings. Besides, because of the lack of Securities and Exchange Commission (SEC) requirements, these more flexible transactions let the company circumvent onerous public offering requirements and access the nonaffiliated market without full regulatory compliance. Thus, these investments prove much less expensive.

In private placement investments, business owners receive cash for equity, and they can choose from a menu of financing options. In some cases, debt and equity can be mixed to create a funding solution. Further, the private placement investment can include all kinds of financing not publicly sold:

*Senior debt*    Lowest cost financing from banks or insurance companies, generally a secured loan on a first priority status by company assets.

*Subordinated debt*    Higher interest rate than senior debt in exchange for higher risk (paid after senior debt is paid), sometimes packaged with warrants ("sweeteners")

*Subscription warrant*    A security that can be converted into or exchanged for a company's stock

*Preferred stock*    Pays a dividend to the holder and usually includes more rights than common stock (in bankruptcy, considered junior to debt) and can be converted into common stock

*Common stock of the company*

Private placement investments, in fact, consist of anything that is not a public offering. Such leeway lets money-raisers exercise the limits of their creativity and negotiating skills. Herein lies the strength of private placement investment, and the main difference between an institutional private placement investment and direct, participatory investment by an angel. The former is primarily debt; the latter is not. Private placement investment usually means a subordinated debt transaction in the institutional market, but for angels it means an equity transaction between an individual and the company, a transaction that brings with it several advantages and responsibilities.

Private placement investment has the advantages of confidentiality and lower cost. First, with their less stringent disclosure requirements, direct investments enable private investors—who keenly prize their privacy—to maintain confidentiality in their financial transactions. Second, reduced cost figures prominently in choosing direct investment, especially in comparison with public offerings. For instance, the cost of a private placement investment—that is, a capitalization transaction handled directly by the company—is markedly less than the cost of a public offering, or even a SCOR.

Also, with most early-stage investing, private placement investment deal structures tend to be equity or equity-related, including the ability to accommodate subordinated debt. Even when subordinated debt or convertible debt is involved, these structures offer convertibility into equity so that the investor can share in the upside possibilities should the venture become successful.

Finally, private placement investment offers flexibility during negotiations between the private investor and the entrepreneur, a flexibility unavailable when purchasing stocks of public companies. Because the ventures are unproven, early-stage investing is the riskiest investment in the private equity class: Many times the technologies are not developed, the management teams unproven, the market not well developed.

For these reasons, the angel investor manages the risk early on, generally during negotiations or during the valuation of the venture, a point that will be detailed in Chapter 11.

## SELECTING THE RIGHT CAPITAL SOURCE

As an entrepreneur or inventor, you must ask if nontraditional resources suit your deal. Exhibit 2.1 helps answer that question.

The first decision involves financing. If a company has working capital, fixed assets, and the like, then more traditional equity or debt sources of capital are in order. However, if an operating deficit exists, or if the company possesses no revenues, only alternatives to traditional financial sources seem reasonable, as illustrated in the chart.

Another decision involves determining whether the business will appeal to an equity or debt source of capital, a decision determined primarily by risk and return. If the business can offer a high return, more traditional equity sources seem practicable. If, on the other hand, the business offers a low risk, debt becomes appropriate, using traditional sources of financing. However, if the business offers high risk with uncertain returns—as do many entrepreneurial ventures because of a weak cash flow, a high leverage in terms of a large amount of debt, a low growth rate, or an unproven management team—nontraditional financing resources remain the only option.

If, however, the business can offer high return and low risk, it can focus on what type of equity or what type of debt to establish. If the debt transaction involves less than $100,000, perhaps private investors might be interested. In more cases, however, private investors get involved in equity transactions. But an established company, or a company demonstrating rapid financial growth, will be attractive to the institutional equity markets and/or public market, making appropriate the traditional sources of capital. But for a start-up with limited growth possibility—that is, a company without the ability to reach annual sales figures of $50 million to $60 million—only nontraditional financial resources seem appropriate.

Examining Exhibit 2.1 should help you establish the suitability of a private placement investment for your venture.

## IS YOUR DEAL FINANCEABLE?

In Chapters 6 and 7 private investors describe what they look for in a deal. Investors' decisions may seem idiosyncratic; their motivations diverse. They are. But this diversity merely reflects their characteristic individuality. Do not overlook their underlying concurrence: They

# Exhibit 2.1 SELECTING THE RIGHT CAPITAL SOURCE

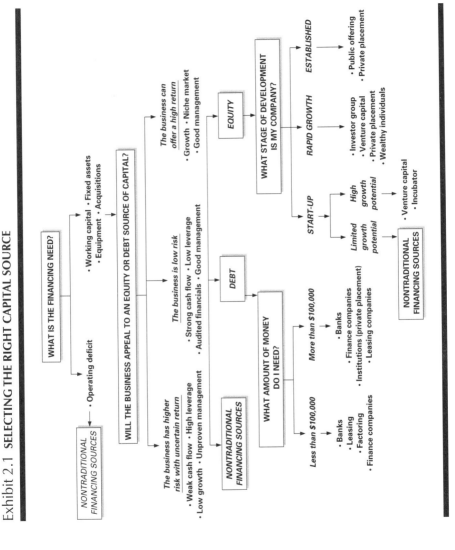

Source: International Capital Resources

share far more than may seem apparent. You will also see that what we advise here fits with what investors say they look for in a venture. What follows, then, are things to think about in making your deal financeable. (See Exhibit 2.2.)

*Management team* experience is crucial. An astute investor has said, "If the critical element in a successful real estate transaction is 'location, location, location,' the critical element in a successful business endeavor is 'management, management, management.' " In determining if your deal is financeable, think first about whether the management team has worked together and has experience in this or a relevant industry. Especially in an early-stage venture, experience in the industry far exceeds the importance of functional expertise. The venture needs someone who understands the industry, its market, and the application of its underlying technology more than it needs a financial expert, operations officer, or advertising maven.

*Market size* must be calculated. Assess the size of the market, specifically, whether the market share is substantial enough to generate the

---

Exhibit 2.2 **IS YOUR DEAL FINANCEABLE?**

- Management team . . . . . . . . . . . . . . . . . . . . . . . . . ✔
   —Requisite skills, driven, worked together, chemistry, experience in industry, pride in enterprise
- Large market size (qualified buyers & unique market niche) . . . . . . . ✔
- Market readiness + need + product appeal . . . . . . . . . . . . . . ✔
   —Is missionary selling required?
- Competition understood . . . . . . . . . . . . . . . . . . . . . . ✔
   —Current–future (3–7 years)
   —Barriers (beyond price)
- Established or emerging industry . . . . . . . . . . . . . . . . . . ✔
- Protected proprietary technology . . . . . . . . . . . . . . . . . . ✔
   —A real solution
- Does it work? . . . . . . . . . . . . . . . . . . . . . . . . . . . ✔
- Production can be currently performed . . . . . . . . . . . . . . . ✔
- Channel economics . . . . . . . . . . . . . . . . . . . . . . . . ✔
   —Demonstrate understanding of cost to bring product/service to market
- High margins (at least 15%, pretax) . . . . . . . . . . . . . . . . . ✔
- Above average profit potential . . . . . . . . . . . . . . . . . . . ✔
- Capital intensity . . . . . . . . . . . . . . . . . . . . . . . . . ✔
- Reasonable projections . . . . . . . . . . . . . . . . . . . . . . . ✔
- Valuation . . . . . . . . . . . . . . . . . . . . . . . . . . . . . ✔
- Clear and believable exit plan . . . . . . . . . . . . . . . . . . . ✔

Source: International Capital Resources

revenues stipulated in the marketing plan. Consider the cost. Are there enough qualified buyers to provide revenues and subsequent return to investors? This calculation needs to be not only accurate but demonstrable.

*Market readiness* should be considered as well. Will the technology or product require missionary selling, the kind that convinces people they need it? Missionary selling, of course, will increase the cost and expand the time needed to bring the product to market.

*Competition* must not be underestimated. Although many people will insist that none exists, everyone has a direct or indirect competitor. More to the point, however, is not the immediate competition but the competition that will surely emerge within three to five years. The discerning investor anticipates the inevitable competition and the resources those competitors may bring to bear on the market. The investor also contemplates the barriers that the entrepreneur can erect to the competitor's entry into the market.

Typically, investors are interested in reducing the risk associated with the investment by identifying investments involved in *established* or *emerging industries.* The ability to analyze financial projections is much easier for an existing industry because data is readily available in order to test the hypotheses and other assumptions associated with the pro formas. In evaluating business plans for introduction to our investor network, we gravitate toward industries that have a track record, as opposed to ventures that will need to invest significant time and financial resources in creating the industry, or an interest in their product or service.

*Proprietary technology* is important in reducing the investor's perceived risk in a venture. If you have developed a technology, investors will want assurance that you have protected it. From the investor's point of view, properly protected technology reduces risk in the venture. Because the deepest pocket often wins, most investors are aware of the shortcomings in patent protection.

*Does the product or service work?* Has the designed service or product demonstrated its function? Is there a working prototype, or are you still operating at the conceptual stage of development? Obviously, the more useful a service or product is, the more financeable it becomes.

Another consideration regarding the financeability of your deal is whether *production* can currently be performed. In other words, will it be necessary to create not only a prototype and a product, but also the machinery necessary to construct a prototype or product? Risk is significantly increased—as is capital requirements—when the production facilities do not exist to manufacture the product.

*Channel economics* demonstrates an understanding of the cost of bringing a product or service to market. Valuation expert John Cadle guesses that roughly 90 percent of all ventures need more money than is presumed. In reviewing a proposal, Cadle points out, investors will always discount projections. Without an understanding of the part Murphy's Law plays, people remain wedded to unrealistic milestones and, thus, to the debilitating conditions that missed deadlines engender.

*High margins* are always desirable to investors. They understand that it will take longer than anticipated to bring a product or service to market, that it will take more money, and that it will take longer to realize revenues. Higher margins offset such adversity, offering a sorely needed cushion.

Concerning above average *profit potential,* within 18 to 36 months, the company in its pro formas must demonstrate with confidence the ability to generate profits that will position the investors to get not only a return *of* their investment but a return *on* their investment. There is a wide range of acceptable levels of profit potential in deals that have been completed in the angel market. But typically investors are looking for a very real opportunity to realize a 20 to 50 percent return on investment per year compounded annually over the term of the hold of the investment. The profit potential must be present in order to provide those levels of return.

*Capital intensity* reflects the investment needed to prove to investors that a product or service will work. In biotechnology, for example, companies may spend years and invest millions of dollars before receiving Food and Drug Administration (FDA) approval to market a product. Significant financial *risk before proof* of concept is available reflects high levels of capital intensity less attractive to angel investors, and achieving a minimum of $10 million in sales per year within five years and growth of at least 20 percent annually constitutes a basis for *reasonable projections.* Research, development, and good manufacturing process (GMP) of a growth hormone, for example, can take up to seven years before permission is granted to test in humans—seven years of preclinical testing to figure out if it works, if it is toxic, if the correct dose is being administered. Add a few more years of separate phases of clinical trials to determine safety and efficacy. Then file a PLA (product license application) and wait a couple of years for the FDA's approval. Finally, the company arrives 12 years later, having spent $200 million—the estimated average cost of bringing one protein to market. Such is the burden and risk that create capital intensity.

On the other hand, being able to develop and bring a product or service to market quickly reflects a less capital-intensive circumstance. Investment will come more easily once the concept has been proven, permitting money to be used to move the product or service into the marketplace. Quick movement to the marketplace spawns a less capital-intensive situation.

*Valuation* is necessary to assess the financeability of a venture. Based on proprietary research conducted by ICR, the average valuation found in 1,275 early-stage transactions—which include R&Ds and start-ups—in California and Massachusetts suggests a mean valuation of approximately $1.5 million to $3.5 million. As ventures progress in the evolutionary life cycle to later stages of development, obviously the valuation will increase significantly. To raise money during the early stages of a company, when its valuation is lowest, more will have to be ceded to investors. This circumstance illuminates two things that influence the financeability of a deal: The investor must feel that the valuation is credible (in other words, it has to fall in line with valuations occurring elsewhere in the market); and from the entrepreneur's point of view, valuation should be based on achieving milestones so that more money than is presently needed is *not* being raised. This prevents giving away more of the company than is necessary when it is at a low valuation.

A *clear and believable exit plan* must be part of the picture. Investors who invest in companies directly, in most cases, will not be able to harvest their investment—especially in equity investments—until those equity investments are liquidated. And while a number of workable liquidation options exist, the plan for liquidation must be explicit. The investor must know whether liquidation will occur through a "claw back"—a sale back to the entrepreneur—or through the merger or acquisition by a public company and the trading of that illiquid stock for publicly traded securities. Liquidation may also occur through the sale of the company to other entrepreneurs, or through an initial public offering.

Simply declaring that one of these days the company will go public falls well short of an investor's expectation because most investors realize that few companies go public. As Cadle reminds us, "The IPO is only one way to gain liquidity—but not the typical way. In fact, probably only 8 percent reach liquidity in this manner." So there needs to be a realistic plan for liquidating the investment, paying it off, and/or providing for return on investment to the investor.

You need to think about all these things in determining whether your deal is financeable and whether—given its time-intensive and resource-intensive nature—the Sturm und Drang of raising private capital is merited.

From our experience in working with more than 490 companies in 1994, we know that added points need to be raised. Do not risk overshopping your deal by introducing your venture to investors before it is ready. Most companies, before meeting with investors or retaining placement counsel, determine that their product or service solves a problem for their customers. Some obtain orders or at least conduct research with customers or potential customers. Many develop a backlog of orders. Also, packaging, or the packaging idea, is developed, a prototype completed, and data from test runs are ready. Finally, progress has been made in developing pro forma financial statements that meet reasonable economic preconditions.

We have already discussed the need for the presence of a growth industry and the need for a strong management in crafting a deal attractive to investors. (Our investors will discuss these things again in Chapter 6.) With management, however, we need to address some less obvious features. Investors need to know that management has made a capital commitment to the venture. This is not to suggest that a reasonable investor would require someone to put up a house as security; even so, the members of the management team should be willing to pledge a substantial portion of their net worth to the venture. In addition, the team must also acknowledge its responsibility in raising the necessary funds for the venture. Though this feat often takes months to accomplish, the task belongs to the team, not to others. Also, team members must be willing to travel to meet with investors. Our experience has taught us that money cannot be raised by proxy or through impersonal contact. Raising money is accomplished only by meeting face-to-face with potential investors.

You must be realistic about raising capital. Give yourself reasonable time to complete the financing; do not allow *desperation* to hover over a deal. Remember this well: In the eyes of an investor, desperation is a deal killer.

Finally, determining the financeability of your deal should form the basis of your *situational awareness*—a term jet fighter pilots use to establish the position of their aircraft, especially in relation to the ground. At such sizzling speed, their lives depend on knowing precisely where they are—even when flying upside-down. While not as breathtaking or life-threatening, your situational awareness—the management team, market, competition, industry, proprietary technology, production, channel economics, high margins, profit potential, capital intensity, projections, valuation, and exit plan—depends on sensing where you are in relation to *your* "ground."

## ARE *YOU* FINANCEABLE?

It is one thing to think about whether your deal is financeable, quite another to ponder whether you yourself are capable of being funded. One of the facts of life in private placement investment is that plans do not get funded, people get funded. Yes, it is important that your deal is financeable, but more important is whether you can inspire the confidence in an investor to write a check. San Francisco investor Raymond Kelly of W&K Investors shares his group's two reasons for investing in Matthew Shoenberg's Sydran Food Services: "The first reason we invested was because of Matthew. The second reason we invested was because of Shoenberg."

Can someone say the same about you? Do you have the traits that will assure an investor that you can accomplish your goal and make good on the proposed return on investment? What it takes is outlined in Exhibit 2.3.

One of the most important traits of a successful fund-raiser is having the vision to create, conceptualize, and communicate a workable solu-

---

Exhibit 2.3  **TRAITS OF A SUCCESSFUL FUND-RAISER**

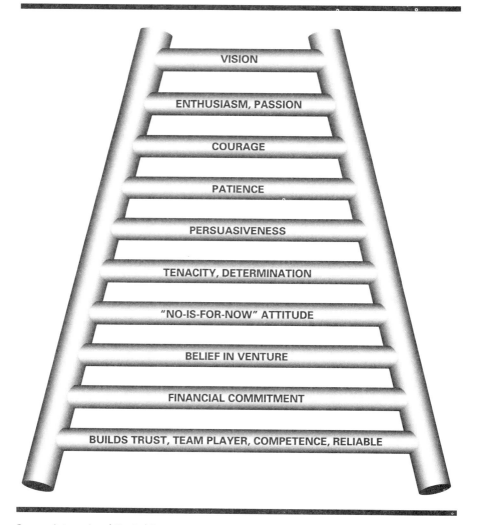

VISION

ENTHUSIASM, PASSION

COURAGE

PATIENCE

PERSUASIVENESS

TENACITY, DETERMINATION

"NO-IS-FOR-NOW" ATTITUDE

BELIEF IN VENTURE

FINANCIAL COMMITMENT

BUILDS TRUST, TEAM PLAYER, COMPETENCE, RELIABLE

---

Source: International Capital Resources

tion to a problem. Sometimes the visionary starts with a blank sheet of paper and develops something new because he or she understands the market or the technology. Other times, he or she diagnoses a unique combination of existing technologies. For example, a recent client has effectively combined CD ROM technology with developments in biochip technology, creating a capability for conducting basic laboratory testing with the same elements in CD ROMs that are used in personal computers. Enthusiasm, courage, patience, persuasiveness, and tenacity—these are also among the traits of a successful fund-raiser. Enthusiasm will enable you to generate zeal for the venture. If you do not exude enthusiasm over your venture, who will? Nor is courage any less imperative, since asking people for money is hardly the favorite pastime of even the most gregarious and bold among us. Also indispensable are the patience to endure setbacks and the ability to remain persuasive. Persuading a person that an enterprise is worthwhile and will generate a fair rate of return demands tenacity, the dogged determination to see the funding process through.

Another trait of the successful fund-raiser involves adopting a "no-is-for-now" attitude. In other words, deal with rejection in a positive light. Refuse to take "no" for an answer. Deflect it. After all, "no" often means "No, I'm not interested now" or "No, I'm not interested in the deal as it is presently structured." Probe. Make suggestions: "What if I were to involve another investor? Might you be interested then?" Or, "If I were to restructure the venture, would you be more inclined to invest?" Plumb your present target for the names of investors likely to think about the deal. Above all, remember not to take "no" personally. Take "no" to mean "No, not at this time." Take it to mean that you have not yet furnished the investor with enough reasons for saying "yes." Above all, do not let a "no" alienate you to the extent that you alienate your potential investor.

A person seeking funding for a venture must radiate confidence. No one can expect an investor to believe in a venture in which the entrepreneur or inventor has no confidence. A lot of the confidence that the entrepreneur sports in the venture can be demonstrated by the percentage of net worth the entrepreneur is willing to stake in the venture. So the entrepreneur needs to commit "sweat equity," that is, forgo a salary, perhaps until the investors receive their money. In this way, the entrepreneur demonstrates financial commitment, a commitment vital to the success of the venture.

Finally, there is the matter of building trust, without which no venture is likely to get launched, much less sail smoothly. Just as you build a database one entry at a time, you build financing one relationship at a time. People become involved only in relationships that improve their self-image. Thirteen-year-old George Washington listed among his 110 "Rules of Civility": "Associate yourself with men of good quality if you esteem your own reputation." Whether young George was capable of such mature thinking at so early an age or simply copying Roman maxims in his notebook, the point remains the same: People are not likely to get involved in relationships that may lower their self-esteem.

Build trust with others by being honest, by responding candidly to all issues. Things can get sticky; make them less so by confronting possible problems at the start. If you have had a problem with alcohol or other drugs, do not wait until the other party's private investigator uncovers the information. Confess—as personal and painful as it may be. A confession can turn a negative into a positive. Be able to look someone in the eye and explain your situation as no one else can.

## IS YOUR RISK FINANCEABLE?

Before embarking on the path to raising capital, the entrepreneur asks three important questions: Is the deal financeable? Am I personally financeable? Is the risk in the deal financeable?

In order to assess the risk of your financeability, our research has identified six areas that investors focus on in their assessment of an investment (see Exhibit 2.4). In our experience, if three or more of these risks arise, a red flag halts the investor.

The first of these is management risk: Will the management team stick together? We've termed this risk "team risk." Do the members of the management team get along with one another? In giving birth to the company, will the team be able to work through the highs and lows of the entrepreneurial experience?

---

Exhibit 2.4  **IS YOUR RISK FINANCEABLE?**

1. Will management stick together?
   (Team Risk)
2. Could market change and impact acceptance?
   (Business Strategy Risk)
3. Is there still growth ahead?
   (Product/Technology Risk)
4. Anything brewing in market that could affect your company?
   (Market Risk)
5. Will manufacturing/R&D work as planned?
   (Operations Risk)
6. Financial performance of venture to date
   (Financial Risk)

Source: International Capital Resources

The second risk involves market change and the team's ability to accept the impact. This risk relates to business strategy and how well the management team has thought through its business strategy and done its homework relative to what's happening in the market and, moreover, the implications this could have for the plan they have outlined in its documentation.

The third area of the risk in your deal focuses on whether growth still lies ahead. Is a visionary leading the early stages in the development of the product or the market, or is someone riding in the tail wind of the lead racing car? Do we really have someone putting the technology together, someone with the courage to be a leader?

Fourth in assessing the risk in your deal stresses the sensitivity of the entrepreneur's ear to the vibrations of the marketplace. What out there might affect the company? Sometimes entrepreneurs get so close to their own technology, so close to the features of their own deal, so close to developing the business plan, to putting the management team together, to raising the money, that they overlook the pulse of the market. Entrepreneurs must not ignore market information. They do so at their own peril. Entrepreneurs can ill afford a business plan that lacks a sense of the market within the last six to twelve months—a time period after which market circumstances practically guarantee a shift in technology.

Operations risk has to do with the extent to which the manufacturing plan can be worked out, and whether the research and development by the company lead to investor confidence. Will the prototype and product that issue from the manufacturing process meet the time frames and cost projections?

Last comes the critical financial risk, a risk that takes different forms: How much money has been invested into the company to date? Has the company raised any money, or will the company need to approach investors beyond family and friends? How much financing needs to occur before there emerges proof of the concept? (This assessment relates to capital intensity discussed earlier.) Another assessment risk concerns the company's ability to generate revenues and/or profits within a reasonable period of time—typically twelve to eighteen months. And what was the financial performance of companies that the principals of the management team have been involved with previously? All of this, as well as the actual financial stability of the managers themselves, will be considered as part of the financial performance of today's venture.

## THE BENEFITS AND DISADVANTAGES OF EQUITY

Since private placement investments are primarily equity, it's best to know equity's advantages and disadvantages. Certainly, the private placement market is booming. Citing Securities Data (a tracker of the financial markets), *Inc.* magazine told us in 1998 that more than $250 billion was invested in these deals during the first three quarters of 1997. "That amount," *Inc.* revealed, "was nearly twice the $128-billion private-placement level of 1993." And in addition to other potent forces, demographic trends include the expected continued increase by baby boomers in investments and savings for at least the next decade. Clearly, the entrepreneurial community has solid reasons for expecting an increasing array of financial options.

Exhibit 2.5 shows, in millionaire households, the dramatic shift in financial services from deposits and loans to investments. Back in 1992, only 31 percent of millionaire households put money into bank deposits; 66 percent put money into equity investments. By the year 2000, 83 percent will be placed into equity investments and only 15 percent put in deposits. According to the Federal Reserve Study of Consumer Financing, First Manhattan Consulting Group, the U.S. Census Bureau, PSI, and Nations Bank estimates, by the year 2010, the number of equity

Exhibit 2.5 **THE SHIFT TO EQUITY INVESTMENTS**

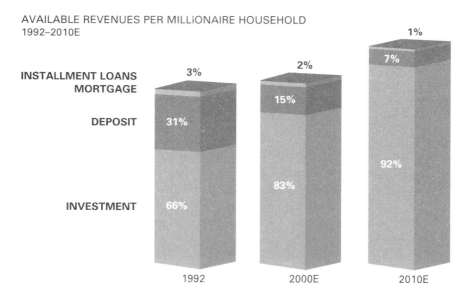

The shift in financial services from deposits and loans to investments is dramatic for millionare households

AVAILABLE REVENUES PER MILLIONAIRE HOUSEHOLD
1992–2010E

INSTALLMENT LOANS
MORTGAGE

DEPOSIT

INVESTMENT

Source: Federal Reserve Survey of Consumer Finances, First Manhattan Consulting Group, U.S. Census Bureau, PSI, Nations Bank Estimates

investments in this market will increase to 92 percent of the discretionary net worth available.

We remain marketing and business development oriented; we try to keep people sensitive to the market. For this reason, we urge entrepreneurs to package their deals in a way that the market is opened to. And what the market is undoubtedly open to are investors looking for equity transactions. Private equity is important for people trying to raise money because that is what investors want. There is money throughout the marketplace, with private equity available for companies at every stage of development.

As Exhibit 2.5 illustrates, equity investments are increasing over time, and thanks to the baby boomers, money is there for these projects too. Wealth is increasing in the United States. Large numbers of people are putting money in individual retirement accounts (IRAs), and they have the ability to invest those IRAs as they see fit. And in most cases, part of that investment will doubtless be in equity transactions. Thus comes an increasing amount of capital for people to make equity investments, creating an increasing pool of capital for companies trying to raise equity.

Since private placement investments are primarily equity, it is best to know equity's advantages and disadvantages. (See Exhibit 2.6.)

First, the advantages. Benefits accrue to the private equity alternative. The private equity infusion of funds means growth capital without servicing a debt. It also means that the venture maintains financial flexibility, which, in turn, enhances the capacity to borrow for funding other opportunities. Further, the private equity alternative permits access to the venture at an earlier date than would be the case in more traditional capital situations. And foremost among advantages is the added value offered by

---

Exhibit 2.6 **ADVANTAGES/DISADVANTAGES OF EQUITY**

| ADVANTAGES | DISADVANTAGES |
|---|---|
| • Capital | • Dilutes ownership |
| • Permanent capital that increases company's net worth, borrowing capacity, and overall financial strength | • More expensive than debt when successful |
| • Enhance credibility | • No means of reversing the transaction |
| • No scheduled repayment | • Give up control/flexibility |
| • No personal liability | • Difficulty finding investors |
| • Help | |
| • Accountability | |

Source: International Capital Resources

the angel investor. In most cases, private angel investors have broader agendas than just return of investment. They look for a deeper involvement—other types of return beyond the financial. Therefore, the entrepreneur can benefit from this broadened agenda by accepting help from the investor, and by being accountable. Finally, there is less market risk, since, historically, the cost of private equity has remained quite stable.

At the same time, however, equity carries its burden of disadvantages. Private equity is expensive, requiring an internal rate of return of at least 30 percent to be attractive. It also provides potential for significant dilution of current shareholders. In a word, equity diminishes ownership. And just as investors bring added value to the company, they often want governance—a seat on the board, perhaps, or an important managerial post. Further, an equity transaction can stretch itself out, taking four to six months, or longer, to close. With an equity investment, investors will require a clearly articulated three- to five-year strategy. Equity will become more expensive than debt if the company is successful. In effect, then, an equity investment offers no means of transaction reversal; that is, you marry your investment partner—unless he or she wants to divorce you. Finally, to reiterate what may be the greatest barrier to persons embarking on a successful private placement: Private investors, prizing their privacy, are extremely difficult to locate.

So problems with the private equity alternative do exist. But before reaching this stage of the venture, there comes the disadvantage preceding all the others: the difficulty of finding high-net-worth angel investors, the individuals involved in private placement investment.

## MAKING YOUR SEARCH FOR INVESTORS MORE EFFICIENT

The difficulty in locating the high-net-worth angel investor generates a critical question: How is the high-net-worth private or business angel investor different from bankers, professional money managers, venture capitalists, and institutional investors? The difference is that the private investor *does not have to invest*. For this reason, the private investor has a different take on things. So the procedures used to sew up a Small Business Administration loan, to secure subordinated debt financing from an institution, or to approach conventional venture capitalists are not appropriate for accessing the private investor.

Therefore, the conventional wisdom and underlying assumptions that drive the search for funds need to be reexamined. International Capital Resources finds that many people approach private investors using the same models and same behavior used to obtain a loan or stir the interest of venture capitalists. But the principles that guide success in finding money among these other markets simply fail with the private investor. Why?

One reason has already been discussed: These investors protect their privacy. Here is another reason, also briefly mentioned earlier: The private investor's reasons for investing are not always exclusively economic. Therefore, the entrepreneur faces difficulty in judging which approach to adopt in trying to locate, attract, and build a relationship with angel investors.

## THE PROBLEMS WITH CONVENTIONAL WISDOM

In locating an angel who can work financial miracles, many entrepreneurs employ the conventional wisdom. Its precepts are predicated on the procedures applied to financing from banks, professional venture capitalists, and institutional investors. Such a strategy is handicapped. What are these precepts and why don't they work?

In their advice for accessing capital, many popular business books suggest networking for your venture in the hope of securing promising referrals by talking to your accountant, attorney, doctor, dentist, or some other adviser. *Networking* is a term widely used, yet it refers to a concept often misunderstood. Networking is overworked; more important, networking works indirectly. Instead of approaching the investor directly, networking lodges faith in the hands of someone else, hoping that he or she will be able to help.

Another tenet of conventional wisdom proposes that you concentrate largely on people who understand your industry, in the belief that staying abreast of it will link you to people familiar with your type of company. This presumably qualifies them as investors for your venture. But industry specialization is only one consideration in an investment decision; many other things can influence a private investor's preference. Remember, we said that the private investor's agenda can be significantly more diverse than merely considering internal rate of return or industry experience and specialization. For example, investors may show more interest in investing in a business geographically close to home. Or the investors may be interested in a venture outside the industry in which they have spent the last 25 years. Or they may be looking for something exciting and fun, perhaps a change from what has long since become drudgery. This type of investor may be looking for something new and different. Thus, overreliance on industry sources narrows rather than widens the pool of prospective investors.

Still another principle of conventional wisdom promotes faith in such intermediaries as finders, brokers, and investment bankers, who should be able to provide the names of parties willing to invest in your venture. But investment bankers charge a fee—in many cases a front-end fee—against the promise of a fund-raising best effort. Moreover, much of the front-end fee of investment bankers comes not from developing contact with investors but from preparing documents, which normally costs more money. In 1993, according to the highly regarded VentureOne of San Francisco, 191 companies raised $6.9 billion through IPOs. Investment bankers earned fees of more than $450 million collectively on those deals alone. Chiefly at the earlier stages, ICR recommends that you focus on direct contact with the investors, initially more efficient than conducting a search through intermediaries.

Conventional wisdom also advises that you advertise. Just peruse the Mart section in the Thursday afternoon edition of the *Wall Street Journal*, it says, and you will discover numerous business opportunities advertised there, thinly disguised as solicitations for investors. These types of classified advertisements supposedly provide another vehicle that entrepreneurs can rely on in order to generate investor contacts. But be warned: In many places, advertising a private placement investment is illegal. This restriction has been eased in some states, for example, in California. The California Corporate Code's new 25102(n) statute permits small business entrepreneurs to advertise for wealthy angel investors. But restrictions have not been eased everywhere. Even where it is legal, the entrepreneur must be cautious. An advertisement for a private placement investment that reaches inappropriate or unqualified investors could instigate legal problems about the way these investors were solicited. By definition, a private placement investment is the limited offering of securities to a small group of private investors with whom the entrepreneur has an *established relationship* and whom the entrepreneur *believes are appropriate and qualified* for that investment opportunity. So be careful with advertising, regardless of the extent to which others may engage in it.

Last, conventional wisdom advises entrepreneurs to turn *finally* to family and friends, people who know them, have the money to invest, and retain a genuine interest in supporting the entrepreneur. Family and friends should be the *first*—not the final—source you entreat after you have personally invested a substantial portion of your net worth. Many people eventually appeal to family and friends after networking, canvassing industry, and ferreting out investment bankers. Family and friends and one's own resources should be the initial sources of capital at the earlier stages of financing a venture.

On close examination, then, conventional wisdom may be conventional, but it hardly qualifies as wisdom. In Chapter 3, our strategy offers a better way, a plan that works.

# 3

# A Strategy That Works

*In practical life, time is a form of wealth with which we are stingy.*

Italo Calvino, *Six Memos for the Next Millennium*

## AN "INEFFICIENT" MARKET DEFINED

Early on, the investment banking business tagged the private capital market as "inefficient." When investment bankers or venture capitalists portray the private placement investment or angel market in this way, precisely what do they mean? Why "inefficient"?

As these investment bankers or venture capitalists quickly point out, no professional analysts are available to tout the offerings or issue research reports—activities characteristic of major investment houses in their effort to increase interest in stock offerings. The closest thing to this activity in the private market may be the *Private Equity Review*—which has merged the *California Investment Review* and the *Investor Connection*—founded to provide just such information about activity in the geographical area within which International Capital Resources practices.

Largely, however, market information on private offerings is limited. For one thing, no SEC requirement forces disclosure of such offerings, a notable dispensation for private investors who, above all else, prize their privacy. Moreover, by the very nature of the transactions, the market is inefficient and inconvenient for buyers as well as for issuers and sellers. Were you choosing to sell a publicly traded stock, for instance, you could pick up the phone, call your broker, get a bid on your stock, and sell it—none of which is an option with a private placement investment. You possess, instead, an illiquid commodity. Finding another angel investor whose idiosyncratic investment criteria match your own becomes problematic, not unlike trying to sell your outlandish, custom-built hot rod. Who is likely to match the affection you feel for that machine? Crafting it was one thing; marketing it, quite another.

So entering the direct investment market becomes expensive, often prohibitively so. Professional assistance in private placement investments may include a finder to locate fellow investors with whom to share risk and an attorney to keep you within the legal bounds of a venture—restrictions on advertising, for example. Furthermore, in private placement investments, no liquidity exists. Unloading your stock may rush you headlong into restrictions: You may be bound by terms and conditions requiring you to hold the stock, or you may confront tax implications of dumping stock too early, thus having to pay excessive taxes on capital appreciation or capital gains.

Also, the conditions of the exchange itself remain fuzzy, undefined. How do you transfer a privately owned stock from one private investor to another? Transferring privately owned stock activates a different type of transaction from that of holding stock in a public offering. Also, you may find yourself having to go back to the company in order to transfer documents to another party. Moreover, oftentimes there is no company history, leaving all financial information about the venture resting on "blue sky," that is, exclusively on projections. This circumstance leaves the investor unable to accomplish a fixed analysis, even through due diligence. Therefore, the time dedicated to due diligence remains unspecified, relinquished entirely to the subjective values of this type of analysis. Finally, entrepreneurs, with the aid of their securities attorneys, tend to draw out these transactions, making them more expensive, complicated, and time-consuming.

Therefore, in this inefficient market, the problem arises of how to maneuver it more proficiently.

## A STRATEGY THAT WORKS

In accessing the affluent, hard-to-find private investor, ICR advocates a strategy different from the conventional suggestions masquerading as wisdom. In contrast, our answer to proficiently searching for investors is shown in Exhibit 3.1.

### Build a Capitalization Strategy

Many companies fail in their capitalization strategy because their initial capital is insufficient to support operations through to the next milestone. Raise *only enough* funding to accomplish that next step in the venture's development. This strategy will save the company from surrendering too much when its valuation is lowest. Many companies raise too much money too early, while not spending enough time to understand their financial requirements. This understanding requires analysis and forecasting of cash flow and timing the offerings so that achievement of the

Exhibit 3.1   **HOW TO INCREASE EFFICIENCY IN THE PRIVATE PLACEMENT PROCESS**

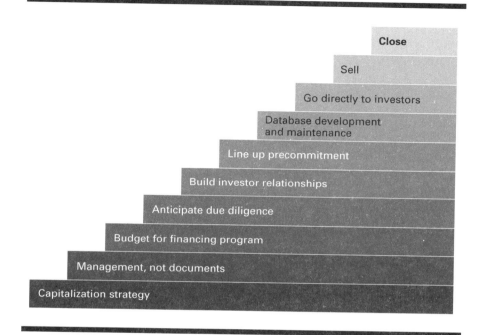

Source: International Capital Resources

next milestone represents a significant step down in the investor's perceived risk in the venture.

Reducing the perceived risk associated with the venture improves the valuation in the following rounds, letting the company raise more money while ceding less of it. Recently one entrepreneur took a company public, raising $23 million. He confided to us, however, that by the end of the process he owned less than 5 percent of it—a perfect example of failing to develop a sound capitalization strategy. To his deep regret, he surrendered too much of the company when its valuation was low. (Valuation is fully discussed in Chapter 12.)

As you develop your capitalization strategy and establish clear milestones, you need to understand the correlation of *stage of development* with private capital sources and the amount of capital required at critical stages in the development of the venture. Coopers & Lybrand completed a study in 1994 that looked at 328 manufacturing and service companies that successfully achieved sales of $1 million to $50 million in the period between 1989 to 1994. They found that it took an average of 28 months for successful companies to pass from seed and start-up through survival on to the initial market growth stage.

One of the interesting findings is the correlation between the amount of capital needed at each of those stages and the source of the private capital. (See Exhibit 3.2.) During the seed and start-up stages, these companies successfully raised on average between $75,000 and $150,000 from those investors who had an affinity for the entrepreneur and the founders. Typically, these individuals included family, friends, neighbors, acquaintances, business associates, professional colleagues, and providers of professional services to the entrepreneurs, who often were also investors.

During the survival stages, generally, these ventures successfully raised $200,000 to $210,000 from individuals and investors, a group that typically includes suppliers and distributors, future suppliers and distributors, employees, potential employees, and customers—all people with an affinity for the technology or product. Add to this gathering those other individuals, such as manager-investors, who invested in the venture and took an operational management position. These are the people who form the backbone of individual participatory investment.

Last, during the initial market growth stage of their development and financing, these companies typically raised $450,000 to $500,000

Exhibit 3.2  **CORRELATION OF STAGE OF DEVELOPMENT WITH PRIVATE CAPITAL SOURCE**

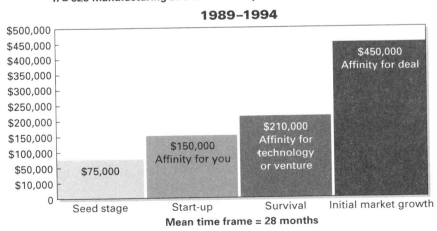

*n* = 328 Manufacturing and service companies achieving $1 to $50M sales

**1989–1994**

Source: International Capital Resources

from nonrelated individuals and investors and groups with an affinity for the deal. These likely were private placement investments or direct public offerings, institutional venture capital investments, or bank loans and credit lines arranged by the principals.

This chart (Exhibit 3.2) on the correlation of stage of development with the private capital source provides a road map, complete with stopping-off points along the way. You should avoid trying to tap family members and friends at a stage of development requiring an amount they cannot contribute, say $500,000. Likewise, why approach manager-investors for an amount in this range when they typically invest only $100,000? The idea is to gain a sense of the best source for capital at each stage of the development of your venture. As you develop a capitalization strategy, keep in mind the amounts of capital typically being raised at these pivotal points in a developmental-stage company.

## Focus on Management, Not Documents

Although development of the professionally prepared business plan (see Appendix B) is important to funding, only implementation of the ideas contained in it bear value. We emphasize the importance of the Investment Opportunity Profile over the business plan as a marketing tool during the initial stages of investor development and as a way to inspire, as well as assess, investors' interest in the venture. And while we affirm that investors invest in people, not documents, this does not make business plans unimportant. In the beginning, you want to focus on management, but eventually you will need documentation to enunciate your vision. Documents may not be crucial in the early going, but be assured their time will come. Never minimize their importance.

But before preparing documents, you should create a number of company boards, particularly a board of directors or an advisory board. A respected board of directors is one of the most important credentials that a private company seeking funding can possess, and it is central to potential investors being able to distinguish the "pedigrees" from the "mutts."

If you have trouble developing a board of directors because of issues relative to the liability exposure of directors and officers, an advisory board is an alternative that will allow you to bring people into the organization, provide counsel, gain the benefit of the board relationship while lessening their legal exposure.

In addition, identify respected technical advisers and establish professional advisory relationships; they are indispensable to a winning team. Assembling a credible fund-raising team and establishing constructive and cooperative relationships among its members should also be a high priority. The team will include not only the entrepreneur, founders, managers, and board of directors but also the attorney, accountant, or certified public accountant (CPA), advisory board members, technical advisers, investment bankers, and any placement agent intermediary or finder assisting in the transaction. Even more important—and this is reiterated by private investors—you must assemble a credible management team instead of placing faith in the capability of documents alone to generate investor interest. (See Exhibit 3.3.)

It's also important to develop a complete set of references you can use with your investors to prepare for the due diligence process. To clarify, sometimes you need technical advisory support. Technical advisers possess different proficiencies. For example, some advisers can provide support in developing the business plan, or in completing a competitive analysis for the marketing section, or in assisting in obtaining patent protection.

Next, though perhaps less recognized as part of the team but in our experience absolutely critical, is your including any lead investors or investors initially interested in the deal among your resources and reference list. This kind of thinking helps you use all the resources available in building the most effective team with which to move forward. Once you've exhausted your own resources and that of family, friends, and referrals, consider a placement agent or other resources for investor introduction as an important part of the fund-raising team with which to build your organization, so you do not spend too much time marshaling investor interest and support.

Finally, it will pay to remember that venture documents are like milk: They spoil with time. An experienced entrepreneur carrying only

Exhibit 3.3  **A WINNING TEAM FOR THE PRIVATE PLACEMENT**

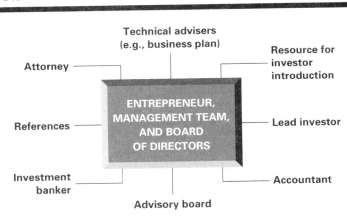

Source: International Capital Resources

a "B" plan will always be financed over a novice with an "A" plan or product. Remember what we have stressed about funding: Business plans do not get funded; people get funded.

## Budget for the Financing Program

It takes money to raise money. This means building a budget to raise money. While every exuberant entrepreneur believes that skilled professionals will line up to work on commission for the privilege of being associated with his or her venture, good help willing to work "on the come"—that is, on commission—is hard to find. Worse, you'll get what you pay for—nothing.

In fact, many entrepreneurs exhaust their resources developing their product and spending money on attorneys and consultants in pursuit of venture documents. But money needs to be set aside to raise capital. Entrepreneurs commit a common error in using all their money for product development and for documentation, leaving no money to raise money.

Another risk unfolds here: Working "on the come" creates dependency on the commission for remuneration. In many cases an intermediary will operate outside your direct control during fund-raising. The concern is that since intermediaries work on commission, pressure will mount to persuade investors to close. The intermediaries may make inappropriate promises to investors, misrepresent the opportunity, or, in their exuberance, fail to disclose risk. This last circumstance especially adds to the hazard of employing people who work solely on commission.

In Exhibit 3.4 we outline expense items typically associated with raising capital which include a number of different expenses usually paid up front as well as fees that follow the completion of the transaction.

Estimates indicate that $10 million is required to get 0.5 percent of the mind of the U.S. market. Similarly, you will need financial resources to gain consciousness of the affluent, high-risk investors' market. So develop a budget, detailing the anticipated up-front costs of raising money and a realistic schedule allowing six to nine months to close the transaction. Remember to calculate these costs into your forecasts. Running out of money before raising capital or setting up unreasonable, overly optimistic funding schedules will create an atmosphere of desperation that will accompany you like a shadow in your discussions with investors and finally work against your financing goal.

For the entrepreneur new to raising capital, costs can be shocking. While raising private capital is less expensive than going to the public marketplace, costs still loom. However, no direct correlation exists between money spent and money raised. Some entrepreneurs may spend $5,000 to raise $1 million, while others will need to spend $25,000 to raise the same amount.

---

Exhibit 3.4  **EXPENSE ITEMS IN RAISING CAPITAL (6–25% of capital raised)**

| UP-FRONT EXPENSES | BACK-END FEES |
|---|---|
| • Development of a financing strategy<br>• Business plan, financing proposal, profiles<br>• Financial projections (accountant or CPA)<br>• Legal security documents (disclosure documents, terms sheet, investment agreement, stock purchase agreement)<br>• Printing<br>• Capital search<br>  —Profile<br>  —Travel<br>  —"Advertising"<br>  —Presentation materials<br>  —Telephone<br>  —Seminars<br>  —Postage<br>  —Printing<br>  —Other | • Investment banking<br>• Finders' fees<br>• Brokerage fees (e.g., sales commissions, underwriting fees, due diligence, processing costs, red-tape fees)<br>• Legal fees<br>• Offering fees<br>  —State and federal |

Source: International Capital Resources

To be sure of covering start-up costs, budget 4 to 7 percent of the amount to be raised in your capitalization program, figuring that during the first few months costs will outstrip investment capital raised. Then budget an additional 6 to 8 percent to cover the back-end fees. As any seasoned capital development professional knows, it costs money to raise money. It is "pound foolish" to operate on a tattered shoestring when a small investment can help you achieve your capitalization goal.

## Anticipate Due Diligence

Anticipation is a wonderful thing. It works wonders in all aspects of life. In tennis, for instance, being able to anticipate where your opponent's shot will land enables you to get in position to control the game. But tennis is not the only activity in which anticipation works to your advantage. In managing financing, for example, anticipating due diligence puts you in a position to accomplish your goal. Due diligence is the analysis you can be sure will be conducted by the investors and their advisers in order to determine your venture's strengths, weaknesses, future profitability, competitive position, and identifiable and possible risks.

Typically, the investor and/or agents such as attorneys, accountants, or private investigators perform due diligence in these cases. These are typically sophisticated and experienced businesspeople who will evaluate not only the venture but also you and your business and personal background.

An example of a recent due diligence case illustrates the point. A company was offered at a $1.6 million acquisition price, then was subjected to due diligence by one of ICR's partners. The principals of the venture stated that there was a net worth of approximately $1 million, plus off-balance-sheet assets of $600,000. The CPA conducting the due diligence requested the company's financial statements and tax returns. Subsequent analysis by the accountant showed operating losses of more than $800,000 for the previous 18 months, fraudulently prepared tax returns, and a $400,000 tax liability. Due diligence revealed the real value of the venture to be only $500,000.

The lesson for you is crucial: Know your own company thoroughly and hire competent personal advisers to assist you in preparing for due diligence.

Due diligence typically is best approached with full disclosure by admitting to yourself in advance those areas of the venture that reflect the strengths but that also unmask weaknesses and expose risks. Only by this procedure can you anticipate the questions that are sure to come and be able to address them honestly. So prepare in advance of meetings with investors all information necessary to support your answers. This becomes imperative, because during due diligence nothing less than your credibility is at stake.

In order to help you to anticipate the questions normally associated with due diligence, we have included a due diligence questionnaire in Chapter 13. The questionnaire represents the experience of clients who have successfully confronted due diligence. The questionnaire will prompt you to think about the questions and discuss them beforehand with the principals and the management team. By doing so the group can concur on appropriate answers.

As Exhibit 3.5 indicates, many factors go into investor due diligence, the preinvestment research that will verify your proposal's viability for receiving financing. This preinvestment research will scrutinize the skills and background of your management team, check references, examine the appropriate industry sector, interview customers and suppliers, assess product realization, study the potential of growth in the market and potential competitors, consult with technical advisers and other investors before investing, valuate, explore financial projections and other business attributes, and test the matchability of the deal with personal investment criteria.

We will have more to say on due diligence in Chapter 13—though from the investor's point of view. However, ICR partner and due dili-

---

Exhibit 3.5  **DUE DILIGENCE, PREINVESTMENT RESEARCH TO VERIFY PROPOSAL VIABILITY**

- Management team skills and background
- Reference check
- Industry sector research
- Customer/supplier interviews
- Product realization
- Market growth potential and competitors
- Consultation with others before investment
- Valuation
- Financial projections in investment proposal
- Other business attributes
- Fit/match with investor's personal criteria

Source: International Capital Resources

gence expert Jeff Ferries advises entrepreneurs not to be shy in conducting the same procedure on investors that investors conduct on them. Inquire about the investors' investment objectives and their track record of investments with companies of similar size and within the same industry. Ask questions about other investments in the industry that could present a conflict of interest. And clearly define what ongoing role the investor may want to play in the venture.

In further conducting due diligence, you should obtain references of the other investors and follow up on what the paperwork reveals. Also be clear about the financial terms of the investment before signing an agreement. Use professional advisers whose experience in anticipating problems can keep a bad situation from becoming worse. Use advisers who understand that you want to do the deal. (Avoid deal breakers.)

Ferries sends this pointed message to entrepreneurs: Be assertive in your due diligence of investors!

## Build Relationships with Prospective Investors

Even 13-year-old George Washington understood that people are motivated to acquire relationships that improve their self-image. Investors have different motivations for investing, just as they have different motivations for declining the opportunity. Still, people invest in people. This seems to be the sense of it: "I'm investing in you. If the association uplifts me, you have a better chance of gaining my contribution to the venture." By the same token, a transaction they think will lower their self-perception will keep them on the sidelines.

So in raising capital, you need to move outside meetings and toward building successful relationships with investors and their advisers; proceed beyond the one-dimensional professional level. The gimme-your-money-and-get-lost syndrome will no longer suffice—if, in fact, it ever has. *You always get the capitalist along with the capital.* To cultivate a relationship with investors, you must add value through the relationship. Properly managed, even investors who initially turn you down can end up providing feedback on your offering as well as guidance on your development and presentation. They can simultaneously provide you with a cost-effective way to cultivate investor referral. Again, those who refuse early may well become investors at a later, less risky stage of the venture's development.

In raising capital, also get to know prospective investors who inquire about your venture before you have contacted them. In 1994 more than $124 billion was donated to philanthropic causes, most of it by individuals, a substantial portion of which was raised by professional fund-raisers. As any successful fund-raiser will tell you, the key to getting a check is matching the donor with the cause. You see, there *is* such a thing as a $250,000 lunch!

To raise funds, gather information on prospective investors before any contact so that you can determine whether a match exists between them and your investment. Good research takes time, so if you cannot handle this yourself, private investigators with access to on-line databases can be an inexpensive and efficient resource for gathering and packaging the necessary information preceding your meeting with prospective investors.

So just as you build a database of investors one name at a time, you build funding one relationship at a time. Take the time to understand the personalities of these investor contacts; find out what they expect out of their relationship with you. Accelerate this process by getting comfortable with their advisers. Take the time to understand their concerns: for example, the intergenerational transfer of wealth. Learn about their favorite charities and pastimes. Expand your relationship within the investor's family. As we have pointed out, spouses are increasingly involved in investment decision making. You and your firm may even be able to speed the investment education of the children of these middle-aged private investors, children who have reached an age when investments may have begun to pique their interest.

Assembling profiles of possible investors becomes another way of building relationships. Three types of profiles exist: demographics, psychographics, and—our choice—biographics. Demography categorizes information by gender, race, age, geographic locale, and so on. Psychographics measures such things as values and attitudes: "How do you feel about the job the president is doing? Excellent? Good? Fair? Poor? No opinion?" Or "What's your opinion of the NRA? Favorable? Unfavorable?

No opinion?" Psychographics aims at the individual's thoughts and feelings, opinions often extrapolated for a look at their broader implications.

The third type of profile originates from the new field of biographics. It is based on the research techniques of case studies and content analyses that assess the personal history and lifestyle of the individual. A biographical profile gathers not only names and addresses—where people live can tell you a great deal about them—but also professions, positions, memberships, family histories, personal histories, financial positions, and investment histories. This is the kind of information ICR has collected in its database, the kind of information that lets it function successfully as a matchmaker as well as figure out the best ways to contact potential investors.

As John D. Rockefeller Jr. concluded, "The more you know about the person you are asking for a gift, the better is your chance of getting it."

## Line Up Precommitment

The entrepreneur can increase efficiency in finding investors by lining up a commitment from them before spending time and money on preparing documents. Private placement investments involve two types of documents: (1) the business plan and (2) the private placement investment memorandum or risk disclosure document. Basically, the business plan proposes reasons *for* investing, while the risk disclosure document suggests reasons *against* investing.

Ironically, many entrepreneurs incur $10,000 to $25,000 in legal fees to prepare a risk disclosure document—even *before* building interest in the venture—which presents investors with reasons why they should *not* invest. Interestingly, ICR found in its own study of a sample of nearly 600 private investors that 50 percent were willing to invest *without* a business plan. This reflects a substantial difference between the informal, private investor and the venture capital community, which usually does insist on a business plan. Therefore, it makes little business sense to be overeager about preparing an in-depth business plan and hiring consultants. Nor does it make sense to enlist attorneys and accountants to prepare private placement memoranda before finding out whether any investors besides yourself are interested in your deal.

At ICR we have found the Investment Opportunity Profile (IOP) to be *the* treasured tool in stimulating investor interest prior to doling out money on documents. The IOP, an investor-oriented executive summary, supplies the investor with enough information to decide whether to look at a complete package of documents. After submitting an IOP to a number of prequalified investors, the entrepreneur will feel confident about spending time and money on more documents.

In a published survey, The Capital Network made a dramatic finding about investors in a network: Unsolicited plans rarely receive funding. The IOP helps improve this low funding rate. An excellent summary tool, the IOP was developed in close cooperation with investors in the ICR network and includes the information investors say they need. The IOP, then, speeds up qualifying the investors while it assists in developing confidence about precommitment. But what precisely do we mean by "line up precommitment"? What is its operational meaning? How do you accomplish "precommitment"? You do so by making certain that you are talking to real investors. Again, the Investment Opportunity Profile becomes strategic. The IOP helps in developing confidence about precommitment and at the same time speeds up the qualifying of investors.

Developing confidence about precommitment leads us directly to the business of qualifying investors. And how is that best accomplished? Based on our experience, the way to get frank answers is by asking frank questions—of the investors themselves. Who better to answer them? Exhibit 3.6 outlines those questions: Has the investor previously invested in deals that address this market? What is the dollar amount he or she has invested within the past year in this type of deal? How typical is that amount? What degree of familiarity has he or she with this particular industry? What motivation is involved? What does the investor feel he or she needs to know about this particular investment opportunity? How much capital is available to him or her? Will he or she coinvest? Do the criteria match the deal? How long will the investor's due diligence take? What most successful investment

---

Exhibit 3.6 **KEY QUESTIONS FOR QUALIFYING ANGEL INVESTORS**

- Has investor invested in deals that address this market?
- Dollar amount of investment of this type made in last year? Typical investment size? How many per year?
- Familiarity with industry?
- Motivation to invest?
- What does investor need to know about the opportunity?
- How much capital is available?
- Does investor coinvest with others?
- Does investor's criteria match parameters of your deal?
- How long does investor's due diligence process take?
- All-time greatest investment investor would like to make again?
- Preferred security or deal structure?
- Time until liquidation?
- Is investor willing to meet in person?
- Has investor read the plan?

Source: International Capital Resources

would the investor like to make again? What security or deal structure is preferred? How much time is expected to reach liquidation? Is the investor willing to meet in person with the entrepreneur? Has the investor read the business plan?

Are these questions *easy* to ask? No. *Must* they be asked? Absolutely. These are the questions that must be asked if the deal has any chance of moving forward.

## Aggressively Manage Database Development

The cost of developing a proprietary high-net-worth investor database goes beyond those expense items listed in Exhibit 3.4.

During the last three years, for instance, ICR has invested more than $300,000 in developing a proprietary database of more than 8,200 high-net-worth investors. On average, ICR spends more than $10,000 a month to service current and new contacts and to maintain a system of up-to-date information on investors. These funds are used to conduct a number of programs that generate investor inquiries. Expense items beyond those cited in Exhibit 3.4 can be added when you attempt direct contact with new investors, including access fees, networks, on-line services, conferences, and the purchase of directories.

Aggressive database development and maintenance practices begin with using multiple sources to build your proprietary high-net-worth listing. Database development involves gathering pertinent information quickly and thoroughly on investors who have been located through investor contacts. We have already discussed ways of accessing investors directly; in later chapters we will provide more detailed information on contacting those resources.

Also, aggressive database development means qualifying the investors whose names you permit to be listed on your proprietary database. In our experience, the best way to qualify individual investors is by examining individual wealth data and characteristics—as opposed to relying on more generic statistical categories, such as what you might find in census data. Many times an in-person interview is the only way to obtain sensitive information, such as: previous investment behavior, financial holdings and portfolio (especially that segment of the portfolios placed into private equity), current status in a profession or industry—whether, in fact, they are entrepreneurs building a company or have previously done so—and, finally, net worth excluding home and automobile.

Another practice in database maintenance has to do with editing the database by hand on a daily basis, at least at first. Addresses, telephone and fax numbers, spelling of names, and other data eventually should be converted to a relational database platform, using software to assist in database management. Individuals building the database must be persistent in their contact with the investors on the list. Many ventures establish a small private newsletter as a way of staying in touch with the investors whom they have identified and with whom they hope to be working in the future.

More important, once the database achieves a large number of investors, it is no longer practical to manage that much data manually. So a point emerges when a relational database program has to replace the three-ring binder.

We will have more to say about building and maintaining an investor relational database in Chapter 9.

## Go Directly to Qualified Investors

The search for direct, private investors can be speedily accomplished in a number of ways. Trying to keep the securities instruments as simple as possible is one commonsense approach. Anticipating the due diligence questions—especially those coming early in your interaction with investors—is another. Be clear about your position, that is, whether you are seeking equity or debt, and what valuation you place on your venture.

Deal directly with the people who have money to invest. You have two options here. First, conventional wisdom suggests secondary research, suggesting that entrepreneurs new to raising capital should survey the public sources of information on affluent individuals. Poor advice. These public resources include real estate directories that list property values and the people who live on those properties, *Martindale-Hubbell Law Directory*, social registers, Junior League directories, lists of wealthy individuals in different geographical locales, *Who's Who*, and other directories and databases.

But there is a better way.

The second option—our choice—emphasizes primary research, which amounts to a market test of your investment opportunity. Don't rely on the resources everyone else uses. Instead, build your own proprietary database of prospective investor leads. Investment forums, meetings, and networks provide the opportunity.

Each year more than 60 major venture forums, conferences, investment meetings, and operating investment networks in the United States bring together entrepreneurs and investors. They are listed in Exhibit 3.7.

In these forums, conferences, meetings, and networks, individuals meet directly with investors, receive valuable feedback on their ventures and offerings, discover investor interest in the entrepreneurs' transactions, and obtain the critical contact information needed to follow up on prospective investors.

Various other forums and services present alternative resources for accessing high-risk private investment capital.

## Exhibit 3.7 INVESTMENT FORUMS, MEETINGS, AND NETWORKS

### Venture Forums and Conferences

Arizona Venture Forum
Florida Venture Capital Conference
Greater Midwest Venture Capital Coalition Forum
International Business Forum
Mid-Atlantic Venture Forum
New York Venture Capital Forum
North Carolina CEO Venture Forum
North Coast (Ohio) Growth Capital & Technology Showcase
North Jersey Venture Fair
Oklahoma Investment Forum
San Francisco Bay Area Venture Forum
Utah Venture Forum

### Investment Meetings

Atlanta Venture Forum
Connecticut Venture Group
Dallas Venture Capital Group
Houston Venture Capital Association
Information Industry Association's Investor Conference
Long Island Venture Group
Missouri Venture Forum
New England Venture Capital Association
New York Venture Group
Northern California Venture Capital Association
Pennsylvania Private Investors Group
Toronto Venture Group
Western Association of Venture Capitalists
Western New York Venture Association

### Investment Networks

The Capital Network
Environmental Capital Network
Georgia Capital Network
Investors Circle
Kentucky Investment Capital Network
LA Venture Network
Mid-Atlantic Investment Network
Northwest Capital Network
Pacific Venture Capital Network
Private Investor Network
Seed Capital Network
Technology Capital Network
Tennessee Venture Capital Network
Venture Capital Network of Minnesota
Washington Investment Network

**Open Forums**   Keynote speakers or presenting entrepreneurs highlight these extended breakfast, lunch, or dinner gatherings, which, besides offering question-and-answer exchanges, enable entrepreneurs to meet directly with investors.

**Panel Forums**   Panels of experts, a moderator, and presenting entrepreneurs are the features of these extended breakfast, luncheon, or dinner gatherings, which also offer time for entrepreneurs to meet directly with investors.

**Deal-mart Meetings**   Business plan submissions are used to screen entrepreneurs and businesspeople seeking financing. A mere handful of entrepreneurs meet with investors and/or venture capitalists, giving short, formal presentations. Entrepreneurs and investors have time to meet directly.

**Newsletters**   More than 3,000 financial subscription newsletters in the United States cover financial topics. Of these, about 10 to 20 percent relate to equity investment and/or early-stage capital investment. These newsletters provide information about important events where entrepreneurs can meet directly with investors. And these newsletters provide articles about fund-raising, letters from people who have been funded or who are seeking funding, case histories of transactions, and of businesses that have participated in various forums and conferences, and information about the organization or group that the newsletter is associated with or published by. For example, International Capital Resources publishes the *Private Equity Review,* which describes early-stage venture capital transactions occurring in northern California. The *Private Equity Review* is read monthly by more than 8,900 accredited high-risk private investors interested in this specialized area of investing. Its circulation has been increasing at the rate of 5 percent per month for the past two years. Newsletters read by investors provide a superb resource for finding out how to get in touch with appropriate investors.

**Association Membership Directories**   Usually available free to members and at a minimal fee to nonmembers, these directories list members along with professional and contact information.

**Referral Services**   These services formally and informally refer members and nonmembers to professionals qualified to meet the interested party's needs.

**Venture Fairs**   At fairs, prescreened entrepreneurs and businesses seeking funding set up booths and exhibits. Often involving large numbers of people and lasting more than a day, these fairs feature keynote speakers, presentations, special events, and social gatherings.

**Conferences**   Targeting a special industry or group, organizations set up booths and exhibits in convention halls. Conferences can involve large numbers of people. Presentations form an important part of these conferences, which may last two or three days.

**Seminars**   Seminar audiences are carefully targeted. Subjects focus on investing, raising capital, joint ventures, building partnerships with investors, business planning, and the like.

**Clinics**   More in-depth than seminars, clinics focus on a special audience, which takes a role in the proceedings. Thus, interaction is the key, leading to helpful advice targeted to the interests of the participants.

**Computer Networks**   Computer networking relies on databases linking investors and entrepreneurs seeking financing. Specific information about both parties offers the possibility of matchups. Chapter 8 has a list of computer matching networks operating in the United States.

**Computer Bulletin Boards**   Users seeking advice or information can access other entrepreneurs and investors as well as upcoming events and advertising of services.

Government is also getting the message about the efficiency of going directly to the investor. For instance, California's Commissioner of Corporations and others who appreciate the challenge of raising capital have helped enact laws that offer opportunities for private placement investment. Recently, a concerted effort by the SEC and the State Department of Corporations in California (SDC) has struck a balance between the need to protect investors and the need to offer emerging growth companies flexibility in their capital-raising activities.

While we have cautioned you about advertising, be aware that new laws are coming on the books. The California legislature has taken the lead in the United States with its innovative new program, enacting section 25102(n) of the California Corporate Code, mentioned in Chapter 2. This section allows entrepreneurs to advertise for angel investors following a simple, inexpensive procedure. (Section 25102(n) also grants an easing on dollar amount and number of purchasers, an action that may reverberate nationally.) Some believe that regulation is unfair to small companies, that there is no empirical evidence that small offerings are any more fraudulent than large offerings, and that, in general, compliance is strangling capital formation. However, this new law opens the way for angels—whatever their qualifications or wealth to earn their wings and halo—to use their own judgment in assessing the risks and rewards of an offering, just as the multimillion-dollar institutional investor does.

## Sell

You must invest time in the investor if you want the investor to invest money in you. The high-risk investment represents nothing less than a sale. Make no mistake: The private placement investment is a sale, and a sale involves obtaining a decision. Attracting a group of affluent, sophisticated coinvestors to write checks for high-risk ventures—in some cases far below investment-grade securities—relies on your ability to cultivate relationships.

However, mailing out business plans cold and following up with telephone calls *do not* constitute a sales strategy. Selling has changed in the 1990s. Many entrepreneurs cling to the notion that selling is beneath them, that it is too manipulative, but such thinking hinders their soliciting the high-net-worth private investor market. It behooves entrepreneurs to enlist their best efforts in this part of the strategy.

We have suggested that selling is different from times past because of the buyers, the regulations, the investment decision-making procedures, the presentations and promotions, and the packaging of investments. All are different.

First of all, high-net-worth investors today are very sophisticated, educated, and experienced. New laws, licensing regulations, and consumer- and investor-protection statutes and practices stifle old-fashioned exuberance. Worse, during the late 1980s and early 1990s, a number of brokers and their representatives were accused and convicted of duping clients. Considering the publicity that accompanies criminal wrongdoing in the sale of limited partnerships, closed-end funds, and other types of high-risk investments, investors have become justifiably cautious when they approach high-risk/high-return investments.

Investment decision making today belongs in many cases to committees. And at least as significant in private transactions is the influence of a spouse. In fact, in a recent study, ICR concluded that one of the major reasons for nixing investments is a spouse who does not feel comfortable with the deal.

Presentations are different as well. Today they include multimedia, portable computers, and communications supported by fax, desktop publishing, and other technological innovations. This electronic support has replaced much of the early face-to-face sales interaction. With technology spewing out such extensive documentation, due diligence can be carried on long before person-to-person meetings and presentations take place. And though no one asking for money should ever be farther than a handshake away, this modern communication technology may let prospective investors draw their own conclusions before the entrepreneur's closing sales presentation.

Today, the sale in these types of investments is not made by an investor-development person or salesperson, but becomes the final step in a meticulously orchestrated public relations marketing and venture advertising strategy. However, these circumstances do not make the basics of selling obsolete. The principals still need to know their venture and be able to explain their financing proposal. They must use sales and promotion and packaging techniques, plus learn the art of asking questions to get the answers they want. Like it or not, they must cultivate the ability to manipulate.

As Exhibit 3.8 illustrates, selling is a process. So here is the checklist you need to manage. First, make sure your presentations are face-to-face. Maintain a positive mind-set. If someone rejects you, don't be thin-skinned; realize that rejection may be because the risk is too great *now*. Enter the investor(s) in your database for later consideration. Be closely informed about the investor and be prepared by using Appendix B in this book to answer any questions might arise. Remember to pick the best person (not necessarily the CEO) to present your case to. Also remember to preview and practice the presentation before soliciting the investors. Two heads are always better than one; three are better than two; so present as a team, and during the presentation maintain eye contact, positive body language, and be selective about word choice. Of like importance is the clarity of your vision, of what you're trying to accomplish with your transparencies, and of the connection between your presentation and the investor's values. Don't ask for the money too quickly, but remember to ask for it. Don't underestimate the courtesy of a follow-up note. And don't forget to update your database.

Further, selling remains an activity; therefore, if there is no activity being managed, the result is no sale. Fundamental to the sale is under-

---

Exhibit 3.8 **SELLING PROCESS**

- Face-to-face
- Mind-set (attitude about money, rejection)
- Informed (venture, investor)
- Be prepared for questions/objections
- Select "best" person to present
- Preview before soliciting
- Present as a team
- Eye contact, body language, and word choice
- Content: clear vision/value connection
- Timing: do not ask too quickly
- Ask for the money
- Send a thank-you note or give a follow-up call
- Update database

Source: International Capital Resources

standing the *funnel* and the *pipeline*. The funnel represents the need to have a large number of targeted prospects interested in the deal, affluent enough to afford it, located reasonably close to you so that you can follow up, and savvy enough to understand your message in contacting them.

The funnel works like this: You need about 100 contacts in order to identify 10 interested parties. You need those 10 in order to get into 5 meetings with prospective investors. Those 5 meetings will lead to 3 presentations, from which you can initiate negotiations and finally close 1 investor. Then you will need the next 100 contacts so you can start over again. And, as we warned in Chapter 2, successfully raising capital involves being able to deal with rejection while persisting in your objective.

Once you have identified a qualified, interested prospect, the pipeline comes into play. You must begin to manage the prospect, moving the deal forward daily, if not hourly. Critical in managing the pipeline is fulfilling investor inquiries, getting documents to interested investors in a timely fashion, and getting the right documents to them based on *their* requests. Inherent in this step is listening closely to what the investor is asking for, as opposed to what *you* think the investor must need.

You must understand and manage the funnel and the pipeline in order to position yourself for the close.

Since sooner or later the handshake(s) will occur, Exhibit 3.9 delineates what the principles are behind the close. Basically, closing simply involves asking for the decision. For most people, trying to close a deal becomes a specter on the horizon. But in order to get into the position to ask for a decision, you're going to have to invest some time in the investors and listen closely to what they have to say. Remember, you can't

---

Exhibit 3.9 **THE PRINCIPLES BEHIND THE CLOSE**

- Ask for the decision.
- Invest time in the investor. Listen!
- Do not rush the close. By doing so you come off as desperate.
- Private investors do not have to invest. Focus on their interests, criteria.
- High-risk illiquid story securities are not bought, they are sold!
- Understand the sales "funnel": generate leads and manage the "pipeline" (selling process).
- Always know where you are in the sales process.
- No sales activity = no close.
- Prepare exhaustively for every investor interview.
- Do telephone follow-up with investor after all meetings.
- Participate actively in negotiation.
- Put any offer in correct legal form.

Source: International Capital Resources

rush things without coming off as desperate. Remember, too, that the key differences between private investors and traditional investors is that private investors don't have to invest. Therefore, doesn't it make sense to focus on *their* interests, on *their* criteria? And don't forget that what you're selling here is a high-risk, illiquid story security. So keep in mind that high-risk, illiquid story securities are not bought; they are sold. And what is selling? Successfully closing and asking for the decision.

## Manage the Close

In order to manage the close of your transaction, you must understand the sales process. Selling involves a minimum of eight activities: (1) prospecting, (2) qualifying, (3) building rapport, (4) making the presentation, (5) overcoming objections, (6) using trial closes, (7) closing the sale, and (8) following up.

The close is only one link in the chain, but, as the penultimate step, it depends on your having successfully managed the previous steps. To successfully manage the close, you must understand its single purpose: getting a decision.

Important in the relationship between the sales process and closing is knowing how near you are to a close. Therefore, you need to understand the steps in the sales process to close at the right time. Not surprisingly, if you do not know where you are in the sales process, you will not get to the place you want to be—closing the investor. Closing is the result of moving the investor to a decision. Therefore, if there are no sales, you have not positioned yourself to obtain a close. An indicator of whether you are positioning yourself for a close will come from monitoring your selling activity.

It is important to have a clear vision about the venture—its present and its future. Ask yourself what the value of the investment is to this investor. Fund-raisers understand the values of the people they contact. They understand, as should you, that different investors have different values. Approach each accordingly. Be able to explain the connection between your venture and the personal values of the investor.

Once a qualified, interested investor has been identified, you should request an appointment, normally by phone, to describe the investment directly to the investor. After setting the appointment, confirm it with a letter.

If you are inexperienced and alone in your venture, bring along your investment banker, your attorney, your accountant, and other people important to the closing meeting. Do not go in alone. Always present as a team; the power of a team effort works. Always practice and preview the close with your associates before you meet with the investor. Get a sense of exactly how the team will move to the close. Your team should review the business plan, other venture documents, and data on the investment. Principal authors of the material should attend the meeting with the investor to answer questions. In other words, prepare exhaustively for every investor interview and closing as if these were your *only* opportunities. If you do not, they will be.

Select the best salesperson to effect the close; do not close simply because you have the time or because you are the CEO. When the team meets with the investor—preferably at the investor's office—members should express their appreciation for the investor's time and trouble but move quickly to the business at hand. Explain how the investor's investment will be used and how much money is needed. Review the proposal page by page, answering any questions.

Exhibit 3.10 lists the elements of a successful presentation to investors.

As we indicated, essential to any close is having the guts to ask the tough questions. These critical questions should include the following: Are you an accredited investor? Is this deal of interest to you? Do you have the liquidity to make this investment? What portion of your portfolio are you putting into high-risk ventures? What is your minimum investment? When can you invest? What might be your financial capability to participate in the next round? Has our documentation made clear what the administrative steps are in putting your money into the transaction? These are the difficult questions. But they must be asked.

---

Exhibit 3.10 **PREPARING FOR THE INVESTOR PRESENTATION**

1. Qualify investors.
2. Present investment opportunity in bite-size pieces, and explain how these pieces fit together.
3. Focus on return on investment.
4. Present your story logically:
   - Overview
   - Your moneymaking track record
   - Basics: what, when, how, how much
   - Describe the market opportunity
   - Demonstration
   - Close with emphasis on your unique position in the market.
5. Use multimedia in your presentation.
6. Present realistic, defensible pro forma financial statements and assumptions. Present an accurate, realistic profit-making scenario.
7. Q&A—Be sincere, enthusiastic, professional, and listen to investor's comments, questions, and pay attention to nonverbal clues.
8. Practice over and over, every chance you get.

What qualities make a private investor a true prospect? The list is brief: investing capacity, interest in your deal, congruity between his or her preferred level of activity and the level of activity comfortable for you. In addition, the true prospect will have a tolerance for risk, a willingness to spend time on due diligence, an openness to developing a relationship, and an interpersonal response to the entrepreneurial team.

Near the end of the meeting, ask if you can call on the investor again to answer any questions and to learn of a decision. Set a date and time for a return visit. Thank the investor once again. Here are some things to keep in mind: Ask for the money face-to-face. Do not ask for it in a letter or over the telephone. Asking for money also demands that you justify your request, but accept a rejection gracefully, using it as an opportunity to clarify the investor's *inevitable* objections and concerns. Again, prepare for those objections and concerns by knowing your venture. Remember that the private investor does not have to invest.

The essence of the close is asking for the money. So be certain the investor understands the procedure for investing money in the venture. Do not, however, rush the close. Rushing the close, that is, attempting to close before completing all the other steps in the selling process, will result in your being perceived as desperate—and, as we have warned, desperation can quickly quash a deal. Timing the close well means not asking too early, but this does not mean that you should avoid an early close if one is in the offing.

Initiate return calls to the investor and any follow-up meetings only by mutual agreement. Keep communicating until you receive that final decision. But regardless of the outcome of the meeting, always send a thank-you note. This will keep the door open for future contact. Once the investor has been closed, acknowledge him or her by expressing your appreciation in person and in writing. Reaffirm directly to the investor that the investment will make a difference in the venture.

Finally, update your database with the information you have drawn from the meeting.

Another principle behind the close—and we've mentioned this before—involves investing time in the investor and time in developing a relationship if you want the investor to invest money in you. Private investors do not invest unless asked. In the investment process, they expect gratitude, respect, appreciation, dignified treatment, thoughtful use of their time, sincere interest in them as people, homework done on their background, some involvement in the venture, a focus on their interests. In short, they expect planning, time, attention. Attending to these details will bring investors into a meaningful relationship with the principals and increase the chances of an investment in the venture. Significant angel investments rarely come from strangers. Whether old or new, these investors have become friends.

## DREAMERS AND DREAM-MAKERS

As we declared at the outset, funding is an arduous task. But a lesson we have learned along the way may encourage you in your search for angels. Investors and entrepreneurs are people on opposite sides of a transaction, though they have more in common than might be obvious. For what is the real difference between founders with the dream of commercializing their idea into a $100-million-a-year company and the dream-maker who anticipates a return 20 times over an initial investment?

Let us demonstrate this point. One study of venture capital firms showed that only 6.8 percent of 383 investments placed into venture capital portfolio companies between 1969 and 1985 returned ten times or more the capital invested. More than 60 percent of those investments lost money or failed to exceed savings account rates of return. SBA studies have shown that just 50 percent of all start-ups survive their first year, and only 10 percent survive a decade. The statistics for investment failure in the venture capital industry run higher than the failures made by private investors.

The primary reason for such statistics rests on the obligation of professional venture capitalists to invest the money under their management. Fund managers must invest, causing them to become entangled in bad investments as they stretch for a clear winner. Private investors, on the other hand, do not have to invest. From this fact arises another: Experienced, prudent, private investors concentrate on avoiding a bad choice instead of trying to strike gold on the two, three, or four investments they have made.

But regardless of the number of investments, regardless of whether the investor is a self-made millionaire or an inheritor of wealth, each, like you, is a gambler and a dreamer. You share dreams and common ground on which to build a relationship.

It is difficult to reach high-net-worth, private investors. The competition for the attention of those with impressive personal wealth is brisk. The key, as with any marketing program, is to target qualified prospects and to use a mix of sources and resources to find them.

After diligent targeting and sourcing, meeting high-net-worth, direct investors amounts to plain hard work, persistence, and attention to detail. Moreover, your approach must entertain as well as incite interest. Consistent application of the principles set forth in this chapter will serve to develop investor awareness of entrepreneurs and those ventures that merit such attention. Sooner or later the persistent entrepreneur will capture the interest and investment of these high-risk investors when they are seeking new investments following a liquidation, or simply when they are in the mood for a change.

In conclusion, deals are the dependent—not the independent—variable. That is why the product must fit the customer and why the dreamer must be matched with the right dream-maker. Investors come to a situation with a portfolio, an asset allocation strategy, and an idiosyncratic tolerance level for risk. Except in some cases—following a windfall, perhaps, or an inheritance, a transfer of retirement pension assets, or sale of a business or stock—the investor will deal only within the context of that investment strategy. Take a lesson from this chapter: Focus on the customer, keeping in mind that in today's competitive market, the customer is the investor.

# Part 2

## The Angel Investor

# 4

# Alternative Sources of Capital

*We are at our human finest, dancing with our minds, when there are more choices.*

Lewis Thomas, "To Err Is Human"

## THE IMPACT OF POLITICAL AND ECONOMIC TRENDS ON THE ACCESSIBILITY OF CAPITAL

Capital is the coal that stokes the fires of entrepreneurship in the United States. No capital, no start-up. No capital, no expansion. This everyone knows. Particularly for start-ups, the more traditional sources of debt—credit unions, S&Ls, banks—have become less workable alternatives for raising capital. Moreover, despite all the federal programs—within just the SBA, for instance—not enough is being done to bolster this important macroeconomic element in our capitalistic society.

For the SBA program, for example, applicants must display more than just good character and management skills; they must demonstrate a history of earnings and a cash-flow record. Moreover, without collateral, and generally without a one-third capital contribution to the total cost of the project, applicants simply will not get the loan. The White House Conference on Small Business put it succinctly: "Small companies still face complicated state and federal requirements." What we have, then, is capitalism without the capital.

Even as the government has increased appropriations for SBA loans with the Small Business Guaranteed Credit Enhancement Act of 1993, even as it has permitted a capital gains exclusion for certain small business stock investments with the Omnibus Budget Reconciliation Act of 1993, and even as it has eased the burden of financial institutions lending to small business with the Capital Availability Program, capital continues to shrink. Adding to this shrinkage has been the increased investment of financial institutions in government securities.

However, some political and economic trends will influence the future attractiveness of higher-risk, early-stage investments. The government's tax incentive bill, for example, contains provisions that can stimulate investment growth. As the top marginal income tax increased to 39.6 percent, the ceiling on the capital gains rate on all asset classes was retained at 28 percent.

Besides, the IPO market is vigorous and looks to remain so. According to Sandy Robertson, chairman of Robertson, Stephens, and the manager of a number of venture capital funds, three macroeconomic trends are at work—and we will note a fourth. First, stock offerings are re-equitizing the economy, compensating for the de-equitizing in the 1980s when buyouts and mergers subtracted huge numbers of stocks. For example, Robertson cites that from 1980 to 1990, equity subtracted from the market totaled more than $500 billion. This trend has shifted since 1991 but still totals only $86 billion, leaving a substantial overhanging demand. Replacing debt on balance sheets of more established companies can make for a strong investment.

Second, low returns in the debt markets have shifted capital to equity markets; that is, new equity issues are soaking up the dollars pouring into mutual funds and pension funds. As Dan Levine of the *San Francisco Business Times* says, a massive psychological shift has taken place among investors in the stock market. Because of low interest rates and the rise of defined benefit plans such as the 401(k), the average investor has been transformed into a Wall Street powerhouse. Just look at the growth of Charles Schwab & Co. And keep in mind that 40 percent of all equity and bond investments are being made directly by the investor over the phone or through the mail—without the assistance of a broker.

Third, the quality of issues is strong and price/earnings ratios are beginning to rise toward the higher levels they hit before the 1987 crash. The IPO market shows signs of life. According to *The IPO Reporter*, 707 IPOs in 1993 raised an astounding $41.5 billion. According to a January 1999 *San Francisco Chronicle* article, "Internet Firms Topped IPO list in '98," it was another big year for IPOs, though not the banner year of 1997. In 1998, nationwide, 379 companies held IPOs; in 1997, there were 524 new issues. So the market did constrict. Furthermore, the top ten IPOs were all Internet-related. The only aspect to increase last year was in dollars raised. Thanks to some blockbuster deals, U.S. companies raised $33.4 billion from their IPOs, compared to $29.6 billion in 1997. At most, the stock market's recent dizzying gyrations may have caused some managers to delay or withdraw offerings. We do see a reduction in offering prices. However, by adjusting valuations, the IPO market will be kept alive by the more responsible underwriters. Also, as long as money keeps flowing into mutual funds, the IPO market will remain alive, though only larger, high-quality deals will likely be transacted.

A fourth macroeconomic trend is at work. While the tax benefits traditionally associated with R&D partnerships have largely been removed, debt vehicles for structuring transactions remain. In the event a loss occurs, the investor retains the ability to write off a substantial percentage of the loss. Also, provisions in the Omnibus Budget Reconciliation Act of 1993 have placed a capital gains tax ceiling on investments in risky start-ups when money is left for longer than five years. The act, having squeaked by in the House by two votes and having needed the vice president's vote to break a 50–50 tie in the Senate, drops the tax on capital gains from 28 percent to 14 percent upon liquidating stock in small business stock holdings or selling the company. This decrease applies to stock issued after the date of the bill's enactment, August 10, 1993.

The Omnibus Act serves as an example of useful government intervention. However, government action resembles the ringing of wind chimes. A occasional breeze can strike a pleasant note, but we can hardly expect to enjoy a sustained melody. So while here and there the government has become more responsive to the problems of capital availability, it is the market that drives public policy, not public policy that continuously drives the market.

## ALTERNATIVE SOURCES OF CAPITAL AND HOW THEY AFFECT EARLY-STAGE INVESTMENT

As Exhibit 4.1 illustrates, the array of alternative sources of financing offers many choices to the entrepreneur or inventor.

---

Exhibit 4.1 **MAIN, ALTERNATIVE, AND NEW EARLY-STAGE FINANCIAL SOURCES**

- Business angels—private placements
- Academic institutional research financing
- Venture capital (industry specific)
- Bootstrap financing
- Self-finance: savings, loans, credit cards
- Licensing technology
- Royalty
- Joint venture
- Venture leasing
- Family, friends, colleagues, and associates
- Economic development programs
- Transaction financing
- Strategic alliances
- Corporate investments (one new fund/week)
- Private equity funds
- Direct investing by financial institutions
- International financing—immigration investment
- Direct private offering
- Incubator-based financing
- Community loan development funds
- Barter investment

Source: International Capital Resources

**Corporate Investment and Strategic Alliances**  These methods involve entering into a contract to do business with a much stronger and better-known business partner. The shared prestige can boost the start-up's credibility. When properly structured, this strategic relationship benefits suppliers, customers, vendors, and distribution sources. It is a venture with complementary customers or technology. Corporate alliances involve long-term relationships, synergy with an existing product line, related products to feed into distribution, shared risk, industry contacts—all aspects encompassing resources beyond the funding itself. Moreover, corporate investment is more affordable than venture or institutional capital, resulting in a higher valuation and more equity than what comes from traditional or early-stage funding. Corporate investors, however, may not accommodate an exit strategy. U.S. companies are completing approximately 5,960 joint ventures or strategic alliances per year with foreign and other U.S. companies; the majority of these transactions involve only two companies and are joint ventures. Strategic alliances, however, take a long time to formulate.

**Lease Financing**  Lease financing possesses an inherent edge in raising funds because you use the equipment you lease as collateral. Advantages to leasing include avoiding a down payment. Leasing is an installment purchase that, at the expiration date, offers a few options: The lease may be extended; the leased items may be bought at par to their market value; or the lease ends.

**Licensing**  This method of financing involves entering into a contract to provide technology or a product or some other commodity to the licensee. The licensee, in turn, will provide a fee and/or a royalty based on revenues for specific benefits (e.g., rights to distribute within a defined territory for a specified time). The second party is granted the right by the owner of a product to manufacture, sell, or use it in some way.

**Franchising**  Similar to licensing, franchising requires the franchisee to pay for the right to sell the service or product of a franchiser in exchange for a fee and portion of the income from sales or profits. The franchiser may supply expertise, as in the case of McDonald University. Franchises involve virtually every kind of business. The franchiser may sell a single franchise or franchise a geographical territory. This alternative capital resource requires no debt service or loss of equity in the company. One firm sold ten franchises for $25,000 each, raising $250,000 to fund further growth. Also, the franchisees assume all costs for opening, staffing, and running new outlets as well as assuming all contingent liability. Franchises are responsible for 50 percent of total U.S. retail sales, although overcrowding has recently slowed the franchising movement.

**R&D Arrangements**   Like other alternatives in this list, R&D arrangements offer variations. Basically, however, an R&D limited partnership grants research and development funding to a company perfecting a technology. The limited partners stand to gain through tax benefits and substantial royalties. Depending on the details of the agreement, the company responsible for developing the technology also has options: to eventually buy the technology, to develop *and* market the technology, or to join with the limited partners to form a new company. R&D is an effective way to get promising technology off the ground.

**Venture Capital Firms**   These sources are professional investors, independent middlemen who chiefly manage and invest other people's money. These investors tend to be institutions, including pension funds, insurance companies, universities, and corporations. Although most wealthy private investors have abandoned professional funds, a number of family endowments still invest. (As pointed out earlier, professional venture capital firms are not the best source of funding for small companies or start-ups.) Professional fund managers seek bigger companies that may develop into $50-million to $100-million businesses within three to five years. To generate returns to investors, these funds must work with fewer, larger deals, those with "superstar" possibilities that can cover the losses from the high percentage of failures inherent in investments. These funds try to outperform the venture capital industry, and rarely get involved in deals smaller than $3,000,000 to $7,000,000.

**Cash Management and Tax Strategies**   Cash management activates immediate cash flow, involving techniques detailed elsewhere in this list, such as bartering and factoring. Cash management techniques often enlist tax strategies to create cash, such as taking tax deductions for depreciation of fixed assets (computers, perhaps, or other equipment and furniture).

**Private Placement Investment (Exempt Offerings)**   The private placement investment is the issuance of treasury securities of a company to a small number of private investors. A private placement investment is an offering of senior debt, subordinated debt, convertible debt, common stock, preferred stock, warrants, or various combinations of these securities. (The private placement investment is discussed later in this chapter, under "The Appropriateness of Your Venture for a Direct, Private Investment.")

**Government Financing (Loans and Grants)**   Small business is big business in America, responsible for a whopping 39 percent of the gross national product (GNP), half the workforce, and more than half the sales. Begun in 1953, the Small Business Administration—an independent agency of the federal government—has become the largest long-term source of financing in the country. Through 7(a), the SBA's General Loan Program, loans are made by private lenders with the government guaranteeing 70 to 90 percent of the loan up to $750,000. The 7(a) Loan Program accounts for 90 percent of the SBA's loan business. (The SBA generally defines "small" as having under 100 employees if a company is engaged in manufacturing or wholesale; if in retail or service, a company's annual sales must not exceed $3.5 million. These definitions qualify 98 percent of all businesses in the United States.)

The SBA array of programs includes the 502 Local Development Company Program, directed in rural areas to long-term, fixed-asset financing, and the 504 Certified Development Company Program, directed to long-term, fixed-asset financing through nonprofit certified development companies (CDCs). CDCs are companies sponsored either by private interests or by the local or state government. Other SBA programs operating under 7(a) include the GreenLine Program, the Vietnam-Era and Disabled Veterans Program, the Handicapped Assistance Loans, the Women's Prequalification Loan Program, and the Low Doc Loan Program for loans under $100,000 to companies with less than $5 million in annual sales and fewer than 100 employees.

Also operating under the aegis of the SBA is the Small Business Investment Company (SBIC) Program. About 200 active SBICs operate in the United States. This program is the only entity under U.S. banking legislation that can lend money *and* own equity in small businesses. SBICs borrow the capital that they, in turn, must lend only to small businesses that operate on a thin margin. However, SBICs like to see assets that can be liquidated if the business fails, and they require entrepreneurs to invest a substantial portion of their net worth and/or postpone salary. SBICs will engage in some subordinate debt. Coupons are typically 10 to 12 percent with a five- to seven-year maturity.

SBA loans can cover inventory, machinery, working capital, and acquisition of commercial property. In applying for a loan, the small business owner must meet the requirements of both the SBA and the lender, having to supply among other documents a current profit and loss statement, a balance sheet, a schedule of business debt, a current personal financial statement, a business plan, and collateral. The government rarely lends money directly to the entrepreneur, and the SBA provides no grant money for business start-up or expansion. Most lenders opt out on anything less than $50,000.

**Bartering**    Bartering, the trading of products or services without the use of money or its substitute, has become a popular business practice. Bartering involves the exchange and subsequent good use between two companies of each other's slow-moving or "dead" inventory or services. What accrues to each company is a commodity that may generate added capital. More important, bartering conserves cash. Though bartering is not for every business—such as those not needing additional customers—those that engage in it find new customers through barter newsletters and member directories.

**Commercial Finance Companies**    These firms handle riskier lending transactions and are open to higher leverage than banks. Most have an asset focus, for example, receivables, inventories, and fixed assets. Commercial credit companies typically charge interest rates of three to five points over prime, and all require substantial collateral and/or personal guarantees.

**Banks**    Traditional banks are creditors, specifically short-term lenders, granting 30- to 90-day loans. They also may lend over longer periods (more than five years), but banks *are not* investors. Banks generally require excellent credit ratings and a perceived ability to repay the borrowed money. Depending on the circumstances, they may also require a large percentage of self-financing.

**Initial Public Offerings**    IPOs are generated when a privately held, usually emerging, company complies with requirements and regulations, then registers with the SEC, makes disclosures to the public, and issues shares for the first time. Investors receive a share of company profits through the issuance of dividends but permit the company to retain control—unless that control gets transferred to the shareholders. As a public company listed on an exchange, the company must comply with relevant federal and state laws.

**International Sources of Capital**    No longer the exclusive purview of large corporations, international trade has flowed increasingly into the ken of small businesses. International sources of capital have blossomed as a result, running the gamut from local commercial banks to the federally, state-, and locally funded Center for International Trade Development. In addition, the SBA's Export Working Capital Program, like the SBA's other programs, guarantees 90 percent of a private sector loan up to $750,000. Though not exclusively for international funding, the Department of Commerce's Minority Business Development Agency (MBDA) funds Business Development Centers across the country. The Department of Commerce also supplies nonfinancial aid through its National Trade Data Bank (NTDB), which contains international information valuable to exporters. What we have mentioned here hardly scrapes the top layer of options open to the international businessperson who, unfortunately, faces daunting regulations and requirements.

**ESOPs**   Employee Stock Ownership Plans involve an internal buyout of a company in which the employees buy shares and thus buy ownership. Hence, equity capital is raised fairly inexpensively by a knowledgeable and dedicated workforce, as it operates in its new capacity as company stockholders. Each employee's share of stock thus becomes the company's contribution to the employee's retirement fund.

**Management Buyout**   This involves another type of internal buyout of a company in which the management buys shares and thus buys ownership. Such a buyout may have been generated by the management's concern for remaining in control of the company's future instead of having it bought by outsiders. Like employees who buy ownership, managers know the intimate workings of the company, putting them in position to leverage-up the company.

**Incubator-based Financing**   Incubators provide support within a close geographical locale for seed, start-up, and other early-stage companies looking to expand. Such support can come not only in funding but also in the form of a physical plant, office management, and marketing services. Corporate- or university-based, incubators help companies raise capital, offer technical assistance, and perform valuation. A fully functioning incubator could house a number of growing companies sharing a common business, for instance, in software. They also might share space and equipment and even professional guidance. The stage of development of incubators varies widely from state to state.

As the *New York Times* reported in January 1999, the number of incubators operating in the United States reached 550 in 1998; of these, 30 offered services but no physical space ("incubators without walls"). Forty-five percent were located in urban areas, 36 percent in rural areas, and 19 percent in suburbs. Forty-five percent had no particular focus, but one-quarter of the incubators focused on technology. Ten percent were dedicated to general manufacturing, 9 percent to other specific industries, 6 percent to services, and 5 percent to minority-owned businesses. That a few incubators merely sustain "failed" entrepreneurs, as investor and author Geoffrey Moore (*Crossing the Chasm* and *Inside the Tornado*) has pointed out in an interview with *The Red Herring*, good incubators, he reassures us, "attract . . . key resources—advisers, partners, investors, and visionary customers." Incubators, he has explained, "give a structure to the bottom levels of basic needs so that entrepreneurs can focus on the higher levels."

**Asset-based Loans and Factoring**   Asset-based loans are virtually self-explanatory: loans granted on the basis of a company's assets, chiefly the company's accounts receivable. The accounts receivable become collateral. A lender provides funds as products are shipped, expecting to receive a percentage of the value of those accounts. The accounts themselves will continue paying as they normally do—to the company, however, not to the lender. The company uses a predetermined portion of the actual payments by the accounts to repay the debt. In this way, the "royalty financing" allows the owner of an early-stage company to sell a portion of the revenue stream rather than hurrying to give equity in the company or burden the balance sheet with debt.

In factoring—a type of financing based on accounts receivable—the factor (lender) accepts direct responsibility for the company's accounts, taking responsibility for the credit risks and collection of the receivables. Factoring is more expensive than accounts receivable financing, although both require extensive bookkeeping and neither comes cheap.

**Self-finance**    Self-financing often supplements institutional financing and may be required by a funding institution to assure a dedication to and interest in the company, invention, or venture. Self-financing may include the use of credit cards, whose interest rates vary widely. According to a 1997 study implemented by Arthur Andersen's Enterprise Group and National Small Business United, approximately 34 percent of respondents indicated the use of credit cards for initial financing of the start-up. A good personal credit record will determine how much money a credit card company is willing to offer. Credit cards do offer one of the quickest and easiest means of obtaining credit.

**Community Development Corporations**    Nonprofit organizations—staffed by civic and business leaders and sponsored by individual citizens, church groups, and even bankers—may submit applications to become community development corporations. These community loan development funds—established to improve community life—even have begun equity investing. Eligible CDCs must have established 501(c)(3) tax-exempt status. The CDC must describe its proposed collaborative partnership with neighborhood residents, local businesses, and financial institutions. A government agency then designates which groups qualify, granting their contributors yearly tax credits of 5 percent for ten years. The designated CDC launches employment and business opportunities within a geographical area for low- and moderate-income individuals. The CDCs require scheduled progress reports. Established CDCs use past performance as a criterion for a venture's receiving more funding.

**Small Corporate Offering Registration (SCOR)**    As William D. Evers makes clear in his "Primer on Securities Law Issues for Non-Lawyers," SCOR offerings "represent an abdication by the SEC . . . to the states of jurisdiction over public or private offerings of $1 million or less." Forty-eight states have SCOR statues for public offerings. The 50-question Form U-7, currently under revision, is the required disclosure document. In many states, financials must be audited. Connected to SCOR is the federal rule known as Reg. A, which is expensive. Because of "SEC review and the required precision of offering detail for 'full disclosure,'" Evers explains, "legal fees [reach from] $25,000 to $60,000." Further, he notes, these figures do not include filing fees and "Blue Sky clearing." (For a discussion of all legal matters connected with small business, see Appendix A.)

Thus, with all the nourishment that small businesses bring to the economic dinner table, it is no wonder that the government understands the need for supplying some coal of its own to stoke the economic fire. Despite the government's best efforts and good intentions, however, its very nature precludes it from playing the role of venture capitalist. Venture capital involves more than capital; venture capital involves adding value to the money invested.

Rather than just throwing money at a company as the government does, investors help a company by knowing about growth and having extensive contacts in the business community. Venture capital means having extensive research resources with which to analyze the market as well as having financial resources to analyze projections and evaluate valuations. So, unable to influence early-stage ventures because its premises are flawed, the government is not designed to be a venture capitalist. Government programs are designed only to throw money at businesses, not furnish critical added value.

Nor are the venture capitalists themselves likely to offer the necessary degree of added value. As David M. Flynn observes in "The Critical Relationship Between Venture Capitalists and Entrepreneurs: Planning, Decision-Making, and Control" (*Small Business Economics*, 1991), "Venture capitalists (VCs) are less involved with their affiliated new venture organization than may be necessary for long-term survival." Entrepreneurs may properly dominate the early stages of a venture, explains Flynn, but in the venture's ongoing development, the VC might add expertise that the entrepreneur lacks. For example, technical skills may concede to administrative skills so the enterprise can survive. Thus, Flynn urges a higher level of involvement in ventures on the part of the venture capitalists. But the question remains: Will venture capitalists be willing?

In addition, the person trying to raise capital has a dual burden: compliance with federal SEC regulations as well as compliance with the regulations of the state Department of Corporations and Commissions. Even when the SEC has tried to reduce the cost and complexity associated with raising capital in private transactions, the states have chosen to take a more aggressive stance on their statutes. State regulations prevail, causing the nagging bottlenecks that have blocked capital in early-stage investment.

## BUSINESS ANGELS AS THE BEST SOURCES OF CAPITAL, ESPECIALLY FOR EARLY-STAGE INVESTMENT

We know that professional venture capital performs an excellent service, placing billions of dollars in American companies, creating jobs, expanding the tax base, and even putting a billion dollars into early-stage deals. But for the early-stage venture, venture capitalists impose rigid criteria, leaving numerous companies unable to qualify. Thus, as venture capital is the real contributor to later-stage deals, angel capital has become the indubitable contributor to early-stage deals, the resource for the majority of companies. The primary source of capital is the direct, private investor—even though these angel investors possess an inimitable advantage: They do not have to invest.

A problem arises for many people who think that finding a securities firm to underwrite their efforts on a "best-efforts" basis is a guarantee that money will be raised. The problem is that once a firm commits, it has to convince its brokers to sell that offering to their customers. The entrepreneur who chooses a direct public offering by enlisting a securities broker has managed to entail only front-end fees to create documents in line with a public offering. But the transaction still requires that *somebody else* has to sell the offering. So the entrepreneur's faith lies in brokers who must convince their customers to buy it.

In the January 1995 issue of *Entrepreneur*, David Evenson sends this sobering message to those hoping for an IPO offering: "Getting an underwriter to say it will take you public can be a hollow promise unless there's broad-based support within the financial community." Obviously, brokers should have been integrated early enough to harvest their feedback, enthusiasm, and commitment. Broad support must come from those who will analyze the opportunity and provide written reports.

## THE APPROPRIATENESS OF YOUR VENTURE FOR A DIRECT, PRIVATE INVESTMENT

As we have explained, the private placement investment is the issuance of treasury securities of a company to a small number of private investors. This investment is an offering of debt, stock, warrants, or various combinations of these securities. While the greater number of private placement investments to institutional investors involve debt securities, exempt offerings of direct, equity, and/or debt investing by private investors are common. These private investors often become involved in a venture in order to limit the downside risk associated with illiquid investments. These participatory investors also begin with transactions requiring less money. Moreover, these transactions move quickly compared to a public offering, are more flexible due to the lack of SEC requirements, and are much less expensive.

A more practical and useful definition of the private placement, however, is any deal you *legally* can put together, then write up and reach agreement on. As Exhibit 4.2 shows, legal definitions for the private placement do exist: cash for equity; all types of offerings not publicly sold; issuance of treasury securities to a small number of sophisticated, private or institutional ventures; the circumvention of onerous public offering requirements and access to nonaffiliated market without full registration compliance. But because this is a highly illiquid security that is not bought, it must be sold. So be warned: The expectation is unrealistic that investors—high-net-worth, sophisticated investors—will beat down your door to buy a highly illiquid, "story" security in the current lucrative publicly traded stock market. Therefore, rather than overly structuring the security and the transaction prematurely, have a more open mind, take a more negotiable, flexible posture. Then gather a circle of investors and bring in the assistance you need—legal, accounting, and so on—to structure an agreement acceptable to all the parties involved.

Let us clarify a highly illiquid "story" security. Selling a "story" security is a concept that you are selling blue sky. That is, what you are selling is a story, a compelling, believable story. Your task is to find people who believe the story. Once you accomplish that, you can reach a legal agreement on the financing of the story.

Is your venture suitable for an individual participatory investment? Think about two things: first, the kind of financing typically appropriate to your venture's stage of development; and second, the sources of such financing.

That you are accurate in the assessment of your company's development is an underlying assumption. But without some understanding of how these stages are defined, it will be difficult to define your stage of development.

---

Exhibit 4.2  **PRIVATE PLACEMENT, LEGAL DEFINITION**

- Cash for equity
- All types of offerings not publicly sold
- Issuance of treasury securities to a small number of sophisticated private or institutional investors
- Allows company to circumvent onerous public offering requirements and access nonaffiliated market without full registration compliance

Source: International Capital Resources

## Stages of Development Defined

*Seed*   A venture in the idea stage or in the process of being organized.

*Research & Development*   Financing of product development for early-stage or more developed companies.

*Start-up*   A venture that is completing product development and initial marketing and has been in business less than two years.

*First Stage*   A venture with a working prototype that has gone through beta testing and is beginning commercialization.

*Expansion Stage*   A venture that is in the early stage of expanding commercialization and is in need of growth capital.

*Mezzanine*   A venture that has increasing sales volume and is breaking even or is profitable. Additional funds are to be used for further expansion, marketing, or working capital.

*Bridge*   A venture that requires short-term capital to reach a clearly defined and stable position.

*Acquisition/Merger*   A venture that is in need of capital to finance an acquisition or merger.

*Turnaround*   A venture that is in need of capital to effect a change from unprofitability to profitability.

When entrepreneurs are asked their company's stage of development, confusion often reigns. Without knowing how to define the stages, entrepreneurs will waste time targeting the wrong investors. This is especially true in the earlier stages of development, because the earlier the stage, the higher the risk.

For example, a seed company is looking for a small amount of capital (between $50,000 and $250,000), and needs to think through its concept and develop a prototype. Market research has begun but is not yet finished. The business plan is in development and the management team is being formed. Compare a start-up. The start-up is a year-old company, legally structured but already in business. It may be test marketing its product or service and may even be bringing in revenue although not yet making a profit. Management has been assembled and is starting to form. The business plan has been completed, and the company is prepared for manufacturing and sales. It lacks only capital.

The differences in stages of development are substantial, and investors' tolerances for risk vary widely. It pays to differentiate your stage of development to target those investors interested in one or another stage of development. This is true because to varying degrees all investors are risk-averse.

But it is no accident that the primary transaction structure used by angels is the private placement investment. The benefits of this investment are shown in Exhibit 4.3.

First, since angels prize their privacy, confidentiality is an attractive feature of the private placement investment. Second, from a legal point of view, there are fewer and less onerous disclosure requirements, which is good because complying with state and federal disclosure requirements raises the ante. The benefit for the entrepreneur in incurring less cost spills over to benefit the investor. Thus, in the private placement investment or exempt offering privacy is protected and money is preserved.

Flexibility is also demonstrated in transactions with an institution—an insurance company, a pension fund, or an independent third party such as a later-stage venture capitalist firm. In these transactions, private placement investment will accommodate subordinated debt. This is attractive to entrepreneurs because senior debt capability is left unencumbered. This means that if the company proceeds apace, it can obtain long-term bank debt. Subordinated debt provides the cash, is essentially less secured, and has a subordinate position to senior debt, but does not close off acquiring long-term debt as the company increases its cash flow and develops assets. From the entrepreneur's point of view, the accommodation of subordinated debt becomes another attractive feature of private placement investment.

Likewise, from the investor's point of view, subordinated debt commonly has convertibility when the terms and conditions are negotiated; convertible subordinated debt, or convertible debenture, offers some protection on the downside of a failed company. For example, if a proprietary technology in the venture is resalable at a later date, or if the company folds and the technology is liquidated, once senior note holders are taken care of, the subordinated note holders will be able to recover some of their money. This provides insurance on the downside.

---

Exhibit 4.3  **BENEFITS OF A PRIVATE PLACEMENT**

- Confidential
- Flexible
- Less costly
- More than capital
- Rapid time frame
- Accommodates smaller transactions

Source: International Capital Resources

And convertibility, combined with a subordinated debt, permits sharing on the upside if the company is successful.

If the company is successful, investors convert the principal of the note into stock. Even the interest becomes convertible—if it has not been paid over time or has been held in abeyance. With success, investors will be able to convert to stock and share in the capital appreciation by having previously negotiated a purchase price. Since the company is successful, the price of the stock is higher. The investors will be able to purchase the stock at a lower price and in time liquidate it for appreciation and a return on the investment. If the company is not highly successful—does not go public or is not acquired—but experiences a reasonable degree of success, the investors' debt can be repaid from cash flow. Hence, they will get their principal and their coupon or return on interest. If the company fails, the investors are in line to get some of their money back when the company's assets are liquidated.

All this provides flexibility. Debt can be used in several ways: subordinated debt, convertible subordinated debt, equity, debt and equity, or even royalty financing. In royalty financing, individuals do not take an equity position, nor do they get a note for their money. Instead, they develop an agreement in which portions of the revenues of the company over time will be paid back until a multiple return is reached—perhaps two or three times the original investment. These kinds of transactions are common in the restaurant business, for example, so that the owner will have no partners or note to pay off. Without thus burdening the balance sheet, the valuation of the venture from the bank's point of view expedites a loan. In effect, a portion of the cash proceeds from the business will divert to the investors until they secure a predetermined return on their investment. Gradually they slide from the picture. Flexibility appeals to entrepreneurs and investors alike.

Seed is a riskier investment than a start-up venture but holds the promise of a greater return. In a recent study of 200 companies and 500 financings by venture capitalists from 1978 to 1988, 41 percent of start-ups provided returns to investors compared with 35 percent of seed investments. However, successful seed deals provided an average of 19.4 times the money invested, compared with 9.7 times the money invested in start-ups. Besides, the hold-time was not significantly different: 7.2 years for seed deals to provide returns, compared with 6.4 years hold-time before harvesting returns from start-ups.

Another benefit of the private placement is that it is less costly than other types of offering, for example, a public offering. The private placement is less costly in time and money. The entrepreneurial team can expect to spend in a public offering 900 hours of its time in completing an IPO, whereas the private placement can be completed much more quickly, allowing the principals more time for running the business. In addition, significant variations occur in the cost associated with private placement: front-end fees and back-end fees.

To avoid surprises, the total cost for a private placement when handled by the entrepreneurs and the principals of the venture themselves—costs of preparing and duplicating documents, binding, mailing, phone calls, follow-up meetings—can be anywhere from 3 to 5 percent of the total amount raised to a high of 12 to 25 percent depending on whether intermediaries (license broker-dealers, investment bankers, and the like) are involved. So while a private placement is *less* costly than a public offering and other types of offerings, there *are* costs.

But the great advantage of a private placement comes with what the investor offers the entrepreneur beyond capital. Private investors bring much more than money to the deal; whereas in the venture capital industry, many of the venture capitalists have become money managers and are not spending much time with the companies in which they have invested because those companies are in later stages of development. Early-stage companies really need a lot of hand holding and angel investors are motivated to nurture new ventures as part of their hedging strategy to mange the downside risk in the deal. Thus, it becomes incumbent on the entrepreneur to take advantage of what angels bring to the enterprise.

Still another advantage of the private placements is its quick implementation. The time frame for private placements is, for the shortest, three weeks, and for the longest, nine months. The range of the time-frame is wide. But if a management team is ready to raise capital, has committed itself to the venture, has put aside some financial resources, and is willing to commit the necessary time to the venture, things can happen quickly. And if the venture meets the criteria we have outlined, has developed the capitalization strategy, has been properly managed using the advice and counsel we have provided—particularly with regard to efficiency in the private placement process—a private placement can be concluded in a relatively short period, reasonably in about three months.

Finally, a significant difference between angel investors and institutional investors is that institutional investors currently under management—because of the larger size of the funds—are gravitating to later-stage deals, which means they are gravitating to larger deals. Meanwhile, individual angel investors are typically investing smaller amounts, and investing in smaller rounds. This way an individual investing $25,000 or $50,000 or $100,000 becomes a significant player in the transaction. In this way, the private placement accommodates the smaller transactions which, in fact, are the hardest transactions right now to get financed in the venture capital industry. (See Exhibit 4.4.)

Exhibit 4.4  **COMPARISON OF ANGEL AND INSTITUTIONAL VENTURE CAPITAL FINANCING SOURCES**

- 250,000  Angels invest annually (potential 2,000,000)
- $20–30 BILLION   Annual investment
- 400,000–500,000  Companies trying to raise capital
- $3.5–4 BILLION  Seed, R&D, and start-ups
- 30,000–40,000  Early-stage transactions
- 90% of transactions less than $1M
- Mean investment $30,000 to $50,000
- Mean investment share, 1st round 20%

- 500 Professional venture capital firms
- $35B   Under management
- $11.4B  Total investment
- $1.1B   300 Early-stage investments
- $7B   1,089 Information technology firms*
- $2.6B   426 Healthcare firms
- $4M   Mean investment ($3M to $7M range)
- $15.2M  Median valuation
- 41%   Average equity share

* Software, networking, communications, and electronics.
Source: International Capital Resources

## PROFESSIONAL VENTURE CAPITAL AS A FUNDING RESOURCE FOR EARLY-STAGE COMPANIES

According to the National Venture Capital Association, in 1997 $11.4 billion in private equity financing was completed by venture-backed portfolio companies, due largely to the increase in funding size ($3 to $7 million). Thus, the total size of investments by the venture capital community is increasing, largely because these portfolio companies are working with later-stage companies, companies that need larger blocks of capital. Moreover, as funds get larger (because more pension money and other institutional contributions go into them), they focus on later-stage financing, which, by virtue of their being later-stage, are larger.

And because of this larger financing and the increase in size of the funds, the activity in the venture capital industry looks as if it is going up, but the venture capital industry still is not working on the early-stage deals. So, although it looks as if the venture capital industry is reviving, the fact is that each financing and, thus, financing as a whole, is increasing; the industry continues to invest almost exclusively in later-stage deals, which require more money.

Supporting this conclusion is the fall in seed and first-round financing of venture capital investment. Only $1.1 billion was invested in 300 early-stage investments, which is approximately 10 percent of the total amount invested compared to 26 percent invested in early-stage companies back in 1993. So as you can see, the amount has decreased. During this time, premoney valuations rose to a median premoney valuation of $15.2 million per transaction in 1997, a significant increase in valuation, indicating that later-stage companies were, in fact, the targets of this institutional investor group.

This means that early-stage deals are currently a bargain. These valuations in early-stage deals are dropping; therefore, private investors are buying up bargains, by investing in these ventures at very low valuations. This points out that, conversely, the venture capital industry is paying too much, as they drive up the price by fighting over a limited number of attractive later-stage companies.

This forecasts grave consequences for the venture capital industry: It is heading for a bust—exactly as happened in 1989. When the portfolio-backed companies begin competing with each other, they keep investing exclusively in the same industries. Thus, since there are only so many deals within those same four or five industries—and since only about 2 to 5 percent of those deals are any good—they are all fighting over the same poor deals. As a result, the entrepreneurs are sitting back, letting them fight, watching the valuations on their deals turn up, up, up.

The more money the portfolio-backed companies pay on a deal, the less internal rate of return they will realize. We already know that a high percentage of their deals will fail and that those that do come through have cost too much. This practically insures a poor return for fund investors five to seven years from now, when half of these portfolio companies will have quit the industry. Therefore, angels are buying into earlier-stage companies at significantly reduced valuations—and for good reason.

Thus do we find a significant problem in the making while we simultaneously witness an emerging opportunity for astute private investors.

What we see is about 90 percent of institutional venture capital money going to companies in stages of development beyond seed and start-up. It is no wonder, then, that entrepreneurs are looking away from venture capital until later stages of their developing companies. As a NVCA publication declares, "Most of the venture-capital funds invested across the country were received by companies already through at least one round of financing." It boils down to this: Angel investment runs the critical first leg of the relay race, passing the baton to venture capital only after a company has begun to find its stride. Venture capitalists focus, as the numbers presented reveal, on expansion and later stages of development, when their contribution is most effective. In this way venture capital investment complements rather than conflicts with private investment.

## COMPARISON OF ANGEL INVESTORS WITH PROFESSIONAL VENTURE CAPITALISTS

Entrepreneurs should realize that early-stage investing by professional venture capital will form only a small part of their investment strategy. Arthur Rock, a founder of Intel, said in *Fortune* that venture capitalists are now portfolio managers, "more interested in creating wealth than in creating companies." Another Silicon Valley veteran has dubbed "venture capital" an oxymoron. Still another CEO warned entrepreneurs not to look on investment bankers as their friends, calling them "gatekeepers" as they screen out what to them is just another deal. For entrepreneurs to rely too heavily on that particular resource is a mistake, when, in fact, there remains a larger resource willing to assume a greater risk. The angel investor—patient and interested in adding value to smaller, higher-risk transactions—stands ready to nurture a company through the early leg of the relay. Then the professional venture capital community becomes a more suitable contributor by virtue of its fiduciary responsibility to those institutional investors who have entrusted their money to money managers.

But examining the people who constitute the private investment market is difficult because of their penchant for privacy, the lack of sophisticated measures for accumulating data, the lack of disclosure requirements by the government about private placement investment, and the costly nature of doing qualitative research. Even the job of compiling information through interviews and surveys and then analyzing their content is work. Because of these difficulties, discrepancies appear in the size and capability of the angel market.

An overview of the major studies of the business angel capital market (Exhibit 4.4)—our own work, the early work of Dr. Gaston, the more current work by Dr. William Wetzel, the studies conducted by the MIT Venture Capital Network and the University of California at Irvine—suggest that there are approximately 250,000 to 300,000 active angels each year. The annual investment of this group will range, depending on the individual studies looked at, from around $20 to $30 billion a year.

Upward of 400,000 to 500,000 companies are attempting aggressively to raise capital at any given time, and ultimately about $3.5 to $4 billion of the angel market is going into seed, R&D, and start-up stage transactions. Approximately 30,000 to 40,000 very early-stage transactions are being concluded in this market. Ninety percent of those transactions are typically for less than $1 million, with a mean investment per investor of $30,000 to $50,000 and a mean investment share in the first round of the financing of approximately 20 percent of the equity.

Venture capital firms, since they are listed publicly in directories, are inundated with requests for capital. To private investors, however, public listings are anathema. If they list anywhere, they list with confidential private networks. Thus, angel investors receive less deal flow. This gives them more time to peruse the deals that do come in, and, since they do not have to invest, they become more selective. Private investors, after all, seek a profit on every investment. Professional venture capitalists, on the other hand, accept that a percentage of their deals will fail, some unable to recover even bank account returns. The reason? The professional venture capitalist *has* to invest.

By ICR's definition of preseed, seed, and start-up, "early-stage" represents the riskiest investment; often it means investing in no more than an idea. Some may insist that we overrepresent the activity of angels in this market, but a look at the numbers should settle the matter: 14 percent of seed and start-up deals out of 256 deals in the venture capital community. Seed and start-up investments in the angel market amount to 30,000 transactions. Entrepreneurs will tally more for their time, trouble, and money from an angel investor than from the professional venture capitalist, who better serves as a near-distant, instead of initial, funding source.

Exhibit 4.5 presents an overview of the main difference between business angels and venture capitalists. When we cross-compare busi-

---

Exhibit 4.5 **MAIN DIFFERENCES BETWEEN BUSINESS ANGELS AND VENTURE CAPITALISTS**

| Business Angels | Venture Capitalists |
| --- | --- |
| • Concern with firm success | • Concern with exit strategy |
| • Own money | • Other people's money |
| • Smaller equity share | • Larger equity share |
| • Mean # investments = 4 | • Mean # investments = 23 |
| • Small business experience | • Academic credentials |
| • 80% started a company | • 38% started a company |
| • Part-time investor | • Full-time investor |
| • Entrepreneurial manager | • Financial manager |
| • Value-adding, active investor | • Strategic investor, not hands-on |
| • Focus on entrepreneur | • Focus on concept & rapid growth potential |
| • Location important (80%) | • Location important (60%) |
| • No industry experience 59% in inv. | • No industry experience 29% in inv. |
| • ROI objective minimum 30% | • ROI objective minimum 40% |
| • Generalist | • Specialist |
| • Short due diligence & negotiation cycle | • Long due diligence & negotiation cycle |

Source: International Capital Resources

ness angels with venture capitalists, business angels seem to be concerned more with a firm's success, while venture capitalists seem to be more concerned with an exit strategy. Business angels are using their own money; venture capitalists are using other people's money. If we look at how private investors are handled, the mean number of investments they make a year total four; the mean number of investments a venture capital firm might make swells to 23.

Thus, angel investors are part-time—although active and value-added—investors, whereas institutional people—almost strictly hands off—are full-time. Angels—80 percent of whom have started a business—value small business experience; venture capitalists—only 20 percent of whom have started a business—value academic credentials. The business angel focuses on the entrepreneur, while the venture capitalist focuses on the concept and rapid growth potential.

Other differences abound. To 80 percent of the angels, location is important, while location matters to 60 percent of the venture capitalists. Business angels will invest in a company when the angel has no business experience in that company's industry 59 percent of the time, whereas venture capitalists will invest only about 29 percent of the time in industries where they have no direct experience. Thus, you have a better chance in the angel market because about twice as many business angels invest in industries they do not understand or have direct experience in. So you can have a larger number of people to go to because they may not understand the Internet, but they do understand the market.

The angel investor, a generalist who anticipates a minimum ROI of 30 percent, contrasts sharply with the venture capitalist, a specialist, who presumes a minimum ROI of 40 percent. Finally, the business angel requires a short due diligence and negotiation cycle; the venture capitalist, a long due diligence and negotiation cycle.

## PROFESSIONAL VENTURE CAPITAL: HELP OR HINDRANCE TO YOUR FUNDING SUCCESS?

In their 1990 article in the *California Management Review,* "Does Venture Capital Foster the Most Promising Entrepreneurial Firms?" Raphael Amit, Lawrence Glosten, and Eitar Muller suggest that start-ups backed by venture capital have a much higher failure rate than those financed by individual investors. Venture capital is spread thin, say the authors, and venture capitalists negotiate tough deals that drive away the ablest entrepreneurs, those who know the value of their projects. Hence, they conclude, we can expect higher failure rates among firms seeking venture capital than among the total population of new firms.

One reason for the high rate of investment failures among venture capital investments may be that inferior deals go to venture capitalists because of their more aggressive valuation stance. In other words, entrepreneurs with less confidence in their venture may be willing to take less money for their company. Compare the entrepreneur or inventor who, encouraged by the venture, would rarely sacrifice so much.

For example, suppose a venture capitalist offers an entrepreneur an investment of $100,000 but wants 50 percent of the company. The venture capitalist is thus declaring that the venture is worth $200,000. The entrepreneur with no confidence in the venture, with no belief in the venture's viability in three to five years, will accept the valuation. If, however, the entrepreneur does have confidence in the venture, why would he or she surrender what may be worth $1,000,000 within a comparable time frame? As the article's authors surmise, "The most able entrepreneurs will not find the prices offered by the venture capitalists sufficiently attractive." Since angel capital is accessible for promising deals, the entrepreneur need not compromise.

Confident entrepreneurs should confer less on the venture capitalist because they believe in their venture's future value. Venture capitalists are aggressive in their valuation because it serves them to manage the downside risk and increases the possibility of achieving their targeted internal rate of return. If the venture capitalist can persuade the entrepreneur to relinquish 50 percent of the venture, for example, the venture capitalist can afford a less successful transaction than either would like, but still provide a reasonable return for the venture capital fund's investors. The venture capitalist will suffer far less than the entrepreneur. At this rate of valuation, chances are the venture capitalist will get back the original investment.

Amit, Glosten, and Muller put it bluntly: "[T]he most promising entrepreneurs will not seek venture capital financing. . . ." That the entrepreneur is better off in the early-stage deal with the direct, private investor than with the venture capitalist seems axiomatic.

In sum, a wide range of financing possibilities awaits; each has its strengths and weaknesses. Some options apply to certain companies, while others would not be suitable. The difference lies in stage of development. Once you are clear about your stage of development, you can evaluate what will work for you. Still, for people lost in the capital gap, only one resource seems practicable: the direct, private placement made by the angel investor.

# What Do Private Investors Look for in a Deal?

## THE HIGH-NET-WORTH INVESTOR MARKET

Private venture investors represent a virtually invisible segment of the venture capital market. These investors form a diverse and diffuse population of individuals of means, many of whom have created their own successful ventures. By providing early-stage financing for start-up firms and equity financing for established firms, these investors fill a void in the institutional venture capital market. They look for products and services in markets with significant growth potential while requiring rewards equal to the risks they incur. They surprisingly—in our estimation, unwisely—may invest in the absence of a business plan. They will insist on clarity about when and how they may cash in their investment. And they surely look for competent management, a point we cannot emphasize too much.

Another point we come to is how dependent this market is on individuals with high net worth, the "wealthy," those who possess something beyond high incomes. A person with a high income may be affluent but not wealthy. Only high net worth determines wealth. In Chapter 1, we discussed how some entrepreneurs mistakenly judge investors solely on their income, while income alone has little to do with what counts in these early-stage, high-risk transactions. By focusing on income, one can forget how quickly it can become outstripped by expenses.

Income alone, then, does not signal a potential investor. Entrepreneurs should not rely on brokers' lists of investors for two reasons: Brokers' lists are based on income, not wealth; and these lists contain information available elsewhere. These lists will not lead entrepreneurs to the investors who make high-risk investments, however much entrepreneurs and their brokers wish it were so.

However, an investor's net worth is much more difficult to plumb than income, particularly net worth exclusive of house and car. A person's net worth is attainable only through interviews, which accounts for the reason that databases become so valuable. By combining net worth with income data, a helpful database, such as the one operated by International Capital Resources, turns up those individuals who meet the standards for such transactions. Private discretionary capital of high-net-worth individuals accounts for a sizable resource for investment.

In Chapter 1 we also noted that only a specific segment of the high-net-worth market is worth targeting for high-risk deals, a market composed of a diverse pool of investors. The principal group for investing in high-risk deals has a net worth of $1 million to $10 million. Net worth of less than $1 million or greater than $10 million will not be a target for high-risk investments. People with a net worth of less than $1 million do not meet the qualifications for being involved in this type of investment and can trigger legal problems. Such investments are simply too risky for them. For those with a net worth of more than $10 million—the roughly 10,000 wealthiest families in the United States—investing is accomplished through family offices that bear fiduciary responsibility, the representatives of which are less inclined toward these types of high-risk investments.

Accredited investors make up the group of incomes ranging between $100,000 and $200,000 or more per year. This is the group typically considered *affluent*. Again, they are *affluent*, but they are not *wealthy*. Someone with an income of $100,000 might have no net worth. However, if only income data is available, entrepreneurs should look for those with a gross income of between $200,000 and $1 million. This income level offers far better prospects of those having the necessary discretionary funds to make these types of investments.

There are affluent market segments that provide unique asset garnering. The inheritance boom and the unprecedented assets of a mature market combine to make the most tantalizing accumulation of wealth in the history of the world. According to PSI's 1995 Affluent Market Consumer Survey, affluent market segments exist that provide unique asset garnering opportunities for individuals seeking to raise capital. The thing to realize is that the high-net-worth market is highly segmented; it is not a monolithic market, just as the angel market is not monolithic, but rather a series of types. (See Chapters 6 and 7.)

In studying this affluent or high-net-worth market, we discover the following segments: the "young affluent" and "low-end affluent" (people with a net worth of $100,000—excluding their primary residence); the "retired affluent" and "career affluent" (those with a net worth of more than $500,000); "established wealth" and "senior corporate executives" (those with a net worth of between $1.4 million and $5 million); "business owners" (whose net worth ranges across other segments, from a low of $500,000 to a high of $5 million); and "active wealth" (those whose net worth tops $5 million).

Obviously, segments of this market are more inclined than others to early-stage investing. Because of their age, need for income and security, and time remaining to garner capital appreciation, early-stage investing—with its longer-term horizons and higher risk—are much less attractive to the retired affluent than to other affluent market segments. Clearly, then, the retired affluent are less of a target for early-stage investing. The young affluent are in the earlier stages of acquiring homes and material things and therefore probably are less inclined to engage in early-stage investing. In addition, the young affluent, more concerned with the time investment of family and career, become much less available to provide the time-intensive dimension of added value that these early-stage companies require. Nor are the young affluent readily available to devote the necessary time to hedge the downside risk associated with this type of investment. So an economic element and a time element make it less appealing. The low-end affluent will not yet have the discretionary net worth. So the entrepreneur's camera lens naturally narrows on established wealth: those looking for socially responsible deals; and on active wealth, those actively placing money back into the economy. Likewise, senior corporate executives are investing in their industries because they understand the opportunity, just as business owners are looking to invest and diversify and grow beyond their businesses. Finally, the career affluent are seeking to broaden their retirement portfolio through capital accumulation over time. Obviously, it is these latter segments that deserve the early-stage entrepreneur's store of energy.

## THE INFORMAL, HIGH-RISK, INVESTOR PROFILE

Just who are these investors? What profile fits the hard-to-find, affluent, private, early-stage investor? In Chapter 6 we profile specific types of angel investors. In Exhibit 5.1, using the results of survey questionnaires and follow-up interviews, we sketch the generic informal, high-risk investor from ICR's study of more than 600 private investors.

These individuals are typically males around 48 to 59 years old. Age, in fact, influences investment. We see in the age range of 46 to 55 an inclination to redeploy some of their income, particularly toward growth potential. In the 56 to 65 bracket (which reaches a bit beyond our overall age profile), we see a much more active portfolio management, in which these investors trust their own judgment, not that of brokers, particularly in investments into private business ventures.

Returning to our profile in Exhibit 5.1, these investors typically have postgraduate educations and extensive management experience. In

Exhibit 5.1  INFORMAL, HIGH-NET-WORTH INVESTOR PROFILE

- 48–59 years of age, male
- Postgraduate degree, often technical
- Previous management experience; started up, operates, or sold a successful business
- Invests between $25,000 and $250,000 per transaction
- Prefers participation with other financially sophisticated individuals
- Strong preference for transactions that match with technical expertise
- 60% prefer to invest "close to home"
- Maintains an "active" professional relationship with portfolio investments
- Invests in 1–4 transactions per year
- Diversification and tax shelter income are not the most important objectives; however, ROI is rarely the only objective
- Term for holding investment is 5–7 years
- Looks for rates of return from 22.5% to 50%. Minimum portfolio return 20%
- Learns of investment opportunities primarily from friends and trusted associates. However, majority would like to look at more investment opportunities than present informal referral system permits
- Income is $100,000/year minimum
- Self-made millionaire

Source: International Capital Resources

fact, they have probably owned and sold their own companies. And because they can aggressively negotiate strong discounts, they are interested in earlier-stage deals. They see potential in these transactions for high returns through capital appreciation.

Their investment strategies vary: One segment invests between $10,000 and $50,000; another segment invests from $100,000 to about $250,000 in a deal. A very small percentage invests less than $10,000; a very small percentage invests more than $250,000. Typically, these investors pool their money, or they invest with a syndicate of coinvestors who ponder hedging strategies and managing risk, two things we will discuss in a later chapter.

These investors also have a propensity for manufacturing ventures, particularly those that overlap their previous industrial experience and expertise. Finally, the misconception persists that angels invest only close to home. Our study found that about 60 percent wanted to invest geographically proximate to their homes, but 40 percent felt this was not a major consideration.

We will see in the composite sketches of types of private investors featured in Chapter 6 that despite their diversity much unites them. Investors are like DNA molecules: Although everyone's DNA is assembled from the same nucleotides, everyone's DNA is different. Individual investors, too, are different, reflecting a market of splintered segments comprised of distinct individuals. Therefore, no monolithic overture to them will suffice. Entrepreneurs must approach investors individually, in terms not only of personal demography but also of idiosyncrasy. Thus, a careful measure—something beyond an array of mere market statistics—illuminates the informal, high-net-worth investor as both individual and member of a select group.

In correlating segments of ICR's proprietary database (with more than 8,400 listings) with the size of investment angels make, we provide an example for the entrepreneur and the investor of the typical investment size. (See Exhibit 5.2.) Twenty percent invest less than $25,000 per deal; about 40 percent invest $25,000 to $99,999; 25 percent invest $100,000 to $250,000; and about 15 percent invest roughly $250,000 *per deal.*

## ADVANTAGES OF DIRECT VENTURE INVESTING

The question arises: Why do these people get involved in the market in the first place? They get involved because this type of investing—direct, early-stage, private equity investing—offers them some unique advantages. One of the advantages is no middleman. This type of transaction is based on their own due diligence, their own assessment, their own intuition, their own intelligence and analytical skills to identify a winner. One very attractive advantage is the possibility of hitting a home run in this area, and we've given a number of examples of the high returns possible. (See Exhibit 5.3.)

Exhibit 5.2 **SIZE OF ANGEL INVESTMENTS IN ICR DATABASE**

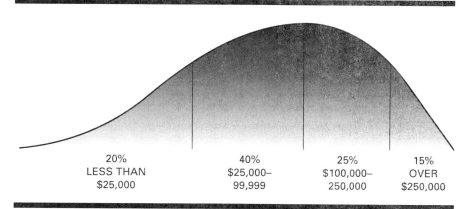

| 20%<br>LESS THAN<br>$25,000 | 40%<br>$25,000–<br>99,999 | 25%<br>$100,000–<br>250,000 | 15%<br>OVER<br>$250,000 |

Source: International Capital Resources

Exhibit 5.3  **ADVANTAGES OF DIRECT VENTURE INVESTING**

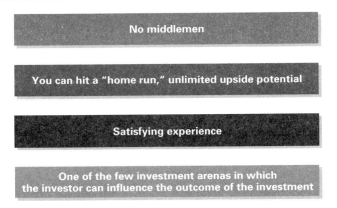

Source: International Capital Resources

And because you can hit a home run, the upside potential on these investments is unlimited. It's not like a loan that will return your capital plus a little percent interest. For example, if you own 30 percent of a company and it becomes an AOL, you potentially stand to make millions on your investment. So beneath the surface bubbles the incentive to hit it big. Another aspect involves many executives late in their career who are bored with the businesses they own or are no longer challenged by their career. For them, direct investing can satisfy by once again being in the early stages of a company's development, a development that can require the investor to wear many hats, become involved in a number of different activities, and confront a number of challenges missing in the larger, more structured, bureaucratic organization. And last, and perhaps most important, by getting deeply involved, the investor influences the outcome of the investment.

## THE PRIVATE INVESTOR'S CRITERIA

The private investor in this select group has investment criteria. As Exhibit 5.4 suggests, he or she is steeped in the excitement and the fun of this type of investing. To the investor, these feelings figure as prominently as return on investment. Lest you have forgotten, it is fun to make money.

These private investors search for investments that include a proprietary advantage, that is, a unique technology, a significant competi-

Exhibit 5.4 **PRIVATE INVESTOR CRITERIA**

- Exciting, fun (it is also fun to make $$)
- Proprietary advantage or unique technology
- New features recognized competitors don't have that result in significant barriers to competition
- Cost advantage
- Something investors can understand (not too complex)
- The possibility of new markets
- Potential for fast growth and share of the market
- Potential for ROI, 5–10 times investment with solid financials, BS, IS, CFS, and assumptions spelled out
- History of profitability, if applicable, or a borrowed track record
- Not just an invention, but a plan for profit
- A management team with the following attributes:
  —Perseverance
  —Decency
  —Competence
  —Track record
  —Personal financial commitment of their own net worth
  —Burning desire to succeed
- Comfortable with level of active/passive involvement required
- In their price range (affordable loss)
- Geographically close (within 300 miles)
- Allows for incremental funding based on performance
- Allows for due diligence
- Must have a clear exit strategy

Source: International Capital Resources

tive advantage that can act as a barrier to competition. And private investors look for other qualities in their investments, such as a cost advantage. They also want to understand the industry, or at least understand the underlying technology. They will be acutely conscious of whether the venture—its product or service—is something they can identify with and become excited about.

In addition, their investment decisions often hang on a salable product or service entering a receptive market. Private investors will scrutinize the possibility of new markets—behind which must exist a driving force—and a potential for fast growth, leading to a significant share of the market. This clearly defined market for the company must be without large players already firmly entrenched. Management can be changed; the market cannot.

Private investors also look for solid financial forecasts with sufficiently supported assumptions as they seek a return of five to ten times their original investment. With credible projections and supporting assumptions, the investor aims for a minimum return of 30 percent return on investment. They also want to see a history of profitability in operating companies, that is, a track record that demonstrates financial success.

These private investors want to invest in businesses, not ideas; they want to separate business plans from strategy, have a differentiation strategy based on some element beyond cost, for example, creative product engineering, or proprietary technological leadership. The Intel Corporation saga is pertinent here, one of the great venture capital successes of all time. Arthur Rock invested $300,000 in the early 1970s; today that investment is valued at $117 million. The business plan for Intel covered a page and a half. In fact, it was not even a business plan; it was an Investment Opportunity Profile written by Rock to sell the deal. But that was in the "old days." Today lawyers abound, involving themselves in the business planning process. No one needs to be reminded that we live in a litigious society.

The business plan, in particular, is tricky in assessing investor criteria. In International Capital Resources' recent study a large percentage of more than 600 informal, high-risk investors stated a willingness to invest in a venture *without* a complete business plan—a blatantly unnecessary risk! The business plan demonstrates in writing management's hypothesis about those elements in the business over which it claims control. The logic, strategy, and support provided for the plan reflect management's assumption that there exists some cause-and-effect relationship: If management does X, Y is likely to occur. Without a business plan, however, due diligence to determine the feasibility of management's assumptions becomes even more subjective than it is. For example, assessment of the market potential, which drives all cash-flow forecasting, becomes sheer speculation. The caveat is this: Everything that works is simple; but achieving simple is difficult. The business plan is essential because it assesses the true workability of an early-stage venture.

Because experienced, sophisticated investors find risk distasteful, they minimize it in every way possible. Nothing minimizes risk more than the business plan. But the business plan also works to the advantage of the entrepreneur, enabling him or her to achieve two critical goals: recruiting talent and raising capital. The business plan achieves these two goals because nothing better explains the entrepreneur's concept and vision. It helps capture the attention of the investor, defines the argument, and forces him or her to define the opportunity, strategy, resource requirements, and risks of the venture.

The business plan acts as a resume for the venture. In the entrepreneur's absence, it sends a host of messages to the private venture investor, messages about the management team's grasp of reality, its ability to assess opportunity and risk, its clarity of thinking and communication, and its overall effectiveness. The business plan helps the entrepreneur define goals and strategies, while it helps the investor evaluate the company's potential.

The plan should answer the following questions:

- What is special about the venture's technology?
- Who will the customers be, and why will they want to buy the product or service?
- What levels of revenue and profit does the venture expect to reach, and how much capital will be required?
- How will the company be positioned in the industry, and what specific markets will it serve?
- What are the most significant risks the venture may encounter?
- Who will make up the members of the management team, and why is there reason to believe the team will succeed?

If your business plan impresses investors, they will take a closer look at your management team, product, marketplace, financial requirements, and goals. If the investors decide the venture offers opportunity, the entrepreneur stands a good chance of raising the capital required to build the business. Thus, the business plan becomes integral to the astute investor's criteria. While private investors face subjective variables in investment decisions, they can avoid unnecessary risks by engaging in diligent analysis wherever possible. Most investors, then, desire not just an investment but plans for a profit, a carefully thought-out business plan. (See Appendix B.)

The quality of the management team—its perseverance, decency, competence, track record, personal financial commitment, and desire to succeed—rewinds itself in the minds of private investors as few things do. As we pointed out in our fund-raising strategy in Chapter 3, hardly anything is more important. Also indispensable to the team members from the investor's viewpoint is their burning desire to succeed. The spark must glow, else the entire venture soon dims.

In addition, investors need to feel comfortable with a particular level of active/passive involvement. (See "Variations in Preferred Level of Involvement after Investment" later in this chapter.) They look for something in their price range, that is, a venture carrying not only affordable losses but a venture affordable in current and later rounds without undue dilution. For some investors a venture needs to be geographically proximate (within 300 miles). The criteria of private investors must also allow for incremental funding based on performance. Another must involves due diligence on the part of both investor and entrepreneur or inventor, an aspect of investing we will discuss in Chapter 13. Finally, there needs to be a clear exit strategy—an essential point we will come back to in Chapter 11.

## COMMON REASONS WHY ANGELS REJECT AN INVESTMENT

Just as investors ardently scan a venture hoping they find certain features, they assiduously avoid others. These investors have shared their reasons with us, reasons that span the range of weaknesses inherent in this type of investing. For one thing, avoiding a mistake in this type of investing is more important to the private investor than picking a runaway winner. Since these investors make only about one to four investments a year, a single poor investment can collapse heavily on the investor. Unlike a venture capital firm, which makes perhaps 15 investments in a year and can absorb a hit, the direct, private investor must take great care with each investment. Therefore, the philosophy of the venture capital firm does not apply to our private investor.

Obviously, investors want a return on their investments, with a minimum return in today's market of 30 percent. If a venture does not show enough potential, if the margins simply are not there, the risk/return ratio is not adequate to attract investors. In some instances, as we indicated earlier, people get funded, not business plans. Therefore, if chemistry or mutual respect is lacking in the management team, if credentials seem weak, if no track record exists, an investor's rejection is almost sure to follow.

Remember that these people want to have fun making money, so they are looking for something different, not boring. If they do not understand the business; if, for them, the venture is too technical; if they cannot embrace the technology, wrap their arms around it—these too are reasons for not investing. The venture has to strike their fancy. Although not all investors feel the need to have a deep familiarity with the industry, many do wish to invest in areas they know and understand, be it in the technology, the application of the technology, or the market the technology is aimed at. Their unfamiliarity with the business technology or the technology market can be a reason for rejecting a venture. And some investors, especially the socially responsible (described among the types of investors in the next chapter), may not see any value to the venture.

Private investors also reject possible investments because entrepreneurs often overvalue their venture. In a recent study by Coopers & Lybrand, mean valuation for early-stage technology companies was about $2 million. These days, companies coming into ICR's office often boast of valuations ranging from $10 to $15 million. Such unrealistic valuation can lead to a disagreement between the entrepreneur and the investor on the price of the transaction. Some entrepreneurs, aided by the omnipresent spreadsheet program, develop cash-flow projections on which they forecast exorbitant returns on investment. Such forecasts are driven by wishful thinking. These poorly developed assumptions are the reason that private investors reject financial proposals—and, of course, the accompanying ventures along with them.

Private investors reject investment opportunities for additional reasons, referred to in connection with investor criteria. Entrepreneurs who lack the fire characteristic of people who believe in their venture will face disappointment. These investors want to see a spark waxing, not waning. Also, for some investors, the proximity of the venture to their home or business figures prominently in accepting or rejecting an investment. The need for missionary selling can be a reason why investors reject investments. Lastly, these investors must believe there is a market that will support the growth of the venture, that will provide a worthwhile rate of return within a reasonable time.

Finally, rarely will entrepreneurs find investors willing to make direct, private investments to provide salaries or back salaries, or to pay off loans or other debts incurred by the venture. Investors are interested in building mountains, not throwing money into a hole that has already been dug.

## VARIATIONS IN PREFERRED LEVEL OF INVOLVEMENT AFTER INVESTMENT

Different types of direct participatory investors prefer different levels of involvement in their ventures. These levels of involvement fall along a spectrum ranging from less active involvement to more active. (See Exhibit 5.5.) The private venture investor helps to build value. Most direct investments require additional work beyond the money invested. This additional work often translates into being involved in almost every aspect of growing a business.

Also, the level of involvement can change dramatically—in either direction—depending on management's performance and the risk to

Exhibit 5.5  **LEVELS OF INVOLVEMENT IN DIRECT, PRIVATE INVESTMENTS**

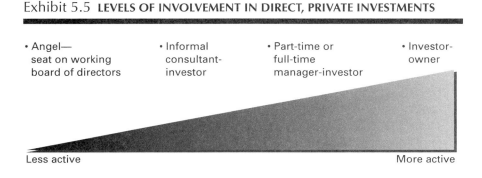

- Angel— seat on working board of directors
- Informal consultant-investor
- Part-time or full-time manager-investor
- Investor-owner

Less active                                                                    More active

Source: International Capital Resources

the investor's investment. Passive angels may settle for a seat on a working board of directors, or they may require detailed financial reports prepared periodically. These persons are not looking for operating management responsibility. Meanwhile, consultant-investors may link their desire to invest with the development of their professional services consulting practice. This type of investor will look for remuneration from an ongoing involvement.

Manager-investors, a new breed of investor discussed in Chapter 8, provide support and industry knowledge, long-term commitment, and deep pockets. As long as the chemistry is satisfactory, well-connected manager-investors investing within a close geographical area typically expect an operational role in the venture. Investor-owners, for their part, are buyers concerned with control. While involvement may be a knee-jerk reaction to the illiquidity of this type of investing, in most cases, it may simply create value through the use of the investors' knowledge and contacts, or reflect a sizable financial commitment. As Andrew Carnegie said, "If I'm going to put all my eggs in one basket, I'm going to closely watch that basket."

But your eagerness for funding should not blind you to the things they will add beyond money. Neither should it blind you to their possible shortcomings. As we will make clear in Chapter 13, you need to perform due diligence on investors with the same scrutiny they bring to their due diligence on you. Do you hire a private investigator? Why not! You should be as discriminating in selecting investors as they are discriminating in choosing you. It is the investors you gather in this round who will be inspected by the investors you wish to bring on in the next round. If these early investors have brought more than money to the table, the easier the task will be of bringing on board more significant investors.

So early-stage investors help form alliances through their connections with larger corporate partners, technology exchanges, original equipment manufacturers (OEM), or other agreements that can help make your company succeed. They assist with equity offerings, financing, joint ventures, and acquisitions. They provide industry contacts with potential customers, vendors, and financial institutions; they assist in strategy, financing, and recruiting issues. They bring the correct knowledge and functional experience needed to grow a business. And, worth mentioning again, these investors offer a multidisciplined external contact network.

## HOW ANGEL INVESTORS CAN HELP—BEYOND CAPITAL

While more passive investments expect profit derived solely from the efforts of others—in mutual funds, for example—direct investing in private, early-stage ventures can entail significant involvement, contributing the investor's added value. In several ways, investors can help beyond their infusion of capital. (See Exhibit 5.6.)

Early-stage investors offer more than money. They offer added value in several ways: recruiting key management; understanding the industry/markets to be served (a network of contacts); serving as a sounding board; devising inventive team-oriented systems; displaying the patience and courage to go the distance; recruiting customers; and, finally, showing the patience, fortitude, and calmness in the face of the emotional roller-coaster ride inherent in start-ups. In the next chapter, we will hear from the investors themselves about the various ways they add value to start-ups.

## PRIVATE INVESTOR MOTIVATION

One motivation in private investment is, of course, return on investment, but it is only one factor of many in the decision-making process. The decision of the private investor to invest always turns on this fact: The private investor does not *have* to invest. Therefore, unlike the institutional investor and the money manager, the private investor market cannot be approached as some monolithic block. Even Stonehenge is not a single giant slab of rock. Like Stonehenge, the private market—despite all its shared elements—is composed of separate entities, exhibiting a complex set of motivations that we need to analyze. (See Exhibit 5.7.)

---

Exhibit 5.6  **HOW INVESTORS ADD VALUE BEYOND CAPITAL**

Alliances with larger corporate partners
through technology exchange,
OEM, or other agreements

Assist with equity offerings, financing,
joint venture, and acquisitions

Provide industry contacts with potential customers,
vendors, and financing institutions

Assist in strategy, financing, and recruiting issues

Bring right knowledge & functional experience
to help you grow your business

Offer a multidisciplined external contact network

Source: International Capital Resources

Exhibit 5.7 **INVESTOR MOTIVATION**

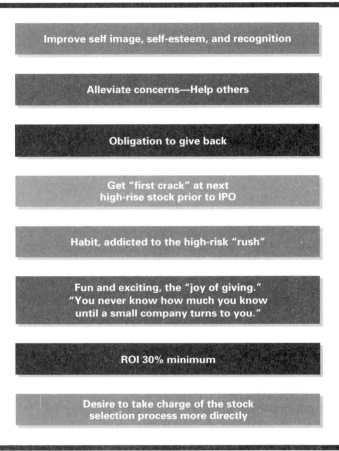

Improve self image, self-esteem, and recognition

Alleviate concerns—Help others

Obligation to give back

Get "first crack" at next high-rise stock prior to IPO

Habit, addicted to the high-risk "rush"

Fun and exciting, the "joy of giving." "You never know how much you know until a small company turns to you."

ROI 30% minimum

Desire to take charge of the stock selection process more directly

Source: International Capital Resources

As Exhibit 5.7 indicates, one significant shared element ironically serves to separate investors: Ninety percent of the millionaires worth between $1 million and $10 million are self-made. Having made it on their own accounts in part for their idiosyncratic natures.

One way they can recapture their successful experience—typically in their late 40s, after they have already "made it"—is by investing in new companies, making investments based on the acuteness of their analysis and intuition. Scoring once again reinforces their self-image. Their judgment, once again proven correct, sustains recognition in the investment and entrepreneurial communities in which they live. This serves as an important motivation.

A particularly fascinating component in the investor's motivation may involve the desire to alleviate misfortune. If the investor's spouse or a child has died from a disease, the investor may hope to be an instrument in research or a cure.

Some investors are motivated by the passionate commitment of the entrepreneur. People committed to a venture can be persuasive; they have enthusiasm and solid entrepreneurial vision, especially when the venture is close to their heart. Entrepreneurs with an ingratiating style, with the investor's concern at heart, and with a passion in their plea, become difficult to shake. The only way to get rid of them, in fact, is to make a token investment or pass them along to another investor.

Motivation also emanates from the feeling of obligation, noblesse oblige, perhaps born of guilt about how a particular fortune was made in the first place. David Rockefeller outdid his father's campaign of giving away dimes, begun in the first place to improve his deeply tarnished image. The compulsion arises to outdo the previous generation, to give back what may have been gained darkly—and then give still more.

What we mean by getting the "first crack" is being a part of the first-round of financing at what investors hope will be the next high rise, private stock leading to an IPO. Many people are familiar with the IPO market. Another way of looking at the angel capital market is to see it as the pre-IPO market. By the time a deal reaches the IPO stage, the big money has been soaked up by the early players. The people attracted to this type of investing, those willing to leave themselves subject to high risk, are those who want to play at that level because this is when the return comes in—not when the stock hits the street and is already being managed by a securities broker and the syndication.

Also there is a habit associated with this kind of investing, not unlike a gambling obsession, the rush experienced just before the check is written. This is another compulsion not to be underestimated.

Another motivation involves the sheer joy of high-risk investments. Possibly adding to a fledgling company's success has returns well beyond return on investment.

Last, however, is the motivating power of return on investment. John Cadle, ICR's valuation expert, offers in Exhibit 5.8 the rules of thumb in alerting entrepreneurs to the levels generally regarded by investors as acceptable rates on return by venture stage. At the seed/start-up stage, for example, an investor is looking for a compounded, annualized rate of return of 60 to 100 percent, while at the bridge-to-cash-out stage, the expected rate of return is measured at only 20 percent.

This leads Cadle to offer some facts of early-stage investment life: First, prospective investors may not share the entrepreneur's level of optimism for the venture's success. Successful, sophisticated venture investors are risk-averse, quick to discount projections in reviewing proposals. Investors also find that management teams of early-stage

Exhibit 5.8  STAGES OF VENTURE CAPITAL

| | Rule-of-Thumb Required Return |
| Description | Internal Rate of Return* |
| --- | --- |
| Seed/start-up | 60–100% |
| Development + mgt. team | 50–60% |
| Revenues/expansion | 40–50% |
| Profitable/cash-poor | 30–40% |
| Rapid growth | 25–35% |
| Bridge to cash out | 20%+ |

*Before applying subjective factors.

enterprises rarely forecast cash requirements accurately. Investors realize that unforeseen follow-on financing is lurking about. Each of these points is detailed in Chapter 11.

Taking charge of the stock selection process has to do with a trend in the brokerage industry to discount brokers and stimulate more active involvement using the information available through various resources, for example, the Internet, trade papers, and magazines. The idea is to take a more active role in managing one's portfolio. This type of investing allows for ways to diversify based on past experience, a way to control the placement of a percentage of one's portfolio, a way to steer a portfolio percentage into other equity areas, perhaps increasing the range of return. People today are doing a thorough job of managing their retirement, of choosing mutual funds for their various retirement accounts. The desire for increased control, using technology and available information, fuels this type of investing, which gets the investor more deeply involved in the selection process and more directly involved in the deal.

## THE ALLOCATION DECISION

An investor's allocation decision is, of course, intrinsically tied to portfolio management. The private investor is not investing an entire life's savings in a single venture. He or she has invested in cash, in liquid investments and less-liquid investment, in real estate, in bonds, and in publicly traded stock. So while this investor is interested in investing in publicly traded stock, he or she is also interested in investing in private equity, which boasts a range of investments, including seed, research and development, start-up, first stage, expansion stage, mezzanine, bridge, acquisition/mergers, and turnaround.

Strong evidence suggests that these investors place a small percentage of their money in higher-risk deals—about 5 to 10 percent of their private equity portfolio. High-caliber money managers will confess that they always leave some money for the client to manage, money for clients to play with on their own. It is this play money that represents investments in higher-risk deals. So it is the individual's allocation decision that influences where private equity investment ends up.

Exhibit 5.9 shows the specific elements that influence the decision to invest in a particular venture.

First, the investment in a particular company must match the investment strategy of the individual investor. If the investor desires income, he or she will invest in a subordinated note providing interest or perhaps in preferred stock providing a dividend. If the capital strategy is to generate capital appreciation and capital gains, the investment will be in a common or preferred equity deal, requiring the investor to hold that position for a period of five to eight years, hoping that the stock will increase in value.

Another factor in the allocation decision reflects the investor's stage of life. Investors in their early 30s are concerned about buying a house, saving for a child's education, buying a boat, taking a grand vacation, or perhaps buying jewelry or art. These investors, in other words, are less likely to have the discretionary income necessary to make these kinds of investments. However, by the time these investors have reached the late 40s to late 50s, the kids are out of school, the house is paid off, and more discretionary income is available. So more discretionary income becomes available at a time when their income has increased or has reached its peak. Thus, the stage of life of investors has a significant impact on the allocation decision.

Additional impact arises from the investor's proclivity for risk. One who can stomach the ambiguity associated with the earlier-stage deals

---

Exhibit 5.9 **THE ALLOCATION DECISION**

- Match investment strategy
- Stage of life
- Risk posture
- Part of business cycle of interest (experience)
- Relative attractiveness of participatory investing
- Net worth, income, liquid financial assets on hand

will likely sport an aggressive risk posture, a willingness to invest in an early-stage deal, preseed, seed, or start-up. One who cannot stomach the ambiguity and risk—despite having the money—probably will gravitate to later-stage private equity transactions, such as a leverage buyout of an existing company, one that has a financial history, or to a mezzanine financing with a guaranteed payoff in 18 to 24 months.

Another aspect of the allocation decision of private investments is the investor's experience in various stages of the investment cycle. An investor is like a physician: The doctor who feels engaged in the early stages of life is likely to go into pediatrics, while another physician might opt for taking care of the elderly. In the same way, a private investor may like to associate with early-stage companies, reflecting his or her earlier successful experience, perhaps as president of an early-stage company.

We know other investors who have had great success in turning around old, staid, bureaucratic enterprises. So if we take an early-stage deal to someone who has been president of a large corporation, he or she may not understand or may feel uncomfortable. There simply may be no grasp of the interpersonal relationships, or the political and emotional dynamics of such an enterprise. Two things have to fit: the stage of the company in the business cycle that the particular investment represents and the experience of the individual investor.

Next in the allocation decision is the relative attractiveness of the participatory investment. As we have indicated, value-added investing means more than supplying capital, particularly for an individual participatory investment that is a time-intensive activity. One of the reasons venture capitalists have moved out of such investments is not only that venture capital funds have become much larger but that those individuals managing the funds do not have the time to sit on five or ten boards. The private investor is looking for that participatory role most likely to furnish the necessary level of involvement. So the relative attractiveness of this type of time commitment—a value-added commitment beyond the element of money—is a prominent component of the allocation decision.

Last, but centrally important to the allocation decision, are the levels of the investor's net worth, income, and liquid financial assets—the tendons of the entire investment process.

## PRINCIPLES OF DIRECT VENTURE INVESTING

Warren Buffett has said that he has no idea what that world of high technology will look like in ten years. Technology is just something, he claimed, we don't understand, so we don't invest in it.

We believe that if the second richest person in the world can follow that principle, we can follow it. As Exhibit 5.10 shows, the first guideline of direct venture investing is to know the business you are investing in. Knowing the business you are investing in becomes a solid hedge against losing your investment. Second, do your own due diligence—do not rely on other people—and focus your due diligence on the management team, on the market, and on the technology. The third guideline is to plan on having sufficient reserves for future rounds to protect your position in the investment. To some extent in the negotiating terms and conditions, providing dilution and protection is possible, although in certain instances it will not be. Still, it is important to remember that if you want to maintain the same ownership share over time, you are going to have to have sufficient funds for future rounds.

One lesson we have learned is that when a sophisticated investor claims to have $25,000 to invest, what the person really is saying is that he or she has $50,000 to invest: The person is keeping $25,000 in reserve to take care of his or her position at a later date.

Another point is to avoid unrealistically high valuations. While the money managers in the venture capital industry clawing for the same deal can afford that kind of luxury, the private investor who is struggling, reading business plans to find one or two in 100 that are viable, must, in order to be protected in the future, make sure that he or she does not get involved in a situation that is overly valued. The real opportunity here at the early stage for taking that high level of risk is to get the appropriate percent of equity. And in many cases investors seek about 20 to 30 percent of the company on the first round of financing beyond self, family, and friends. So if this is the first round of investment, when the company is going to sophisticated investors to whom they are not related, 20 to 30 percent of the company is not an unrea-

---

Exhibit 5.10  **DIRECT VENTURE INVESTING**

- Know the business
- Do your own due diligence on:
  —People
  —Market
  —Technology
- Plan on having sufficient reserves for future rounds
- Avoid unrealistically high valuations
- Understand the liquidity risks

Source: International Capital Resources

sonable amount to be looking for to cover the financing at that high-risk level—particularly when the company as yet cannot boast of revenues.

With the last guideline we suggest that you understand the liquidity risks. So few companies really take the time to think through an exit strategy. But it is imperative that the principals of a company think through a legitimate strategy and have documented that that strategy within this industry is applicable and capable, and that the financial forecasts that have been developed are in fact going to lead to a viable exit strategy.

Understand the true liquidity risks in a situation; understand that, based on our research at ICR, the average hold on these investments is around eight years. Above all, understand that direct venture investing requires a long-term hold—thus, lots of patience. We turn in Chapter 6 to the investors themselves.

# 6

# Types of Private Investors

*I should like to have a more perfect knowledge of things,*
*but I do not want to buy it as dear as it costs.*

Michel de Montaigne

## INTRODUCTION

Every private investor would appreciate having a "more perfect knowledge of things," but operating, at best, with an *imperfect* knowledge of the "dear costs" of things, each has decisions to make—as you are about to discover from their own words. Taken together they form a highly articulate verbal community that talks straight, an information-rich, information-sharing network of idiosyncratic individuals.

In his 1997 *Inc.* article, "My Life as an Angel," Norman Brodsky speaks to what drives these networks of investors: "For me, there's nothing like it—the business of seeing a business rise up from nothing. . . . There's just something unbelievably thrilling about seeing the growth, watching the numbers go up, getting the business to stand on its own. . . . I can't get enough of it." He continues: "[T]hese deals . . . offer me the opportunity to teach other people some of the things I've learned over the years and to share with them the excitement of bringing a new business into existence."

The variety of individual private investors we enumerate in Exhibit 6.1 forms a nexus, a large group within which we differentiate types. Based on our experience, and based on countless conversations and interviews and hundreds of Bay Area Venture Forum investor presentations, we have selected individuals who we feel capture the essence of *types* of angels from among the more than 8,000 listed in International Capital Resources' database. From these conversations and presentations, and from more than 600 interviews with private investors, have emerged patterns of like-mindedness within similar investment orientations.

Exhibit 6.1 **TYPOLOGY OF ANGEL INVESTORS**

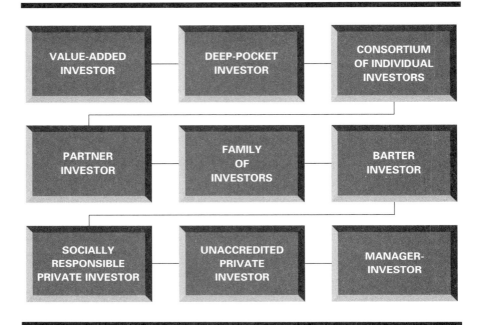

Source: International Capital Resources

To know the types, to glimpse their differing motivations, is to evaluate what investors are looking for and determine whether your time would be wasted or well spent in dealing with certain investor types. Thus, understanding and distinguishing types of investors forms the rationale for this chapter.

In assessing investors, entrepreneurs are dealing with singular individuals, not impersonal structures such as banks. Beneath the facade, all banks are the same. Their criteria for granting a loan fit a single mold. Their ratios, calculations, and protocol are stamped out cookie-cutter style. Their loan-to-risk computations are cloned. On the other hand, no monolithic investment criterion dictates when and where private investors are likely to invest, although they share much, as we have noted. But neither are they of infinite variety. Angel investors fall into types, the types we delineate here. So as you listen to the barter-investor, the value-added investor, the deep-pocket investor, and so on, weave these individuals into generic types of the private investors you will be meeting and asking to invest in your vision.

(One important type of investor in particular has emerged, a new breed of investor responding to a number of different market factors.

This is the manager-investor, so important a group, in fact, that we will treat it separately in the next chapter.)

Our first type of investor is the value-added investor.

## THE VALUE-ADDED INVESTOR

### Value-Added Investor #1

**I either jump into the plan or the plan jumps out of my hands.**

I've been involved in a broad range of industries over a lot of years. This includes the experience of having worked with a company that, when we started, was doing about half a million in sales and grew to $80 million in sales within two years. We have bought up about 21 companies and gone public and done amazingly well. The common thread that runs through all of my activity is my background in building ventures. The financial investments I've made in companies, for the most part, have ranged from $50,000 to $150,000 per company.

Location of the company is an issue for me. If I can't drive to the company within an hour of my base, San Francisco, it becomes a real stretch for me. I have invested in out-of-state deals, but I'm not comfortable with them. Further, industry is not as important as the economic opportunity, the point being that I am a generalist and not a technologist. I look at each case on its own merits. I perform the due diligence. I've invested in both loans and

---

Exhibit 6.2  **VALUE-ADDED INVESTOR**

- Very experienced investors and former investment bankers and venture capitalists
- Storefront venture capital firms
- Short due diligence cycle, require business plans
- Make multiple investments
- Want to help grow business and have fun doing so
- Lead investor. Searches out investment opportunities and makes an independent decision to invest and often suggests investments to others
- Very strong network of coinvestors whom they leverage and who trust their judgment
- Become extremely active and involved, however, only for short periods; problem-solver orientation
- Tend toward industry concentrations
- Invests close to home
- Invests $50,000–$250,000 in either debt or equity

Source: International Capital Resources

equity. I look for an opportunity to advise the companies. That's the reason I do all this, because I like helping companies.

Private investors who spend time with companies are called "value-added investors," which is precisely what we are. I'm a very active investor. For instance, I've just completed a merger for two companies that I've been involved with. I've done all kinds of things with these businesses, which is precisely what I enjoy doing.

I am a *follow-on* investor. I've been in a number of situations in which there have been "deep-pocket" investors who put a million dollars or more in companies that I eventually got into as a follow-on investor—a situation I like to see. I'm not saying that a follow-on investor has to have $1 million in the company, but if there is a major investor in the company, it's nice for me to know, as a follow-on investor, that he or she has a lot more invested in the company than I do, that he or she is going to carry the company through the blips. This is exactly what has happened and exactly what has saved some companies that I've been involved in. So being a follow-on investor attracts me.

For me to become involved in companies at the idea stage, I have to see that each company has a good product, a ready market, and a management team with a lot of experience in its field. If the company has some revenue, I'd prefer to see about $1 million in sales. The CEO is also important in a company that I look at.

And, in my mind, the people in the company have to have, at the first cut, the four *P*s. They have to be *passionate, persistent, pleasant,* and *penetrable.* By *passionate* I mean they have to love the business they're in. They have to live it seven days a week in their heart and their soul. They have to be *persistent* in reaching for the appropriate goals, they have to do it with fervor, but they also have to commit to the follow-up issues associated with any task. And I mention that especially in regard to my recent experience with a person of great vision but no follow-up. The people in the company also have to be pleasant to work with. Compatibility *is* an issue. In fact, treat your investor as your partner. Finally, they have to be *penetrable,* that is, open to advice—extremely important, especially given my involvement with businesses. Part of this is having a collectively logical mind, that is, the people have to be able to think logically through business issues.

I'm at the point in my investing career where I really discourage plans being sent to me. Initially, I want to look at an executive summary. In terms of a nondisclosure issue, you're probably going to find investors who are willing to sign every nondisclosure statement coming to them, or they won't sign even one because of the liability. You can get around that by giving them the executive summary, which typically doesn't have any proprietary information in it. Then you will see if they're interested and carry on from there. I usually review the executive summary, which gives me a real quick idea of what the business is, then turn to the resumes—because those are the people who are going to make it happen. Then I either jump into the plan or the plan jumps out of my hands.

I want to plug something I call *mutual due diligence*. As much as an investor is going to do due diligence on your company, you should do due diligence on the investor. And you should think about what kind of investors you want, what they're going to bring to the table. I think there's a whole host of questions you can ask. From my experience, an organization like International Capital Resources brings together quality investors. By contrast, you have no idea what you will find out there on the street.

One of the sensible questions for an entrepreneur to ask investors is whether they have ever done this kind of thing before. Have they been involved with a company and with the kind of investment they're about to make with you? Because if they haven't been through the downside of working with a business, I don't think you want to be in the position of a trainer. It takes an awful lot of time out of what could be an awfully good company.

## Value-Added Investor #2

**What I ask—and I've learned this question painfully—is whether the venture can survive as a business in the short term, say six months, a year, or 18 months, whatever it takes to get to a positive cash flow.**

I've been on both sides of the table, as a principal, as an investor, both for venture capital firms and for my own account. I've also been on the entrepreneur side of the table raising money. I am an absolute expert in this business, because, after 20-plus years in the business, I've been in more traps and made every mistake you could make as an investor. The trick is not to make them more than once or twice. That's probably why I'm such an expert. This is very much an apprenticeship business. That is, the investor learns by doing.

I focus on a few areas, trying to sift the weak from the strong in investment opportunities. Number one for me is the market. Let me just say up front that the definition of your market is the key. Obviously, as an investor, I want to see that there's a big enough market so that if you have to shift strategy or change course, there's enough room to do it.

Specifically, I'm interested in the appropriate market segment you're doing business in. And if it's the San Francisco Bay Area, fine. Tell us how you're going to capture the San Francisco Bay Area and use that as a model for expansion into other cities. Zero in on your segment and talk about that.

If you've got a product and you want to attract third-party investors, the entrepreneur needs to think about the following: making that product into a business, using the personal skills of your team, creating a distribution network, and multiplying your expertise into similar kinds of products or services. Then mill all that together to make a business that has a chance to grow and to attract third-party capital.

I want a product or a service that offers customers a compelling reason to buy it. That means it needs to be different from whatever else is out there, because you're obviously going to be a small business going against the big guys. But—and this is where I've gotten a lot of arrows in my back—it cannot be so different, so revolutionary, so unique that you have to do a lot of missionary selling to convince people that this is a product to buy. Now, that may be fine for larger institutional investors or venture capital groups that are in seed-development capital. That's what they do. The technology guys and engineers who do due diligence aren't the people who write the checks. The people who write the checks are the purchasing managers, so you need to convince me that the theoretical demand for your product can be converted into dollar orders in the short term.

A second criterion for me is survivability. This, however, is a double-edged sword. When I look at a plan, certainly I want to see a big enough opportunity to make it worth my while, or an opportunity to shift course if necessary. That's great. But what I ask—and I've learned this question painfully—is whether the venture can survive as a business in the short term, say six months, a year, or eighteen months, whatever it takes to get to a positive cash flow.

How are you going to do that? How are you going to sell product in the short term to generate cash internally? I think this is absolutely critical. What is your sales strategy? How are you going to get those orders in the door? What is a realistic sell cycle for your product or service? If it looks like it's two months, it's probably four months. I've learned that the hard way. I've been in some deals where the technology worked, the product was great, the people liked it, but the sales cycle turned out to be four or five times as long as we thought and, as a result, we ran out of cash and had to engage in down-and-dirty financing to bring in capital at a much lower valuation level.

Another factor is financing strategy, an aspect that goes with the survivability. As I mentioned, I will look to see whether the company can generate cash in the short term to survive. Also, have you thought about a long-term financing plan? And I know that's a little difficult when you're scratching around trying to figure out where the next dollar of capital is coming from, but it's important to have, just like you have a marketing plan, a sales plan, a manufacturing plan, a plan to bring in capital in various stages, and a strategy to attract the kind of investor who would be ideal at those stages.

Last, what are your plans to fill out the management team? In an early-stage company, obviously the key person is the founder, the CEO. Few early-stage companies can declare, "We have our whole management team in place." Obviously you don't, and we investors understand that. But I'm interested in your thoughts about how you're going to fill those important positions, such as a salesperson, in the early stage, and what your plans are for bringing on those people in a logical progression.

## Value-Added Investor #3

**I try not to make investments that I don't think the venture community will be subsequently interested in.**

As someone who has been making private venture investments now, I guess, for the last seven or eight years, I believe that most investors are not aware of the tremendous concentration of investments in just a few areas. I was at a dinner with some people from professional venture capital firms—two of the larger Silicon Valley venture capital firms—who admitted to me that in the last three years, more than 80 percent of their investments had been made in the following areas: software, networking, multimedia, and the last area was wireless. And so you can look at presentations made today and 90 percent may fall out of those areas. There may be one telecommunications-related activity and the bulk of the investors will be in other perfectly reputable areas, but areas not very accessible to the venture capitalists.

I'm not sure why the industry tends to concentrate like this. I think it tends to want to put a consortium together and work in areas each consortium can then become expert in. As far as my own investing philosophy is concerned, I find it very difficult to fight these trends, so the bulk of the investments I have been making in the last couple of years tend to fall in those same areas. However, it's the exception to the rule that probably makes for the best opportunity, so I think all of us have to be willing to look in other areas.

I make investments in the $50,000 to $250,000 range. I don't make them outside of the local Bay Area. I've had some bad experiences in trying to fly to Boston or commute to Los Angeles to help make investments. I try not to make investments that I don't think the venture community will be subsequently interested in. And I don't make investments outside of what would generally be called the high-tech area. Formerly, I was a senior executive with a major computer hardware manufacturer, so I'm involved mostly in that industry. Those are the businesses I'm interested in. So I don't want to invest in services, in medical, or in distribution.

## Value-Added Investor #4

**I like to very quickly get an idea of the product, the market, the competition. . . . Then I go right into the people, because the people are the ones that are going to make it happen.**

In being asked what I look for in companies, I always respond that I'm looking for the product and the market opportunity. And once I understand that, it becomes 99 percent management. I've been through enough companies to know that management is the key to making any plan work.

I've had the experience of being part of a start-up company that went public, and I've had the experience of working with a Fortune 100 company, of being responsible for billions of dollars in assets and thousands of people.

But the most fun has really been in helping to grow young companies, which I've done all my life.

I'm very involved in these businesses and spend my time on the most important problems or the biggest opportunities. I try to focus my time on the things that make a difference for the company. I do debt and I do equity deals with companies. The average investment that I've made has ranged generally from $50,000 to $150,000 per company.

The industries I've been involved with have been diverse. What drives me is the economic opportunity more than the industry, but I shy away most definitely from anything exotic. I'm involved in due diligence or I've invested in businesses related to the mountain bike industry, the software that helps make the health care system more efficient, and the coffee business. So I diversify and it's a lot of fun. I am a generalist.

For me, the critical ticket for the laundry is the business plan. Ninety percent of the deals that I look at have business plans and, frankly, the flow, the funnel, has been real big over the years. I've gotten to the point where if I just get the executive summary I'm a happy camper. And if it's of interest, I'll talk with the company.

The companies are located in the Bay Area. I like to get there if they need me. Then I look for a return on investment, which, obviously, ranges. Also, there has to be a variety of exit strategies. One recent exit was the acquisition of the company. Acquisitions are very nice.

Gross margins, I have found, are pretty important; the bigger the margins, the more attractive it is—for a simple reason. There are positives and negatives to large gross margins, but I have found, generally, that with the bigger gross margins, there's more forgiveness for problems that a young company has. In fact, it has saved a few of them.

The projected numbers that you have in your business plans definitely are important, but they're not as important to me as the assumptions that underlie them. I will spend time carefully going through those assumptions, trying to comprehend the depth of understanding and the degree to which the company has grasped all the components of its business. I have rarely found projected numbers actually occurring, so I'll spend the time on the assumptions.

When I get a business plan, I'll first take a look at the executive summary. I hope it's not more than a couple of pages. Then I go right to the resumes. In other words, I like to very quickly get an idea of the product, the market, the competition—all the basic things you put in an executive summary. Then I go right into the people, because the people make it happen. If they pass muster, I'll spend the time going through the plan.

Value-added investors, I think, are really important. I will tell you this: I've dealt with an awful lot of companies; the most successful ones have had value-added investors who have brought more than money to the table and they've helped grow the business in ways that money alone can't.

Also, companies need to do their homework in understanding the market dynamics and understanding distribution. Obviously a business plan deals with the marketing issues, the competition, the distribution, the pricing, the market needs, how to sell, and strategy. But when I sit down with the people in the company, I have found, unfortunately too often, that they do not have the necessary depth of understanding of those issues. If a company doesn't understand its market and understand how to access the market, it's going to face serious problems.

A lot of people running these companies are technically oriented; they have a great idea of the product and its applications. But the issues are broader than that. A common issue I see occurring with companies centers on a naughty F-word: *focus, focus, focus.* The problem is the lack of it. It's easy in the early stages of the business to pursue opportunities as they arrive, and multiple opportunities typically do arise. But it's the highly disciplined businesses that succeed.

In experiences I've had with a few companies I've invested in I learned a particular lesson. It really saved me; it saved a certain part of my anatomy located just below my waist. There was a lead private investor, a major investor who had invested close to $1 million in the company. I felt secure because I knew that he had deep pockets; he had a vested interest in, and a history with, the company, so I knew if problems arose—and they did; they always do—he would keep that company afloat. The lesson is this: Among your private investors, getting one in particular who can bring added value along with a significant amount of money can mean the difference. I think if you have a compatibility and you know your investor, you're going to bring something to the company that's of real value.

Our second type of investor is the deep-pocket investor.

## THE DEEP-POCKET INVESTOR

### Deep-Pocket Investor #1

**Even if you give up a significant chunk of your company to get the right management in place, you'll be way ahead for having done it.**

In my career I've been an accountant, a lawyer, a consultant, a CFO of high-technology start-up companies, and most recently I'm president of a software company. I have been an active individual investor, and over the past 15 years have done 15 investments, roughly one a year, although it's more a matter of accumulating enough money to make the next investment than it is an ability to accommodate them. The rate of investment seems closely related to my earnings from other things. These 15 investments ranged in amount from $10,000 to $90,000. The average is about $50,000 to $100,000.

---

## Exhibit 6.3 DEEP-POCKET INVESTOR

- Built and sold company
- Corporate not technical background
- Emphasis on deal structure to mitigate risk
- Invests only in what he knows
- Prefer that investor(s) hold control, e.g., outside board
- People and plan equally important
- Can be lead or independent investor. Can search for opportunities, makes independent decision to invest, suggests investments to others, welcomes leads from respected colleagues, but always relies on own judgment, & investigation in deciding to invest
- Geographic preference
- Fun is a factor
- Targeted ROI of 50%/year
- Some involvement to make a contribution
- Open to both debt and equity
- $50,000–$100,000 per investment, 1–3 investments per year

Source: International Capital Resources

My experience as an entrepreneur puts me squarely in the middle of individual investors. And when you put up private placement out there and you're looking for 10 to 35 people on a regulation D offering, that's the kind of folks you're going to get. Of my 15 investments, five have been winners, four outright losers—"losers" as in all my money is gone—and five have either not had their outcome determined or have more or less broken even. Of the 15, nine have been in start-up or early-stage companies; three have been in venture capital funds—in which my money was pooled with other people's and then professional management hired us out of the funds—and three have been in real estate.

I have divided my primary investment criteria between those that are *absolutely* essential and those that are *merely* essential. It's like saying in a business plan that you want to have an analysis of the market *and* a description of the people *and* a financial forecast *and* a description of the assumptions. I want good grammar *and* correct spelling. If it doesn't have all that stuff, I'm disappointed, though I may still make the investment.

At the top of my list of criteria is a high ROI—at least 50 percent a year—50 percent a year *after* all of my discounting of time slippage, risk assessment, and everything else. Only in an early-stage deal are those kinds of returns usually offered, which is what drives me to early-stage companies. Sometimes—and I've made this kind of investment a couple of times—you can do a short-term debt instrument that has that rate of return. It happens when somebody has an existing business, an opportunity that requires capital, an opportunity that has the level of risk no bank wants to back. By having something that combines debt and maybe some warrants, or some other equity component as a sweetener, you can get the same 50 percent return and have a short liquidity time—certainly an added attraction.

My second criterion demands exceptional management, especially a solid CEO. Over time I have found that even if the rest of the management team is good, it's really only the CEO that people invest in. And having been a CFO—a somewhat humbling experience—has helped me crystallize the need for a top-notch performer in that position. Generally, an investment becomes a gamble on that individual and, as an investor with some experience, I've decided that, after ROI, there's hardly a more significant consideration in my deciding to invest or not invest. Obviously, if that person changes, the risk of your investment changes a lot, so how committed the management is and how committed the funding sources are become critical. If it's a start-up company, I cannot fund the whole thing out of my own pocket.

One of the common themes among my investment losers is not finding enough financing to take the venture all the way. It wasn't because the idea was all bad. (At least, no one but the people who turned down the investment would say so.) There need to be people with deeper pockets than mine as part of the deal structure, a structure in which my interests are aligned with theirs, so that they don't get a big return if I don't get a big return.

In addition, I prefer that investors as a group have control, certainly control if downside contingency occurs. If the management or founders as a group have control and want to keep control, they'd better have been in business a while and have had some revenue and perhaps even made a profit. If there is a 50-50 split—which is often the case in the early-stage deals between capitalists and workers—I think the capitalists need to have a way of gaining control if milestones are not met.

An essential criterion focuses on local connections. First, all my investments are in the Bay Area; the exception occurs where there is a strong local connection and the company is actually operating somewhere else or considering relocating to that area.

Another criterion of mine in deciding whether to invest is whether the opportunity is available for input to management, typically a board seat. Because of the skill sets I have, I usually can count on people asking for my help to set up accounting systems, or hire lawyers, or write their business plans, or evaluate the deals for them. Thoroughness of the business plan is very meaningful. I run across entrepreneurs—or would-be entrepreneurs—who actually hire other people to write their business plan for them. It's one thing to hire somebody who can do an Excel spreadsheet better than you can, but I have never seen a CEO able to run a company successfully who couldn't describe in writing what the plan was for that company—and do so in a fairly articulate manner.

So I think it is essential for you to write the plan demonstrating an understanding of the market, a careful forecast of the future expressed in numbers, complete with the assumptions for a forecast. Frequently a business plan has page after page of month number 10 as well as month number 24. However, what I'm more interested in is three or four pages of *careful* assumptions *carefully* described, plus prepaid expenses based on the industry average, and the amount of capital required in year number 2—coming from a public offering or other investors. Or else we're going to tap you if we can for another round.

What also gets my attention is a business plan that includes in its terms an action plan from someone who demonstrates that over the next 90 to 180 days, from the time the company receives the money, he or she can enumerate what exactly has to be done to make this business go. The more specific those kinds of milestones are, the more comfortable I am in knowing that I can measure progress after I've made the investment and calibrate how I should react—that is, whether I've made a mistake, or whether I should put money in if I'm asked. This is a very good way both to monitor the investment and to assess how management is doing and what you can do to help them.

I favor a short time to liquidity. I don't think of myself as a long-term investor, but I turn out that way in many of these ventures. A fax company that I helped start in 1988 had a business plan that declared by 1993 we would go public and have $50 million in sales. It's got about $10 million in sales and probably another three years till liquidity—now that it's been in business six years. That's typical. And I've found that there are good enough opportunities in the public stock market that provide liquidity with moderated risk.

If I'm going to have a long-term, definite ending in a private company, I'd better have some chance of liquidity along the way. I don't necessarily want to pull my money out, but the company needs to have a plan for stages of investor returns. I'd like also, as a secondary criterion, to have the possibility of a very high return. Maybe you think a 50-percent-a-year return is high. To me, a very high return means it is an Apple Computer in the making, or a medical device that everybody in the world wants, or a solar energy company, alone among the whole industry, that actually makes something everybody wants.

Also, I look for people who have done it before, hopefully very successfully. This usually means that they are coming out of the same industry, maybe another company, and they're just going into business competing with the former employer. Or in some other way they have been successful entrepreneurs and are working now in something very closely related. And, finally, I look for some downside protection.

I'm quite willing to walk away from investments and lose all my money, but I prefer that there's some kind of second chance at getting part of my money back or parlaying it into something else of value. I think also that the fellow investors need to be able to contribute something besides money. Finally, the process ought to, on a whole, just be fun if it works; otherwise, it becomes too painful to think about.

What most entrepreneurs sell is a story, and what most investors, particularly the more sophisticated investors, want to buy is management. When you're out there selling to people who are investing $15,000, $20,000 at a crack—your friends and members of your family—the story becomes a question of *what* they are buying. If you're going to succeed in raising the money for a larger, more sophisticated investment, and if the company, in turn, is going to succeed, you're going to have to show the more sophisticated investors that you've got the management team in place—or know how you're going to get it in place—and also show that the team has formulated a clear plan of action.

Management is the key to being able to deal with unexpected problems certain to arise. So if you are an entrepreneur with a great idea and a great story but you don't have the management expertise, get it. Even if you give up a significant chunk of your company to get the right management in place, you'll be way ahead for having done it. Qualified management is one of the most difficult parts of a business plan to evaluate because resumes can all be made to look great. How do you evaluate what someone can really do? I have found that I need to do a lot more due diligence every time I review a potential investment. Having done it several times, I have been surprised at instances of outright fraud, outright cover-up in which people were not revealing everything.

Personally, I'm a generalist. If it looks like it can make money, I'll take a look at it. For example, a potato chip plant in Colorado already had an empty building where the company was going to set up its plant, and it was already sourcing the chips from a Texas operation. From a look at the business plan, from all the numbers, all it needed was capital to get machinery in there and start producing, instead of buying, the chips. The company was going to be making money in no time. It was in the stores, a really ready-to-go operation. It already had shelf space and name recognition in the area. But it wasn't telling the whole story.

So how do you uncover that? It's a difficult thing from an investor's perspective. You have to be very careful. It's very important for entrepreneurs to reveal everything and to have integrity, or else you are building in your own doom. You're not going to succeed by hiding things. It all comes back to bite you. So make sure you tell a potential investor the bad news first, and if they're still interested after they hear the potential difficulties, you've got someone that's ready to go through the trials and tribulations with you. But if you're giving only this wonderful story about the future, and the investor buys into that, what happens when the first problem comes along? Now you've got problems beyond anything you have anticipated.

I, by the way, have an entrepreneurial background myself; I haven't always been an investor. I remember someone explaining the difference between institutional and private investing, a distinction sometimes difficult for a private investor to remember: The private investor does not have to invest! Sometimes the story is so attractive that you are lured into it and say, "Wow, this is hot; this really has sizzle." But you have to have that management team to keep the bacon frying or the sizzle fizzles.

Perhaps the greatest disservice that's been done to entrepreneurs is the saying that if you build a better mousetrap, the world will beat a path to your door. It's just not true! The shelves are lined with better mousetraps. If you have the right management you can take an inferior product, make it succeed, and make money. So don't buy into a story that just because you've got something unique and better than what's already out there that you're going to succeed. It takes a lot of hard work and correct management decisions.

In terms of my own investments, as I said, I'm a generalist. Generally, $50,000 to $100,000, sometimes a little more per investment. I've been a public investor and actually was a commodity trader for many years, which led me to understand risk and decide that the risk involved in investment in private companies made sense. In fact, it's kind of the same game. You expect to lose. You have to be willing to accept losses; the wins just have to be big enough to compensate for them. So as a commodity trader, I found that if I could be right 30 percent of the time I could make a lot of money, because I cut my losses short and my winnings were big ones.

## Deep-Pocket Investor #2

**A good CEO without an exit strategy is much better than a poor CEO with an exit strategy. If it's a poor CEO, you know what your exit strategy is; it's called a Chapter 11 or a Chapter 7. So to me the quality of a CEO is the most important thing.**

When I look at a business plan my interest is heavily weighted toward the numbers. I look at projections going out only about three years, because after three years, I've never found a crystal ball that was clear enough to mean anything. The other thing I'd look for in a business plan is a reason to believe the numbers are good. I would expect a write-up saying it's a projection, but why should I believe this projection is solid? I do not want just words; I do not want just numbers. I really think you have to feel ownership of that business plan. You have to believe in it; otherwise, you can't sell it. When you ask for investor capital, you're asking the investor to buy your perception or your business plan.

Companies never go broke if they always have enough cash. Since the only time companies go broke is when they run out of cash, really work on your cash projections, your cash flows. The size of the investment I typically look for is something in the $100,000 to $250,000 class. So I would say I'm a smaller investor.

The enterprise should be projected in the black within 18 to 24 months, or have a reason why it's not profitable within that time frame. If our projections are good only for three years, we had better be in the black 18 to 24 months out.

The president of the company should really consider that his investment in the company is a modest living and his real income should come through stock options. If the president isn't willing to live modestly as he's building the company and figure his payout comes at the end with the stock offering, or stock options, I really question whether this is the person to run the company. I'm not concerned as much with an exit strategy as I am with the quality of the CEO. A good CEO without an exit strategy is much better than a poor CEO with an exit strategy. If it's a poor CEO, you know what your exit strategy is; it's called a Chapter 11 or a Chapter 7. So to me the quality of a CEO is the most important thing.

Also important is that the company be big enough to have an outside control board. I would not be interested in owning control of the company, but the company has to have an outside control board. And I will help in the area of actively recruiting board members, because my firm belief is that if you have a board with experienced businessmen and those members have all run businesses larger than this one, you have increased your chances of success. And getting an outside control board, gathering people who will truly participate, is not that much of a problem, and not that expensive either.

No single customer should represent more than 5 percent of your volume. If you have a customer who represents 20 to 30 percent of your volume, you no longer are making the business decisions; your customers are.

In my investments the majority of the business assets are located within two to three hours of my home. As an investor I want to go out and be able to kick the side of the wall, or kick the desk, and find out where the hell the investment is. I don't want an investment a five-hour plane ride away. You also want to go out and see what other people think of the business, depending on what the business is and depending on whom you'd ask.

Time frame? I'm comfortable with looking at a 10- to 12-year, maybe a 15-year investment, as long as the projections forecast that we can grow by internally generated cash flows. If you're going to show rapid growth, you're going to need additional rounds of investors, and additional rounds of investors may demand more than the first group did. May not, but, in turn, may.

I guess everything boils down to three important things: the quality of the CEO, the feasibility of the projected balance sheet, and the reasonableness of the business plan. The rest becomes second fiddle. If you can get those three things in order, you should be able to get an investment.

## Deep-Pocket Investor #3

**I'm not going to continue looking at a deal where I don't feel very, very comfortable with the people. That's not only a feeling that they're straight, but also that they're honest. And I gotta like them. Otherwise, I'm not going to invest.**

I'll just make one comment up front: I'm a real expert in this business because in the 12 to 14 years that I've been in this aspect of the business, I have personally made every investment mistake you can make. Or I've witnessed the mistakes.

The trick in this business is to learn by doing business and to try not to make the same mistake twice. But oftentimes we get caught up in the entrepreneur's and the founder's enthusiasm. That's as it should be. That's the kind of business this is—more art than science.

My particular background is eclectic: I've been on both the entrepreneur side and the venture capital side. Last year I spent the better part of the year working as the founder of a company and I was humbled by that experience. So I certainly have empathy for people on that side.

One of the things that came out of that experience is a respect for knowing the market. I see a lot of plans stating that the market is $5 million, or it's equal to the gross national product, or it's this or it's that. I would urge you to concentrate on how you're going to get to that market, to zero in on what the served market is. And, like all of these things, there are entries on both sides of the ledger. Certainly there is the focus: You want to have a niche; you want to have a small market; but, at the same time, that market has to be big enough.

Like any business plan, like any good entrepreneur, you can count on shifts in your strategy once you get into the market. So I would urge you to also understand the market and be comfortable with the fact that it's big enough to accommodate the necessary shifts in your strategy. If you're in a very small, very well-defined, limited market, you're not going to have the luxury of shifting your strategy, so you'd better have a concept for a product that is proprietary or has significant barriers to entry.

As an investor in technology, nontechnology, and service companies, and as a board member of seven small companies, I look for what is really different about the concept. Now that difference doesn't necessarily have to be proprietary technology. It can be the different distribution strategy. It can be a different way to service an area that's not now being served well.

I spent most of my life in the corporate rat race, and I left it in my late forties to start my company, not because I had a burning, compelling desire to start a company, but because I'd been running a company in Silicon Valley and, as you sometimes hear, the venture capitalist will terminate a president when the moon gets into a certain position. I fell victim to one of those venture capitalists. I couldn't get a job anywhere else so I started a company.

I had been in the equipment leasing field for a lot of years, so I started in that. I capitalized the company with $1,000 and went after a market that all the big people in the equipment leasing field said was impossible to succeed in, and that was financing start-ups. They thought my concept was that I would take incredible risks and go down the tubes. They were wrong on both counts.

I wasn't taking terrible risks. I wasn't gambling on my ability to discern a good deal from a bad deal. What I was doing was structuring each transaction as a professional financier might structure a real estate transaction. And so I mitigated risk, if you like, with available collateral. I capitalized the company on $1,000 and in the first year, before my own salary, we made about $17,000. So I paid myself a salary of about $15,000—about a third of what I had been making before—so I could show a profit of $2,000. I had this strong compulsion to show a profit.

And 14 years later, our pretax earnings were a million and a half, and I sold it. And, since that time, I've been taking life a little easier, and from time to time, I invest. I have looked at literally thousands of deals because I focused on emerging-growth companies, start-ups in a wide variety of fields, but primarily in high tech (though I had very little high-tech background, it was primarily in electronics, and I never took physics). And I'm still as green in technology as I was when I started. But it isn't a knowledge of technology that helps you determine a good investment.

I don't talk from theory, I talk from practice, practice as an investor, occasionally putting money into deals. There are a lot of similarities between the institutional and the private investor. You know them as well as I do. Don't think you can get by without a good business plan. You can't. It's absolutely essential. It would be like going out in the street without your pants or skirt on. You've got to have a good business plan.

And you have to associate with professional people who will be available as soon as you get into operation: a good CPA, but even before you start, a good corporate lawyer. And you don't need big people. I'm not knocking the big firms by any means, but it's been my experience that when you're very small and not exactly flush with money, the big firm gives you a junior, someone inexperienced. In smaller firms, on the other hand, you get principals, the more experienced people, those with the fire to help you and with a desire to make a name for themselves. When you're dealing with a private investor, you are dealing with principals. So, select your professional advisors with care. They are essential.

I don't put my money into Hollywood, looking to associate with the stars, but I will tell you this: I ran my own business and I function today on the philosophy that I'd spent 25 years in the corporate rat race and liked most people, but, now and again, you come across some real so-and-so's. I vowed to myself to deal only with people I like. I'm not going to continue looking at a deal where I don't feel very, very comfortable with the people. That's not only a feeling that they're straight, but also that they're honest. And I gotta like them. Otherwise, I'm not going to invest.

What are the things that will make *you* likable? Your commitment, your understanding of what you are doing, your analysis of your risks. This is where most people go wrong. They seem to think that the potential investor doesn't want to hear the bad news. If he hears the bad news, he's going to get scared off. I get scared off when my investee demonstrates that he is or she is oblivious to the risks. So I want someone who has taken a hard look at the risks.

Let me give you an example of some of the more subtle things that I think motivate principals and career people. In the leasing/lending industry, particularly with emerging growth companies, it's commonplace to take additional collateral. I'm sure you know what I mean by that: collateral above that which you are leasing, taking the form of cash, perhaps, or cash equivalent.

Now let's create a hypothetical example. This is a young, high-technology company. They have $4 million of the institutional venture capitalist's money in the bank; they have a series of timed CDs, but are not making a product yet. They're going to use that cash to meet the burn rate until the product comes out the door. They want to lease half a million dollars' worth of equipment. I come along and say, "I want a couple hundred thousand dollars of that money and I'll give you an interest rate on it just like the bank; in fact, I'll give you a quarter of a point more and then I will release that money to you as you meet certain benchmarks." Meanwhile, my competitor—a big guy—comes along and offers the same thing but says, "I don't want the cash; give me an assignment of the CD, or a letter of credit drawn on a credible bank like Citicorp or Bank of America."

Why does he do that? I won't say I wouldn't touch his offer with a ten-foot pole; if I couldn't get anything else, I would take it. But he doesn't want the cash, and the reason he doesn't want the cash is because his legal department has warned him that under certain circumstances in a particular state, in a particular city, there might be trouble. They cite a case in 1973 in which a very aggressive bankruptcy trustee got caught holding a cash deposit that, in fact, was part of the bankruptcy estate. They're worried, of course, about the same thing happening to them. So this competitor says, "I don't want the cash; I want a letter of credit." And I say, "Baloney! Give me the cash."

Cash is king to me. If a bankruptcy trustee attempts to do that to me, I will fight him. He isn't stronger. He's not using the money of the estate to launch this legal attack. We're about evenly matched. This isn't the question of the big guy against the little guy. I'll fight it. Well, I did fight it, a hundred times, and it never bothered me. The difference is in motivation. As far as I'm concerned, it's my money, and if I've got a nice piece of cash from the lessee covering it, it does a lot for me. It helps me sleep at night. It also motivates my lessee, because I've got his cash, cash he'd like to get back one day. But doing it the other way would put my job in jeopardy if anything went wrong. I would have made a big mistake.

Another thing, I find that investing with others is the norm for several reasons. We all attract people because of our interests. If you play the violin, you probably know other violin players. If you fool around in the private investment marketplace, you know other people because, generally speaking, you don't play that game unless you like keeping very close to what's going on in the community.

For instance, I knew nothing whatever about high technology. The only reason I formed a company leasing to high-technology companies was because I happened to be living in Silicon Valley. Had I been living in Oregon or Washington, I'd be in fishing boats and lumber—and bankrupt by now. If you like a particular field, you want to keep talking to people who are active in it.

So, if I go into a deal, I will turn to other people for three very powerful reasons. One of them is that I may turn to someone who is closer to a technology I know little about. I'll turn to somebody who understands that field and, very likely, it'll be someone who, like myself, is investing. This way, I gain knowledge of a technology I'm not familiar with. Second, if I think it's a good deal and I know other people who I think deserve it, I let them take a part of it. And third, I'm probably not going to make a cold investment. I'm probably going to want to get involved in one form or another, maybe not actively, but when I put money into a company, I want to help them. It's not like selling insurance, calling on all your friends. I'm not being critical of that field, but, generally speaking, I've identified with a small company, I like the people, I like what they're doing, I believe in them, I want to help them. I don't demand a board seat unless I have a significant position. So I'm going to turn to other people whom I know, but I'm not going to go hunting for money like an investment banker.

Normally, I do want some involvement. I'm not necessarily going to be attracted unless I feel I can make a contribution somewhere. I'm not looking for operating management responsibility. I'm through with that part of my life, and I like things the way they are now. But if the thing is going downhill, I have to realize I am stronger than the individual running the show; I have to get him out and get myself in—something I don't otherwise want to do.

That's why I will not go some distance away. Like carrying an umbrella, I hope it never rains. If I stay close to home, fewer problems seem to crop up. This means that people are absolutely critical. You've got to have confidence that they can do what they say they will do, and that they have got the sticking power to do what they say they will do.

## Deep-Pocket Investor #4

**One thing I do not want to hear is that it's going to be a wild ride and a lot of fun. If I want to have a lot of fun, I'll go fly an F-14.**

I've been investing since 1988. I've done a wide range of investing in several different types of firms. Overall, my investments probably total about $20 million now, including those of my coinvestors. I've invested in insurance, financial services, money management, investment advisory—those kinds of things. I'm pretty diverse. I have no requirements in terms of geography. I've invested in a firm outside the U.S., a firm in New York, a firm in Iowa, where I'm from originally.

I really look for innovation and passion—"fire in the belly." But you can get some sense of that, I imagine, in looking at an executive summary or business plan. I like to sit down with the people, look them in the eye, find out their backgrounds, find out what drove them to this investment and basically what their personal commitments are. I think that that's very, very important.

I try to add value whenever I can, particularly if it's needed. I have been doing this a long time and my vision is usually pretty good and I have found that I can help an entrepreneur substantially if he or she remains open to ideas. One thing I do not want to hear is that it's going to be a wild ride and a lot of fun. If I want to have a lot of fun, I'll go fly an F-14.

On the other hand, one thing I *do* want to hear is that you have an executive summary that tells me what it is you need, what the potential market is, how much you're looking to raise, and what kind of rate of return might be expected with the size of this particular market.

Explain where the technology is coming from, how it's going to be developed. Elaborate on your concept; tell how it is innovative. Explain why your product or service is superior to the techniques currently in place and what the relative cost would be. Tell why it's superior, what the relative cost advantages or disadvantages might be, and just explain a little bit more of what it is. You have to be a little more excited and tell *why. Why* you're at the company, *why* you believe in this, and *why* you are spending the amount of energy that you're expending.

The third investor type is the consortium of individual investors.

## THE CONSORTIUM OF INDIVIDUAL INVESTORS

### Consortium Investor #1

Our group has three investors with quite diverse backgrounds. And because of that, our investment interest is very diverse. One of my colleagues and I most recently founded a multimedia software company in the educational software field. We went through all the trials and tribulations that I'm sure many people have gone through. I started from self-financing through friends to institutional financing and we were fortunate throughout the process.

We finally sold the company to a public software company last year. We learned a lot about what you don't do and what you need to do in order to be successful. One of my coinvestors has gone the more traditional institutional investor route in the retailing field and cofounded a company that received a venture backing and then went public last year. He's been very successful. So from that experience of both self-financing and the traditional institutional venture capital funding, I think we've learned the ins and outs of how to get from here to there from the viewpoint of the people seeking money.

So, we're most interested in talking to people. Our interest in funding is in the $50,000 to $500,000 range. We're looking at seed funding to early-stage funding. Retailing is an area we are very interested in, and the software technology area as well because of our backgrounds. And lastly, we are

Exhibit 6.4  **CONSORTIUM OF INDIVIDUAL INVESTORS**

- Loose confederation of private, individual investors (unrelated, typically 3–6)
- Experience in start-up, running, and selling their businesses
- More passive involvement; seek oversight; sounding board role
- Will invest in technology and product opportunities, as well as start-up companies
- Individuals make their own decisions, may not always invest as a group
- Extensively connected with "deep pocket"–type of angels with whom they coinvest or to whom they refer deals
- Seek some protectable advantage
- Invest $50,000–$500,000

Source: International Capital Resources

interested in consumer-related investments. So that pretty much hits the entire spectrum.

## Consortium Investor #2

**We like to get very close to the entrepreneurs, the people who start the business, the people who have the ideas. We offer them some oversight; we offer them a sounding board, and, of course, we offer them some capital.**

I am an individual investor, working with about half a dozen other people, all of whom have started, run, and then sold businesses, but have continuing interest in nurturing small businesses. We're a loose confederation of investors. We don't have a company structure as such. We respond to each opportunity as we see it.

Our focus is on the people involved in starting a business. We like to get very close to the entrepreneurs, the people who start the business, the people who have the ideas. We offer them some oversight; we offer them a sounding board, and, of course, we offer them some capital.

We generally work in technology-based areas, often manufactured products. We don't do a lot of seed ventures but, in fact, we just invested in a small one last year that turned out quite well for us. We didn't carry it to the prototype stage. We managed to sell it to an East Coast company for a fairly substantial return on investment. Normally, we're looking for return in the area of 10, maybe 15 percent. The days of 20 and 25 percent, I think, are behind us.

## Consortium Investor #3

**As we look at the lower end, at start-ups or seed money, we don't really care if it has the potential of becoming a company. All I really care about is if it has the potential of making money.**

My group is a loose confederation of private investors who look at individual deals, make their own decisions, and may or may not end up investing in the particular deal as a group. Basically, I think we classify deals in two categories. We invest in deals less than $250,000. In bigger deals we have a number of well-heeled private investors that we will bring in, simply pass the deals to, or become coinvestors with.

A difference exists, I think, in the way we, or I as an individual, will approach some of these opportunities. As we look at the lower end, at start-ups or seed money, we don't really care if it has the potential of becoming a company. All I really care about is if it has the potential of making money. That simply could mean that it's a product or technology that, unto itself, is not going to turn into a $50- or $100-million-a-year company. But it may turn into a $10-million product line that GE would love to have, or that some international company feels it can manufacture and distribute more efficiently overseas.

I think Silicon Valley is full of opportunities that are masquerading as companies, but are really product opportunities or technology opportunities that need to be developed and then put together with an exit strategy that makes everybody involved a little bit wealthier. The larger deals are company deals. They generally are things to be looked at much farther along the path; they probably have a proven concept, maybe they've done some test marketing, and have most, if not all, of their staff in place.

On the low end, we typically look at technology deals simply because that's our background. On the higher end, because there's generally more information in place, we look at a broader range of ideas. I look at what I call *value-oriented* opportunities. And, from that perspective, I consider their *protectable advantage.* Typically, protectable advantage means patent protection, technology protection, a lock on distribution channels, something like that.

It may be a great technological idea or a great technology opportunity, but if nobody cares except the inventor, it's of no value. And if somebody does care, the question is whether they will pay, whether it can be done profitably. And probably one of the more important things to me—because I come from a sales and marketing background—is how to get to them. How do you distribute whatever you've got? In that respect, when I look at an opportunity, I will look first at the market, at the marketing aspects of it.

Second, I'll look at the technology aspects of it and, third, at the people. When it comes to the decision-making phase, I reverse that process: Who are the individuals involved? What does the technology look like? And, how are they going to package that technology and market it? Beyond that, I look for people who believe in focusing on the customer.

The fourth type of investor is the partner investor.

## THE PARTNER INVESTOR

> Somebody once defined the survival of the fittest to me as not being the strongest, but finding the niche where you can exist and make things happen. So it's not the "fittest" that counts; it's the "fit."

I've been looking for an investment for eight months. I left my job in January, and I've had this long-term goal to buy into a business. Basically, my career has been sales-oriented and general management, which I think is key to being a successful entrepreneur. I operate where the rubber hits the pavement. I dislike meetings and bureaucracy.

But I do like collaboration and teamwork, and I think that to be successful in the kind of environment we're talking about you need to have—and I think I have these elements—a lean, seat-of-the-pants operating style from running small businesses, extensive direct sales and marketing experience, finance and numbers discipline. And I've acquired that from working on an $80 million leverage buyout, and a lot of calluses from fighting for customers in competitive markets and from navigating the corporate jungle. And you have to have a very strong desire to do a deal, and you have to be very focused about it.

I have a collaborator whom I met at an event hosted by ICR, a collaborator who's been at it for 18 months and he's running out of money—and he's got a lot more money than I do. So, it's a tough slog. As Mr. Benjamin has said, only 2 percent of his deal flow complete transactions, so you have to be focused. The key part of all this is to generate deal flow. You have to develop as much deal flow as you possibly can, and you have to constantly get feedback from the marketplace and refocus your efforts. That's what I've been doing.

There is no path in this process. It's constant invention, reinvention everyday. I have a little model in front of my desk that for me reflects this whole process. I call this model the *funnel strategy.* Basically, the way to succeed is

Exhibit 6.5  **PARTNER INVESTOR**

- Buyer in disguise
- Very high need for control
- Is trying to build network or has developed some coinvestor relationships
- Would prefer acquisition of established company but lacks financial resources
- Lead investor who searches for opportunities, makes independent decision, and suggests investment to coinvestor network
- Wants to be president
- Able to invest $250,000–$1,000,000

Source: International Capital Resources

to employ six ways in closing more sales, or employ six ways in getting more deals going—all of which depends on the size of your funnel. In other words, get more of an effort going; weed out unprofitable prospects. The idea is to fail quickly; get off the stuff that isn't happening immediately because you can burn a tremendous amount of time on wasteful action.

Don't work on the undecided that have little chance of going further. Find better prospects. Increase the speed. I think the key is more throughput. It's all about throughput. It's about replenishing your funnel every week. And don't chase one deal too long; instead, continue to feed the funnel. This is the model I've used to work on deals. I've created deals by answering ads in the paper; I've worked with business brokers; I've networked with people; I've used direct mail, a CD-ROM database, mailed more than 700 letters to targeted businesses located within specific Standard Industrial Classification (SIC) codes, zip codes, and types of businesses.

In fact, out of those 700 letters, I received 40 calls, a 5 percent response rate. I've evaluated more than 100 businesses, evaluating them across a wide range of criteria—from just a quick phone call during which someone runs the gist of the business by me to doing full due diligence. I've made four offers on businesses: One was a manager-investor opportunity, while three were to purchase. I'm in escrow on a deal right now, hoping it will work out.

Since everyone is different, you have to figure out what people want, that is, you have get to people who want to do your kind of deals. It's a waste of time to talk to people who don't. My deal is that I had about $200,000. I also have $140,000 in credit cards that I worked very hard to accumulate over the last few years. Credit cards are being used to finance about 25 percent of the small- to medium-size businesses in the United States today. And if you evaluate what private investors want in terms of return, I want a 30 percent return on the investment from my deal. Credit cards are really the cheapest forms of financing—if you have the guts to do it.

I built up a wish list that I kept on my bulletin board. I'm looking for an international business, a consumer product leading to an ongoing relationship in the business, a business I could bring value to. As an individual investor, I don't have an unlimited supply of money, so critical for me is what value I bring to the party, what value I add to the business.

The business has to be able to respond to aggressive direct sales, respond to strong, capable management. The business has to be local. I want to be able to ride my bicycle to work. I want casual dress. I want it to be part of a "wave" out there, a wave that is home office, aging population, information technology, and so forth. I want it to be fun. I want to be president. I want a good return on investment. I don't want it dominated by few customers or few vendors. I want an exit strategy so I can cash out for cash. In my current deal I got about 70 percent of this stuff. That's the way it goes.

But the really critical piece in terms of keeping the whole thing together is the chemistry and trust among the people involved. Things have to be very good, but things are better if the chemistry is excellent. Everybody has different needs and wants. Understanding this one fact in terms of the whole process, plus being able to deal with rejection, is dead center. Basically, it's not about being the smartest, or having the best product, or looking the best, or even having the most money. It's about getting the right fit.

All those other things help, but somebody once defined the survival of the fittest to me as not being the strongest, but finding the niche where you can exist and make things happen. So it's not the "fittest" that counts; it's the "fit." That's what this process is all about for me.

This type of investing takes persistence; it takes throughput, as much throughput as you can muster and emotionally tolerate. It is draining. You simply cannot do it all by yourself. Firms like ICR can help. You have to delegate. And you have to collaborate. I met someone at an ICR event who has helped me. Now, we meet every three weeks and collaborate on the process and share ideas and share leads.

The next type of investor is the family of investors.

## THE FAMILY OF INVESTORS

**[W]e believe we can contribute not only the funds but also the experience in management, as well as provide the connections we have in the Far East and in some countries in Europe.**

I'm new to the United States. We still have some investments in the Far East—Taiwan, Singapore, and also China. We also have some business connections in Europe. But, basically, we are a family-owned business, a small group. We are interested in information services, computers—both hardware and software—as well as medical industries.

We view investments in amounts ranging from a few hundred thousand dollars to several million dollars for each project. We like to look at the early-stage venture, as early as possible. We believe we can contribute quite a bit of experience, just as we have in the past.

Exhibit 6.6 **FAMILY OF INVESTORS**

- Family money is pooled and a trusted, skilled family member coordinates investment activity
- Very astute investor, MBA minimum, many Ph.D.'s in coordinator role
- Contribute experience, intense involvement for short periods of time
- Group investor likely to invest only if there is group consensus
- Very common among Asian investors in Bay Area
- Invest $100,000–$1,000,000

Source: International Capital Resources

Our company has been in the high-tech business for more than 20 years. We have been handling very complicated processes, such as air traffic control, radar, defense equipment, and small components. So we believe we can contribute not only the funds but also the experience in management, as well as provide the connections we have in the Far East and in some countries in Europe.

The sixth type of investor is the barter investor.

## THE BARTER INVESTOR

**We have an active business today that might dovetail with what you do. We have an infrastructure in place. We advertise for customers, we process customer orders, we warehouse, we ship, we build computers, we service computers in the field. We do all sorts of things: bill, invoice, and collect. All of these things we might be able to add to your business.**

Do you need the money, or do you need what you're going to use the money to buy? Our company operates in a limited area, looking to make investments and participate in your company. So that sets us apart, narrows the scope, if you will. Our business is to try to dovetail with what's out there, something that could be a good fit for us. My partner and I are knowledgeable in starting up companies. We both have done several.

We have a company that operates and provides business-to-business services throughout California. And what we are looking for is investing in an early-stage idea or business that we can contribute money to. But equally as important to us is the infrastructure of the business. We have thousands of customers, we bill them, we collect, we negotiate bank lines, we do marketing—we do all of these things.

Exhibit 6.7 **BARTER INVESTOR**

- Provides what you would have used capital to buy in exchange for equity
- Participative—not passive
- Early-stage preference
- Offers capital and infrastructure (an incubator model)
- Management is most important criteria
- Independent investor who relies on own investigation in deciding to invest
- Venture must have capability to grow to $10M minimum in 3–5 years
- Invests up to $250,000 and frequently supplements with guaranteed line of credit

Source: International Capital Resources

My partner and I are interested in participating in new ideas, in growing a new business. We are interested in the expansion phase of a seed-capital or start-up business, defined by us as a venture with a working prototype ready to roll, what we call a beta test. We are interested in the early stage of testing or initial growth capital. Mezzanine, bridge, or IPO is beyond our scope. So that is not what we are looking for.

We feel a capable management team is necessary, as everybody says, but it doesn't have to be completely formed. Because of our participation, we believe that we can fill some of those holes, give a running start to the company, get it going a little faster than might otherwise be the case.

Quality product or service is of interest to us. Technology advantage is always nice. Proprietary is desirable but not necessary. We like a substantial market potential, a $10- to $20-million revenue target in five years with compatible financial objectives. And this is one of the stumbling blocks that I run into many times with entrepreneurs: The entrepreneur has to agree we are not just building a good lifestyle for that individual. So we have to have an exit strategy within a time frame that we can mutually agree on.

Business categories of interest are communications, the Internet, computer software, and multimedia. Of course, every time I hear of a new business outside these categories, I get interested and I add that to my list. And not so much multimedia CD-ROM games, but multimedia interactive marketing, or some projects we're working with now, such as financial and business services, even light manufacturing or distribution. We're fascinated with the idea of producing a product and distributing it.

Our company is in the computer rental, leasing, and sales business, primarily rental. People always ask what the difference is between rental and leasing. If you think of it as a Hertz rental car kind of thing, as opposed to long-term leasing, that's what it is. Computers cycle in and out of the shop every day. People call and order. We deliver, install, then pick them up when they're through, put them back on the shelf, and rent them to somebody else. The investment of interest to us might have a direct fit with some other business we've had.

We are interested in early-stage companies, ventures in the idea stage, in the process of being organized, a start-up, a venture that has been in business less than two years, that is completing product development, and maybe has some sales. First stage, expansion stage. Everybody has a different definition for these terms, but we're interested in a venture with a working prototype that has been through beta testing and is in need of initial growth capital. Mezzanine, bridge, IPO are beyond our financial capability. We are not interested at that level.

We look for general investment criteria. Of course, first comes a good management team. We invest in key people as much as the product or the technology. That team should have industry experience and be able to execute its business plan. We don't expect you to have all the holes filled, because we are interested in being active investors. We are not passive investors in that sense. So between my partner and me, our backgrounds cover finance, accounting, marketing, and general management, and we are interested in a couple of people with an idea and a good market to pursue. We believe we can fill in some of the holes.

Quality product, service, or technological advantage is important. Of course, the proprietary advantage is desirable but not necessary. Anything very high-tech may be beyond us in terms of our understanding, so we're probably not equipped to evaluate that very well. But applying a technology, a proven technology, to a business is something that we are experienced in.

The product should have substantial market potential, a potential for $10 to $20 million in revenues within three to five years. We say that because of what our experience has been. From a liquidity standpoint, you have to have at least $10 million if you are going to do anything in terms of getting liquidity for your investment after that period of time. Actually, I've rarely seen a business plan that worked out the way I expected within one to two years, but I am looking at an investment growth projection that gives me a feel for the size of the market. Substantiating the size of the market is very important to me. If you can't convince me of that, I don't think you've done enough homework to attract our investment.

We are active managers, so in early-stage deals we're interested in a significant piece of the company for our investment, ranging from 30 to 60 percent of the company. It depends on your stage of development and the capital required. We can provide an incentive for founders. You're going to give us a business plan that says, "Here's what I can do"; and we'll say, "Fine, we'll put some money in," and maybe we have 51 percent at that point. But if you meet the business plan, you earn 20 percent back and dilute us, and so forth.

So we're very flexible in terms of how we go into a venture, but we want a significant equity position in the company. Common stock or convertible preferred, purchase options, licensing agreements, joint ventures—we would consider all of these things. Let me back up a minute on that. We have an active business today that might dovetail with what you do. We have an infrastructure in place. We advertise for customers, we process customer orders, we warehouse, we ship, we build computers, we service computers in the field. We do all sorts of things: bill, invoice, and collect. All of these things we might be able to add to your business, if you think of us as an "incubator" as well.

So, our investment might take two forms: The first is a cash check; the second, or combination of the two, enables us to save you a lot of cash by leveraging off the infrastructure that we already have in our company. And we operate throughout the state of California. Participation in the business, representation on the board, part-time management. My partner and I, or one of us, depending on the needs of a particular investment, would be willing to spend half our time in the early stages of that company.

We are interested in communications, data services, and telecommunications—providing it is not too far out. Also, we're interested in computer software. I would say we're interested in vertical market applications: financial and business services. Our company, even though built on computers, is really a business service; in fact, that's all it is. And light manufacturing or distribution is another interest of ours. In other words, if we can make it, manufacture it, put it in a box, and ship it out repetitively, that's something that's simple enough that we can understand. So that really forms the outline of our investment objectives.

If you want to place us in a potential investment or a company's potential investment, put us in cash terms of up to a quarter of a million dollars. And I would like to think of adding infrastructure equivalent to that amount in terms of saving you cash.

The seventh type of investor is the socially responsible investor.

## THE SOCIALLY RESPONSIBLE PRIVATE INVESTOR

**I think that people who come into this kind of business perceive needs and have values. Those individuals in the nurture capital process are people with a clear sense of values. The companies that have integrity, that have a product, that have meaning to them are the ones that I think really matter.**

There's a big gap and a lot of misunderstanding about what venture capital is. Venture capital serves as the generic term that refers to the full range of direct investments in the private equity class. But, typically, a venture capital firm fills a gap in which you have either a fairly complete management team or a fairly well developed product.

Many times a management team is missing a number of key elements, or a product has just entered the field. But because of their fiduciary responsibil-

---

Exhibit 6.8 **SOCIALLY RESPONSIBLE PRIVATE INVESTOR**

- Nurture capitalist, seeking intensive hand-holding situations
- High need for personal interaction, less able to provide savvy business support
- Seeks to be associated with individuals with "high values"
- Prefers ventures addressing major social issues
- Seeks reasonable ROI while supporting people/ideals consonant with "enlightened" personal values
- Often inherited wealth with extensive investment capability
- Referred investor, relies on recommendations through trusted advisors

Source: International Capital Resources

ity to investors, the venture capital community can't look at the technology and can't look at the company. In this regard, it resembles a bank. This capital gap between the founders, on the one hand, and the banks and the venture capital community, on the other, has fostered what I call *nurture capital*. The terminology speaks for itself. You nurture a company, helping it any way you can. It means a lot of hand-holding, a lot of intimate relationship with that particular business.

It seems to me people often cling to the impression that venture capital is interested only in making money. I don't believe that's true at all. I think that people who come into this kind of business perceive needs and have values. Those individuals in the nurture capital process are people with a clear sense of values. The companies that have integrity, that have a product, that have meaning to them, are the ones that I think really matter.

We end up putting a spin on the developments and technologies of the companies that we get involved with; we add a dimension, a spin, just like spin on the bowling ball spreads it wider than it really is, creating a greater impact on the target.

My perception is that in the United States especially, but around the world as well, very little knowledge exists about what is happening in the petroleum field. Our economy runs on oil, and we are about to see a major transformation, such as we saw here in the 1970s—except that this time the entire world will suffer. In the 1970s, United States oil extraction peaked, and, you may recall, a couple of years later major repercussions occurred. But we possessed the unique advantage of still being able to import oil.

The globe will not have that possibility, at least from oil. About five years from now when production peaks, oil expectations will continue to grow. There are many people working on putting plants in China, for example, and in India, building cars and, sadly, fueling expectation that oil will be available. The trouble is there won't be any oil. This event is a mere five years away and when it happens, we're going to have to import oil. The problem is there won't be any oil to import.

The only source of imports we have is the sun, so my perspective is that solar energy applications are a major area of investment interest for me. And we're going to see a major transformation and the potential and the technology in renewable and in energy conservation and, suddenly, the cost of oil is going to be so high that these investments will have potential for the next century as well.

People claim that there's still plenty of oil out there. Sure enough, there is. But the reality is that while we had gushers in the 1950s, oil is going to be harder and harder to get in the years to come, and the yield we derive for the same amount of effort is going to be less and less. So it's going to be less and less exciting to go after oil. Between 1977 and 1991 we discovered in the United States 5 billion barrels of oil. However, we consumed twice the amount we extracted. It doesn't take an Einstein to figure out that this is a losing proposition. If your business plan doesn't take this into consideration, and you plan to be here five years from now, then you have some thinking to do.

And if you are interested in working with me in terms of investment programs, this is really what drives me. I think that the money will flow if the service is there. Making money is not the goal; profits and return become the score that gets chalked up after the goal has been reached.

The last investor type discussed in this chapter is the unaccredited investor.

## THE UNACCREDITED PRIVATE INVESTOR

**I initially get excited by the concept, but I think ultimately, I invest in a venture because of the entrepreneur rather than the concept.**

I spent 24 years with a Fortune 500 chemical corporation, specializing in real estate development, a major business of the firm. I started as a junior accountant of a subsidiary, then left six years ago as vice president in charge of the company's activities. Since then, I have combined investing in a few start-ups with a financial and consulting practice.

I'd rather try to spread my apples around a little bit more, make smaller investments in a bunch of different companies, companies in which I would like to spend some time in an important capacity. I might like a management role, perhaps a board role; I might like to serve as an interim CFO, though only one day or so a week.

In looking at deals I'm typically going to make an investment in the $10,000 to $25,000 range. I get talked into higher amounts occasionally, but that's

Exhibit 6.9 **UNACCREDITED PRIVATE INVESTOR**

- Less experienced, less affluent private investor
- Looking for a role in earlier-stage situations
- Not a patient investor; plans to get money out in 3–5 years
- Must "really get to know" investee
- "Spreads his apples around," making multiple small investments
- Used to invest in real estate, now has a preference for technology
- Invests close to home
- Has to justify investment to spouse
- Typically a referred investor who is primarily influenced by recommendations from a knowledgeable person
- Invests $10,000–$25,000 maximum

Source: International Capital Resources

where I start out. I don't have to make a deal. People who represent funds have to place a certain amount of money. If I don't invest in a private enterprise, I've got the money in the stock market or in something else. So it's really a question of taking it out of alternative investments.

I typically look for some type of niche, obviously at start-ups. Often I'll go in with a bunch of other investors because that's the thing to do with a large amount of money.

But to me the story is much more important than numbers. The business plan is really important, but numbers usually aren't very reliable no matter how well they're done. So the concept is much more important. People may have an idea of what they want to do with product A and that really makes sense to me. Then they want to continually reinvest and go on. I can understand they want to do that from their perspective. But from my perspective, I would just as soon make the investment in a joint venture, get my money and my return out of it. Maybe during the course of the investment, I'll get sold on continuing in the company, but I don't necessarily structure it that way going in.

I think that in small investments, one of the main things investors have to worry about is being able to justify investments to their spouse. Believe me, the worst thing is to have to explain to your husband or wife why you lost $10,000 to $15,000 in such-and-such a company, the same money you could have used on a luxurious trip to Tahiti, or on a material purchase of some kind. That's probably the toughest sell, the one sell I try to avoid.

I would prefer to be thought of as a friend or member of the family. I want to really get to know the CEO; that's the kind of company I'm going to invest in because I think no matter how you write the documents, what's really important is whether that entrepreneur's going to treat you fairly over a long period of time, whether he or she is intelligent, and will work hard. I initially get excited by the concept, but I think ultimately, I invest in a venture because of the entrepreneur rather than the concept.

One other thing that's important to me in concept is accessible geography. On a business plan, I think it becomes a terribly important sales tool.

The final type of investor—the manager-investor—is discussed separately in the next chapter.

# 7

# The Newest Breed of Angel: The Manager-Investor

## THE MANAGER-INVESTOR

Within five years of the end of World War II, older males began dropping out of the workforce. That trend continues at an ever faster rate, according to the Bureau of Labor Statistics. The pool of men over age 55 is shrinking. Working until age 65 is a distant norm, as more than 30 percent of men between the ages of 55 and 64 are unemployed. Roughly 85 percent of employed males in this same age bracket had been a part of the workforce through the 1950s, the percentage slipping only a little. Late in that decade, however, things began to slide precipitously.

The percentage these days continues its downward spiral, to less than 65 percent employed in 1994. Many in this group feel displaced, some devastated. There are, however, a number of individuals who feel neither devastated nor displaced. These individuals are a new breed of investor—the manager-investor.

Basically, manager-investors are looking for a job. They might have been a casualty of downsizing, might have sold their company, or may have received golden parachutes early and unsuccessfully tried retirement. Now they want to get back in the fray, but they have too much dignity in their late 40s to late 50s to push their resume across a table, or they are too affluent to make such a move in terms of their net worth.

They make direct investments in companies for the purpose of creating an employment opportunity, as well as the potential for a return on investment. The manager-investor deals directly with principals in negotiating the transaction and position. The employment objective can be in management, technical, or administrative areas.

What they're going to do is buy their next job. And, basically, they are going to ride one investment for the next few years. From manager-investors you can expect much longer periods of due diligence and much more assessment of the chemistry with the entrepreneurs to make

Exhibit 7.1  MANAGER-INVESTOR

- Affluent, senior-level executive or former business owner reentering workforce and buying a "last job"
- Focused on making one investment
- Less experienced at direct, participatory investing
- Referred investor who asks questions and reads materials but can be primarily influenced by recommendations from a knowledgeable person
- Very long due diligence cycle
- Less tolerance for risk, so seeks more developed ventures
- Seeks high level of involvement for extended period of time
- Invests $100,000–$200,000, staged investment

Source: International Capital Resources

sure that they feel part of the team. They are determined not to take a hit on the one deal that they're trying to create. Manager-investors are also going to be less prone to stomach the risk because they are looking for a job. And, typically, the amount of money that they can bring to the venture is limited. Also, they want to be very active in the company, perhaps in an operating position. Manager-investors typically invest from $100,000 to $200,000 in staged investments.

The characteristics of the manager-investor are enumerated in Exhibit 7.2.

## Manager-Investor #1

> Now, six months ago when I first began investing, I would have characterized myself as a novice. Over the past six-month period, however, I have grown considerably: I would now characterize myself as simply inexperienced.

I am what ICR has categorized as a manager-investor. This means that any investment I make is into a company I want to play a role in, a role in the pursuit of that company's business activities. It certainly does not mean that I am interested in control. But it does mean I want to be active; I want to be aware of what is going on. From my standpoint, this becomes a necessity.

Now, six months ago when I first began investing, I would have characterized myself as a novice. Over the past six-month period, however, I have grown considerably: I would now characterize myself as simply inexperienced. My bet is that there are a number of people like me who haven't had a great deal of experience in investing in start-ups, so I hope it will help you to know how I pursued this area.

Probably all of you have seen the little company profiles that ICR publishes. These have been extremely helpful to me. They offer within a very short

Exhibit 7.2  **CHARACTERISTICS OF THE MANAGER-INVESTOR**

1. 40s to mid-50s. Mid- to late-career manager or former business owner, seasoned executive, astute business analyst
2. Full-time operational involvement; will provide support and industry savvy
3. $100,000 to $200,000 to invest. Not a deep pocket for subsequent rounds
4. Less concerned about control, more concerned about sharing founder's vision. However, does desire at least some influence
5. Typically well connected both geographically and in the industry
6. Not interested in seed stage, but will consider more developed start-ups
7. Prefers business with demonstrated viability, less inclined toward turnarounds. More concerned with the business than with pro forma statements (e.g., what is produced, who the competitors are, debt on balance sheet)
8. Will require a business plan
9. Will seek to benefit from appreciation on equity, and will seek steep discounts in private negotiations; will aggressively negotiate price; will want potential for above-average returns
10. Will seek long-term commitment, "chemistry" with current management and founder, and geographic proximity to home or desired locale

period of time a perception of what a company does, what its product is, what its marketplace is. These profiles supply an excellent overview of opportunities, letting a person like me zero in on the 10 percent of the deals that make sense to me.

I suspect that I've looked at maybe 50 or so of those company profiles. I probably ask for either additional information or an additional conversation with ICR principals, or maybe product information—sometimes maybe even a business plan, if it's available—on maybe 10 of those 50, having eliminated 40 of them. From there I believe I met personally with six of the remaining 10, having become sufficiently interested in three of the six to conduct more than one meeting.

One in particular I have met with numerous times, and, frankly, some have accused me of making a career out of this one potential investment. But I think I'm in the eleventh hour of that one, and it will no doubt be coming to fruition soon. First of all, I try to take a look at the product and make certain that I feel that it's good, something I can identify with.

Second, I consider whether the marketplace for that product is fragmented, or whether it is dominated by a single or several very large companies. And third, I consider whether this company has any kind of an edge, for example, in its technology. I don't mean that it has to be a technology company, but it may use technology in a way that is more advanced than anyone else—anything, in other words, that might give it the edge. And I check to see if the company has patents on the product, another thing that could give it the edge.

This is typically when I have become serious in discussing the company in depth with its management. Now let me give you three examples of prospective ventures, and tell you how I characterize them. There was a software company that had what I consider to be a very good product and a very good market, not dominated by any single seller or manufacturer of a similar software package. There certainly was and is similar software in the market, but no one dominated it.

My concern with this company was that I didn't feel it had an edge. Additionally, even if they had had an edge, I thought it would slip away very quickly. This may be true of all software; I'm not certain. But I've noticed in the case of Lotus, Excel, and Quattro Pro, that by turns one will come out with a new version containing a few features, then another will match those features and raise the ante two or three features more. Someone else will then match those and raise again. It becomes an unending poker game. I didn't believe that this company could maintain an edge under this circumstance and, therefore, I tended to eliminate it as an investment.

The second company was a medical transcription business. It had a very good product. Medical transcription, I think, is a classic example of a function that should be outsourced from a hospital. It's specialized. The people are highly paid. They're intermixed presently with other hospital employees who have dissimilar interests and goals; therefore, it's a function that is ripe for outsourcing.

In addition, it's a function that can be turned into a cottage industry quite easily with technology. And this company, through its planned use of technology, seemed to have that ability. Therefore, I considered it a good product with a good market and, potentially, with a solid edge. The eliminator in this case had to do with the business plan. The projections had included revenue from a contract, but when I examined the contract more thoroughly, I discovered that the projected revenue wasn't there, changing the forecast rather significantly. This circumstance made my equity investment seem considerably more risky than had been the case, and made my desired reward much less realistic. That's when the deal no longer made sense for me.

The third company, the one I have made a career on, is a chair manufacturer. This is a chair so advanced that it comes with an operating manual. Therefore, the marketing job for this chair has been difficult. And though the company has been in business for a number of years, it has been unable to get the product off the ground. They've also been cash starved for a number of years. Their brochure looks amateurish. They have an instruction video that is "okay." But they don't have the money to advertise. They don't even have a full-time salesperson. Yet, while they've had a lot of things going against them, I continue to view them as having a good market and a product with an edge. The only failing I have discerned is an absence of investment capital, and that's the reason I have spent as much time as I have on this one. In fact, I'm still hopeful of doing something with them.

Now, along the way, there are a lot of things that can eliminate an investor from a deal, even if he's passed these other tests that I've mentioned. First of all, there may be bad chemistry between the investor and the owner, and there's no point in pursuing it if you sense that something is just not right. If you don't communicate well or you don't agree on rather basic strategies and outlooks for the company, there's just no point in forcing yourself into that situation.

Number two, the investment amount that I have in mind has some constraints on it. If the company I intend investing in needs considerably more capital than I will put into it, I can picture myself being stranded nine months down the road in essentially the same position if we haven't achieved breakeven. Now keep in mind that projections are, after all, projections, and an investor like me would like some safety built into them, so if I run into a situation needing a ton of cash, and I'm not prepared to come up with it all, or I don't have the confidence to think I can raise it from other resources, that could be an eliminator.

Also keep in mind my primary objective is to stay active in whatever company I invest in. Last, the business plan is extremely important. I'm not going to spend a lot of time examining it, but the entrepreneur must realize that both the historical financial part of the plan and the projections have got to make sense. If there's anything in there that doesn't hold water, I guarantee you I will discover it. Even a novice will discover it.

## Manager-Investor #2

**I should also mention that in all cases my objective would be not just to invest, but to participate in the formation, management, or direction of the company—either in a board capacity or in a consulting capacity. I like to feel comfortable about what is going on in the company.**

I have been in the search business for several years now. It's only recently that I've found an investment I was satisfied with. It is easier, probably, to eliminate categories of investments than to explain specifically what I'm looking for. For example, it's easy for me to eliminate bioscience and health care fields because I know nothing about them and simply don't want to learn about them at this stage of my life.

I would also probably eliminate retail or consumer activities for the same reason. I like the field of high technology, either hardware or software. I prefer that technology to have a patented or patentable aspect. That gives me some comfort. Alternatively, I would prefer that there exist some barrier to entry by competitors, for example, technology in a way that is not easily duplicated, either by virtue of the heavy capital investment required or by virtue of the skills necessary to implement that technology.

I do prefer earlier-stage companies, preferably ones having a product and a year's worth of sales activity. I like the idea of getting in early, when there is a greater opportunity to influence the company. That way, at least, problems will probably be of your own making—not of someone else's.

I thought that I would always steer away from the idea of investing in an idea or the seed-capital concept. However, I have made an investment just like that: no company, no organization, and no business plan for that matter. I could find very little about the process, which, oddly, was the persuasive part of it all.

I should also mention that in all cases my objective would be not just to invest, but to participate in the formation, management, or direction of the company—either in a board capacity or in a consulting capacity. I like to feel comfortable about what is going on in the company.

I also think that an exit strategy is extremely important. A plan without an eye to an exit strategy would be a considerable negative in my mind.

The manager-investors who speak here speak for many who would fall into this category of angel investor. As we noted at the beginning of Chapter 6, the individual speaks for a type—our method of establishing guidelines designed to make your efforts align with a "more perfect" knowledge of what high-risk investments are all about.

# Part 3

# Resources:
# Finding Angel
# Investors

# 8

# Alternative Funding Resources in Accessing Angel Capital

## HISTORY OF THE DEVELOPMENT OF ALTERNATIVE FUNDING RESOURCES

In earlier chapters we have emphasized the trend toward alternative financing methods. Clearly, the business angel investor represents one of those alternative financing modes—a substantial resource, which we have documented. Today's alternative funding resources ease the access to investors for entrepreneurs and inventors. These resources did not, however, materialize out of thin air. Like everything else we know of, they have evolved.

Historically, alternative funding resources were composed of informal groups of friends, colleagues, and coinvestors—individuals who invested in a deal in a specific industry, at a particular stage of a company's life cycle. Those individuals formed a small circle that pooled its money and shared the mutual responsibility of due diligence. The group also shared the risks inherent in such deals. This informal concept still exists today. It tends to be focused geographically, offering, as always, the benefits of shared responsibilities and shared risk.

Remember that investors are interested in the alternative funding sources—not just entrepreneurs. Why go where there are no investors? As Exhibit 8.1 illustrates, 57 percent of the angels receive their deals from a friend, family member, or coworker; 31 percent receive referrals from professionals; and only 12 percent receive referrals from nonfamily members, who are representatives of the firm seeking financing by cold-calling them. Only one time in ten will someone who does not know you work with you over a phone call. These statistics bear out that cold-calling in this business is less efficient. As we have pointed out, you are not selling stock from a brokerage desk, something you can turn around and sell quickly in order to ease the pain of getting burned.

Exhibit 8.1  **HOW ANGELS FIND THEIR DEALS**

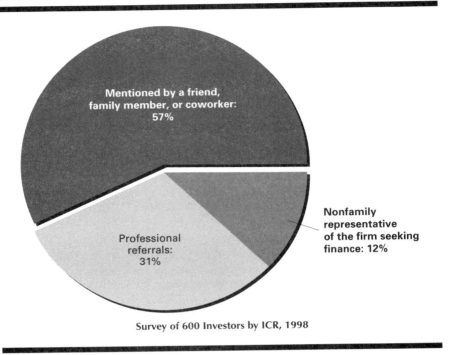

Mentioned by a friend, family member, or coworker: 57%

Professional referrals: 31%

Nonfamily representative of the firm seeking finance: 12%

**Survey of 600 Investors by ICR, 1998**

Source: International Capital Resources

But groups of investors face the problem of skimpy deal flow, a scarcity in the number of ventures and transactions that turn up for consideration.

Exhibit 8.2 demonstrates the depth of this discontent. A 1996 independent study by Harrison and C. Mason found that 33 percent of investors were "dissatisfied" and an additional 10 percent were "very dissatisfied" with existing channels of communication and being able to find out about businesses seeking financing. Such statistics impel a look at alternative funding resources.

In a small group, each person will have gone about developing his or her own deal flow. Regional focus, the angels' propensity for privacy, the small number of people involved—all these account for the limited number of deals. One of the reasons that these groups have traditionally remained small is that, once again, individual investors prize their privacy. As soon as the word gets out that angels are active, they become inundated with deals, few of which meet their investment criteria. Their

Exhibit 8.2  **SATISFACTION OF ANGEL INVESTORS WITH EXISTING CHANNELS OF COMMUNICATION AND BUSINESS SEEKING FINANCING**

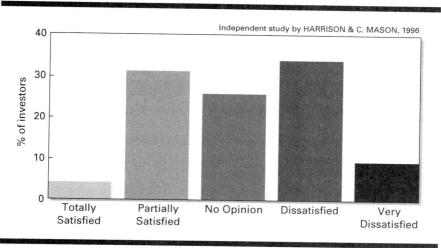

Independent study by HARRISON & C. MASON, 1996

Source: International Capital Resources

privacy is suddenly forfeited, which contributes significantly to the difficulty in finding them.

But the desire to broaden the scope and quality of the offerings has given rise to networks. These networks, driven by developments in database technology and in the personal computer, have spurred many investors to band together. The desire for an increase in deal flow has motivated these organizations and individuals to invest in their communities or in their regions, motivation traditionally reserved by universities, nonprofit organizations, and government agencies in their commitment to regional economic development and job creation.

This interest in community investment and the desire of small, informal networks of investors to increase their deal flow has nurtured a growing industry over the past five years. The investor network is a more formal effort to ease the process linking ventures and capital, while safeguarding the investor's privacy.

In keeping with tradition, most of these networks have been nonprofit. With their computer-based systems, they more easily introduce deals to investors while protecting confidentiality. In this way, the investor can review deals without being barraged by solicitors. As these more formal networks have been able to cluster separate informal groups of investors, significant pools of capital have blossomed.

For example, International Capital Resources' initial effort in creating a network in Northern California has expanded beyond the state; as it has done so, it has cultivated nationwide interest in investing in California. This network has swelled to more than 8,200 investors. Clusters of informal investors from across the United States are now grouped within this network. Besides being connected to ICR's computerized matching system, investors receive its monthly newsletter profiling investment opportunities and providing insight into private placement activity in California. These investors also attend ICR's investment forums—all of which makes easier the networking opportunities between investors and entrepreneurs.

This chapter sketches the history of investor networks from their original, informal beginning to the more formalized attempts to smooth introductions between entrepreneurs and investors.

## OVERVIEW OF ALTERNATIVE FUNDING RESOURCES

Exhibit 8.3 provides an overview of the different types of more formal programs for alternative funding resources and the evolution of the different types of networks.

The only tools entrepreneurs and inventors used ten years ago were directories, the granddaddy of which is *Pratt's Guide to Venture Capital*. Then came the upstart, *VanKirk's Venture Capital Directory*, which lists many of the smaller, "storefront" venture capital firms, and more recently *Galante's Equity Guide*. Typically, these resources list about 650 resources (in *Pratt*), up to about 1,000, the majority of which are institutional resources, not private investors.

Later, with the advent of the personal computer and advances in software, some firms developed software databases. These software databases are interactive, permitting users to query the database for certain criteria that describe their deals, such as how much they need, which industry interests them, and the location of the venture. Using this relational database software generates a list of firms that invest in a particular area. But institutional investors and creditors formed the primary resources of these databases, since information about the informal investor was largely unavailable in the public domain. Frequently, companies avidly publicize their resources and the kind of investments they are interested in. Once again, institutional investors must invest; angels do not have to. Thus, these database developers could easily gather data about more formal resources and arrange them in a database format.

The two big players in database technology are Datamerge and Dataquest. They have not sustained early success, however, because everyone who uses their services bombards those listed. Moreover,

## Exhibit 8.3 WHERE TO START YOUR SEARCH FOR ANGEL INVESTORS

### NEWSLETTERS/PUBLICATIONS

*Environmental Investors Newsletter*          *Private Equity Review*

### INTERNET ELECTRONIC NETWORKS AND INVESTMENT RESOURCES

| | | |
|---|---|---|
| Ace-Net | Financehub | Moneysearch |
| Adventurecapital | Ideacafe | Scor-Net |
| Direct Stock Market | Iponet | Witcapital |
| Edie-Online | Moneyhunter | Yourbusiness |

### COMPUTERIZED MATCHING NETWORKS

| | |
|---|---|
| The Capital Network | North Carolina Investor Network |
| CDA/Investnet | Pacific Venture Capital |
| Investors Circle | Seed Capital Network |
| Kansas Venture Capital Network | Venture Capital Network |
| MIT Venture Capital Network | Venture Connect Website |

### VENTURE CONFERENCES

Capital Conference          The Great Midwest Venture

### VENTURE CAPITAL CLUBS

New York Venture Group          Northwest Venture Group

### DIRECTORIES

*Pratt's Guide*          *Private Fortunes*
*Vankirk*                *Private Equity* Directory

### SOFTWARE

Datamerge          Dataquest          AI Research, Inc.

### INCUBATORS

Accelerate Technology

### FORUMS

Bay Area Venture Forum          Orange County Venture Forum
MIT Enterprise Forum

Source: International Capital Resources

Datamerge's primary concentration is on lending resources, which are not appropriate for early-stage deals; Dataquest focuses chiefly on the equity-oriented institutional investor, who previously had received a much more thorough treatment in *Pratt's* and *VanKirk's* directories.

Concurrent with the development of software databases has been the creation of incubators, a primarily not-for-profit concept growing out of community development efforts and spinoffs from university entrepreneurial programs. Incubator ventures foster the growth of early-stage companies and provide addendum services. People who direct incubators have realized that those early-stage development companies coming to them for guidance also need to raise capital. To get launched, the incubator movement has had to develop connections with capital. Incubator directors—currently numbering in the hundreds across the United States—realized that to serve their clients, they had to set up liaisons with the financial community to help investment in these companies so that they, in turn, could grow their incubators. There was, then, a vested interest in developing a formal mechanism. Thus, incubators also stimulated the movement toward matching networks.

In addition, academic institutions, not-for-profit organizations, and government-affiliated economic-development organizations strove to develop economic investment within their community or geographical region. The concept of networking, which became so popular in the late 1980s, operated on the premise that principal players must be brought together, linking those who need money with those who have it. Typically, the original thrust of the forum and conference movement was educational, beginning as community service seminars and business development educational opportunities offered by consultants. Also, some of the more successful firms performed pro bono work, educating people on preparing business plans and on conducting valuation— activities tied to publicizing their professional practices.

Despite uncomfortable issues created by professional service providers attempting to use these events for their own business development, networking soon took off. Major conferences, such as the Great Midwest Venture Capital conference, have succeeded, with hundreds of millions of dollars being invested as a result of introductions between entrepreneurs and investors. These conferences augment deal flow for investors who attend, providing an efficient way for investors to gain exposure to a wider range of deals. Having entrepreneurs make restricted presentations lets investors compare many possibilities, as well as meet entrepreneurs face-to-face. Forums serve two functions: one, by providing seminars on entrepreneurship and raising money; and two, by providing a forum investors can attend. Institutional investors delivered the primary thrust of the conferences and the forums, although private investors have now begun to get involved, especially the more sophisticated and wealthier private investors.

The rising tide of these forums illustrates anew government's role as a barometer reflecting, rather than a catalyst driving, change. The government is just beginning to recognize that forums hosted by nonprofit groups facilitate the exchange and flow of capital from both respectable institutional investors and astute private investors. Further, forums allow these investors a glimpse of deals they would otherwise be unaware of, and at the same time offer entrepreneurs a golden opportunity to acquire funds they have searched for fruitlessly on their own.

Sentiment for change in the government's attitude about forums appears everywhere. Eighty-seven percent of the respondents to a poll at a 1995 forum conducted by California Capital Access Forum agreed that the Commissioner of Corporations should exempt computer matching networks from being considered publications of advertising. One hundred percent felt that the commissioner's office should provide guidance in this matter of advertising, advertising presently prohibited by California Statute 25102(f).

Through such grass-roots polling and other rising pressures, both the SEC and state departments of corporations are beginning to recognize that laws enacted to protect *unsophisticated* investors from *unscrupulous* individuals inappropriately restrict deals introduced by experienced entrepreneurs, who are principals in the ventures, to seasoned investors, who are highly astute financial analysts with industry track records in this type of investing.

Tracking along with the conference movement came the venture capital club. Venture capital clubs were a specialized spinoff not unlike the small investment groups that comprised associations such as the American Association of Individual Investors (AAII). These clubs brought together a number of novice investors, supplied them with the proper material, and assisted them in building a portfolio. Maybe they pooled their money; maybe they did not. Perhaps they just worked together. They operated much as informal angel networks did but used groupthink to improve their understanding and appreciation of investing. Figuring prominently in the mix was the camaraderie and preference to coinvest and share due diligence.

But because traditional investment clubs emphasized publicly traded stocks, those interested in venture capital did not feel welcome. So there has come the spinoff of the venture capital club movement. There are approximately 100 to 150 venture capital clubs across the country, with typically 12 to 25 members. Members tend to be geographically focused, smaller investors, although the clubs typically include a few more affluent, seasoned angel investors who serve as mentors, as well as participants in transactions. Within the angel investor community, we find a bimodal distribution: One segment invests smaller amounts ($7,000 to $10,000 and $25,000 to $50,000); a second segment invests significantly larger amounts ($100,000 to

$1,000,000) over the course of a transaction. This latter group consists of a different caliber of investors, less inclined to get involved with a venture capital club whose members tend to be at the lower end of the financial spectrum.

Although individuals in a venture capital club could maintain their privacy, the venture capital club publicized its endeavor, which facilitated deal flow to the club. This allowed individuals to share the flow, which increased geometrically, but also share the responsibility of due diligence as well as the investment's risks.

Entrepreneurial associations, on the other hand, are dedicated not to investing but to the craft of entrepreneurship. These associations are composed of people in the process of learning entrepreneurship, learning what it takes to be a successful entrepreneur. They tend to spotlight technical skill development as well as self-development. Organizations such as the Los Angeles Venture Forum typify groups with annual conferences, regular meetings, luncheons, and speakers. Obviously these types of associations are also peopled by many service providers looking for clients.

These associations in many cases are neither true matching networks nor formal networking organizations, although, of course, informal networking goes on. Realizing the added value of helping entrepreneurs find investors, these associations are starting their own computerized matching networks. Knowing investors and entrepreneurs within the community gives them a foot in the door.

These separate movements have contributed to still another: the computerized matching networks, the oldest of which is the MIT Venture Capital Network. Whenever computer technology matches the criteria of an investment with that of the investor, the network sends the investor an executive summary describing the venture. This process preserves confidentiality—the big issue—while creating an added value: Investors receive only those deals that meet their criteria. These networks supply a valuable service, and studies echo the refrain of participating investors: They appreciate the screening and the privacy that these organizations furnish.

Of course, since few charge fees beyond those for the processing of documents, these networks also provide entrepreneurs and inventors with an inexpensive mechanism to expose their deals. And to avoid conflict with securities laws, networks charge no finder's fee. Still, they do endure a rigorous qualifying procedure before being granted their nonprofit status.

Resources currently receiving a lot of popular attention from entrepreneurs are the Internet electronic networks and investment resources, such as Direct Stock Market, Your Business, AdVenture Capital Register, MoneyHunter, SCOR-Net, Wit Capital, Garage.com, IPO-Net, Money-Search, Financehub, ACE-Net, Idea Cafe, EDIE-Online, and others.

However, International Capital Resource's proprietary research indicates that less than $44 million was raised by private companies through Internet electronic networks and investment resources in 1998.

With more than $30 billion being raised in the market, $44 million amounts to a mere drop in the funding bucket. This is a sobering fact for entrepreneurs assessing various alternative funding routes, paths, and mechanisms, because if they are going to spend time and resources on trying to raise capital, they want to make sure they are using an effective resource. Entrepreneurs, we think, can use these electronic resources more constructively for valuable information on structuring their deals, for educational referrals, or for referrals to various technical associates who can help them.

But the concept that entrepreneurs, through an Internet electronic network or investment resource, will meet angels defies everything we have emphasized in this book. Investors prize their privacy; they are not going to list their names, addresses, and contact information on the Internet. To do so would expose them to every crank deal and character out there. Investors just are not going to let that happen. The majority of Internet electronic networks are wonderful research and educational clearinghouses for various types of services, or essentially a massive number of deals in search of investors. But they do not provide true investor resources. Therefore, an entrepreneur with limited time and resources would do much better using resources such as those described in the next section.

We do believe that this new electronic resource is more important today than it was when we wrote the first edition of this book, but it truly is not the resource it is being touted as. In the future, given the trends in securities laws and the other things that may happening, things could change. Things could improve. But right now the Internet is not the best resource on which to focus your limited resources.

Certainly it is easy to become enamored of new technology—colorful and entertaining as it is. But face it: Most of all, it is fetching because it seems to discharge the onerous task of dialing for dollars that so many entrepreneurs grapple with. The bottom line: There is no way to avoid having to find people to ask for money. Money will not be found on Internet sites. What will be found in abundance are information, education, research and valuable resources, and referrals to serve as providers. Thus stands the status of present research.

The latest trend in matching networks is, surprisingly, not electronically supported. Yet it is the most advanced. It is the newsletter. The newsletter accommodates two indispensable aspects missing from the software and personal computer technology that drive all computerized matching networks: direct-response marketing and follow-through. Newsletter matching networks correct both these omissions. Unlike newsletter networks, nonprofits rarely track and support the investor and entrepreneur after introduction, and, when left to their own devices, the two parties rarely reach an agreement—especially in early-stage situations. Nonprofits simply fail to realize that the private investor must be serviced.

What is more, computer networks attract chiefly the institutional investor. Although they serve private investors as well, some private investors are not willing to pay the networks' registration fee, even with a buffering service. Private investors are also reluctant to pay fees for a "black hole" service, one that does not guarantee results or support ongoing communications. Newsletter networks were developed to address this problem and to support financing goals.

In fact, newsletter networks accomplish several things. They build on the hunger for information among investors. According to Hudson Newsletter Directory—the directory of subscription newsletters in the United States—more than 3,000 are flourishing. Of those, about 3 percent are dedicated to investing in the early-stage, private equity, or alternative investment. Moreover, newsletters convey information promptly, just the way investors have been trained to get information about the stock and bond markets. Newsletters let investors study information at their leisure, exposing them to assorted deals—not just those that computer matching software "thinks" they should receive.

Computer software, after all, *cannot* be programmed to match the peculiarities of investor criteria, for investor decisions often emanate from a psychological perspective that computers cannot appreciate. Often we see investors investing in unfamiliar technology, although they do understand the application, a less literal linkage that is incomprehensible to a software matching program. Thus, there have developed newsletter-based networks built on customized printed information, creating a connection that taps a behavior ingrained in investors.

Furthermore, newsletter networks are driven by direct-response marketing. For economic reasons, newsletter networks have developed extensive databases on the investors and their preferences. These databases guide the newsletter publisher in the selection of deals that are profiled and the distribution of different versions of the newsletter to appropriate audiences. But most important, newsletter networks approach their subscription and controlled-circulation subscribers with direct-response marketing techniques.

Direct-response marketing has always been the essence of solicitation and of marketing investments. While deals can be closed only through extensive face-to-face discussions, generating investor interest begins with stimulation provided by compelling direct-marketing programs. So newsletter networks combine database technology, which permeates the computerized matching networks, with the newsletter concept. To this combination newsletter networks add the dimension of direct-response marketing, an added service to investors. So in the newsletter business, we see a more diverse array of participating firms. We see more sophisticated corporate finance firms and firms that understand investment banking transactions. On the leading edge of this dynamic technology in the United States is the *Private Equity Review.*

The newsletter concept of profiling ventures for investors is not new. Public companies have used this vehicle for years. Two currently popular publications are *Sound Money Investor* and *Stock Deck Select,* which describe public companies and provide means for sophisticated investors to get in touch with companies that meet their investment criteria. The main benefit lies in having reviewed a summary describing the companies before requesting further documentation, instead of being matched solely by a computer program that has compared criteria.

The investors who receive *Stock Deck Select* have, in fact, expressed previous interest in particular deals. This previous knowledge forms the basis for the direct-marketing matches. The investors, having first seen the executive summary, express an interest in certain deals and then contact the firm. This differs from some networks, which request filled-in questionnaires from both entrepreneur and investor, then set the computer loose on a matchmaking spree. In this case, investors have never seen the information that has been dispatched to them. In contrast, direct-marketing response adds the element of motivation and prequalification.

BBSs (electronic bulletin boards) constitute a spinoff from computerized matching networks. They attempt to be an electronic version of the newsletter. Because of the development of the so-called information superhighway, and such services as America Online, and other on-line networks, people become aware of the electronic alternatives to the mail, newsletters, and other printed material. Electronic bulletin boards let the user pull down information otherwise handled by the network or printed, published, and mailed out by newsletters. By using personal computers, modems, telephone lines, and software program menus, people can access the same kind of information appearing in newsletters and computerized matching networks.

However, no one has developed a defined and qualified investor database for electronic BBSs. Moreover, our experience at ICR reveals that private investors do not spend time on bulletin boards; they do not surf the Net for deals. Nor do they care to learn about the software programs that would teach them how to use the various files. Those newsletters that do use electronic bulletin boards or the Internet publish into an unknown universe of "suspects," without either the benefit of prequalification or the means of tracking response. Bulletin boards cannot determine if anyone has received the electronically published information or is qualified to use it. In large measure, the population to whom these communications are sent may be as unqualified as it is wide. By contrast, newsletters feed information only to prequalified subscribers, those who have completed an investor application, paid all fees, read company profiles, and requested in writing more information from the company. Quite a difference!

## PERFORMANCE OF THE TOP 20 FORMAL INVESTOR NETWORKS

We have presented an overview of the alternative funding resources. But how much of a capital resource are these alternatives? Our directory (at the end of this chapter) lists alternatives, but let us look here at only the top 20. Amid a stingy market, a market in which early-stage ventures are starving for funds, the top 20 alone have closed for more than $2.5 billion, a sum that elicits a respectful, breathless whistle. These are not transactions merely in the pipeline or in due diligence.

Exhibit 8.4 shows the results of an ICR study of private equity network performance.

Exhibit 8.4  **TOP FORMAL INVESTOR NETWORKS' PERFORMANCE TO DATE**

| | |
|---|---|
| Mid-Atlantic Venture Fair | $1.3 BILLION |
| Investors Choice California Venture Capital Conference | $400M |
| Center for Entrepreneurial Development | $300M |
| International Capital Resources | $221M |
| Oklahoma Investment Forum | $148M |
| Arizona Venture Capital Conference | $72M |
| The Capital Network | $25M |
| Investors Circle | $18M |
| Capital Link | $15M |
| MIT VCN | $12M |
| Band of Angels | $11.5M |
| Rockies Venture Club | $10M |
| Technology Capital Network | $6.5M |
| Great Mid-West Venture Capital Coalition | $5M |
| Canadian Opportunities Investment Network | $3.1M |
| New York New Media Angel Investors Group | $2.5M |
| New Jersey Entrepreneurs Network | $1.5M |
| Pennsylvania Private Capital Group | $1.5M |
| Michiana Investment Network | $1.2M |
| Seed Capital Network | $.5M |
| | $2,554,300,000 |

Source: International Capital Resources

# DIRECTORY OF ALTERNATIVE FUNDING SOURCES

The entrepreneur or inventor needs to employ a strategically orchestrated campaign based on selected resources, appropriateness of the budget, geographical locale, and similar criteria. To this combination of alternative financing mechanisms should be added the requisite networking and computerized matching, the newsletter networks, and other resources. With such a strategy in place, we will be looking at a substantial rise in ventures linked to capital.

## ANGEL WORKS, INC.
9 Longview Terrace
Greenville, SC 29605
864-271-1470
fax: 864-271-2089

Angel Works provides access to one of the largest angel databases in the country. It is a regional office and affiliate of International Capital Resources.

## ATLANTA DEVELOPMENT AUTHORITY
230 Peachtree Street, N.W., Suite 2100
Atlanta, GA 30303
404-658-7000
fax: 404-658-7734
www.@ATLecodev.org

A private, nonprofit corporation, Atlanta Development Authority was founded to promote and implement economic development within the city of Atlanta. ADA represents a partnership of the public and private sectors for the purpose of creating and/or retaining jobs, encouraging capital investment, promoting business and neighborhood development, and expanding the tax base of Atlanta. ADA manages the city of Atlanta's Business Improvement Loan Fund (BILF) program, which is designed to encourage the revitalization of targeted business districts, and provides financial and technical assistance to small, minority, and female-owned businesses.

## THE CAPITAL NETWORK, INC. (TCN)
3925 West Braker Lane, Suite 406
Austin, TX 78759-5321
512-305-0826
fax: 512-305-0836
www.utexas.edu/de

The Capital Network is a nonprofit economic development program designed to introduce investors to entrepreneurs based on their mutual business interests. All introductions between investors and entrepreneurs are strictly confidential. This confidential process is selective and timely, resulting in increased opportunities for both investors and entrepreneurs.

## COUNCIL FOR ENTREPRENEURIAL DEVELOPMENT (CED)
P.O. Box 13353
Research Triangle Park, NC 27709
919-549-7500
fax: 919-549-7405
www.ced.NC.org

The Council for Entrepreneurial Development encourages and assists entrepreneurial development in North Carolina. Members include entrepreneurs, investors, financiers, service professionals, public policy makers, and university faculty who focus on the needs of Triangle area growth companies. CED provides a forum where members share their expertise to create a supportive environment for growth companies in North Carolina.

## ENTERPRISE CAPITAL RESOURCES
James R. Moore
18521 53rd NE
Seattle, WA 98155
206-363-6260
fax: 206-682-4859
www.investorconnection.com

Enterprise Capital Resources provides access to one of the largest angel databases in the country. It is a regional office and affiliate of International Capital Resources.

## ENVIRONMENTAL INVESTOR'S NEWSLETTER
5777 West Century Boulevard, Suite 1070
Los Angeles, CA 90045
310-642-0047
fax: 310-642-0048

The newsletter features public and private environmental businesses in pollution control, alternative energy, and recycling industries. The publication is mailed to individual, institutional, and corporate investors, venture capitalist groups, investment bankers, stockbrokers, mergers and acquisitions principals, IPO underwriters, and pension fund managers.

## ENVISTA
209 Commerce Street
Alexandria, VA 22314
703-379-9200
www.envista.com

The directory is a two-volume, nearly 1,000-page listing of current, detailed information on more than 1,300 venture capital firms. It provides information on contacts, current activity, and total amount of capital under management for each firm. The directory also includes key indexes on funding stage preference, industry preference, and geographic and organizational preferences for listed firms.

## FIRST BOCA ASSOCIATES
Bob Weinberg
2295 Corporate Boulevard, Suite 140
Boca Raton, FL 33431
561-994-3830
fax: 561-994-9757
www.investorconnection.com

First Boca Associates provides access to one of the largest angel databases in the country. It is a regional office and affiliate of International Capital Resources.

## GREAT MIDWEST VENTURE CAPITAL CONFERENCE
c/o ISBD Corp., One North Capitol Avenue, Suite 1275
Indianapolis, IN 46204
317-264-2820
fax: 317-264-2806
www.ISBDCorp.org

The Great Midwest Venture Capital Conference features Midwest equity investment opportunities. The ISBD Corp. (Indiana Small Business Development Corporation), Indiana Business Modernization and Technology Corporation (BMT), and Ernst & Young have joined forces with a coalition of Midwest business development organizations to present the conference in Indianapolis, Indiana. Investor participants receive a conference binder containing executive summaries of each of the presenting companies. Companies in search of venture capital submit detailed executive summaries, which are screened by a committee of business experts. Firms selected to participate are assisted by the committee in developing their 15-minute presentation and their executive summary.

## INTERNATIONAL CAPITAL RESOURCES (ICR)
388 Market Street, Suite 500
San Francisco, CA 94111
415-296-2519
fax: 415-296-2529
www.icrnet.com

International Capital Resources is a focused funding resource, invaluable to the many entrepreneurs who do not have the time and energy to both grow their business and successfully raise capital. ICR has assembled the largest network of business angel, private investors interested in direct investment into early- and expansion-stage ventures. ICR utilizes this database to offer its clients confidential networking capability and to make introductions between entrepreneurs and investors who have similar investment criteria. The Investor Network provides a wide range of different types of funding: venture capital for start-ups, equity and debt capital for acquisitions and working capital for expansion, mezzanine capital for growing companies, bridge capital for special situations, senior loans without equity, and straight loans for small businesses.

## INTERNATIONAL VENTURE CAPITAL INSTITUTE (IVCI)
P.O. Box 1333
Stamford, CT 06904
203-323-3143
fax:  203-348-0622

The International Venture Capital Institute (IVCI) serves as a worldwide liaison of venture networking organizations and small businesses, providing a forum for entrepreneurs and investors. IVCI publishes the *IVCI Directory of Venture Networking Groups (Clubs) and Other Resources.* In addition, IVCI also publishes the *Directory of Venture Capital SEED and Early-Stage Funds,* and its new publication *Directory of Business Incubators in the U.S. and Canada.*

## INVESTMENT EXCHANGE
P.O. Box 12430
Scottsdale, AZ 85267
800-563-5448
fax:  800-563-7492

The Investment Exchange is a publicly owned and operated computer-matching service for investors and entrepreneurs seeking capital. Entrepreneurs seeking capital or selling a business initially complete a Fund-seeker Registration Form and a 200-word Executive Summary of their business opportunity or business for sale. The information from the Registration Form and the Executive Summary are then entered into a computerized investor-base that matches the opportunity to the appropriate investor or purchaser.

## LONG ISLAND VENTURE GROUP
Hofstra University
Business Development Center, Room 217
Hempstead, NY 11549
516-463-6326
fax:  516-463-3907

The Long Island Venture Group, which has been around since 1984, links entrepreneurs with sources for growth, including equity and debt capital, and support services.

## MARQUETTE CAPITAL RESOURCES
E. Jeffrey Lyons
Evanston Business and Technology Center
Northwestern University/Evanston Research Park
1840 Oak Avenue
Evanston, IL 60201
847-866-0420
fax: 847-866-0430
www.investorconnection.com

Marquette Capital resources provides access to one of the largest angel databases in the country. It is the Great Lakes licensee and affiliate of International Capital Resources.

## MICHIANA INVESTMENT NETWORK (MIN)
300 N. Michigan
South Bend, IN 46601
219-282-4350
fax: 219-236-1056
www.Indianachamber.com/SBDC

The Michiana Investment Network helps match entrepreneurs with investors in the Michiana business community. MIN is a not-for-profit organization coordinated by the Small Business Development Center. A noon luncheon series provides a forum for small businesses seeking capital. At each quarterly luncheon entrepreneurs give short presentations about their services, products, investor opportunities, and funding requests. The purpose of the presentations is to give possible investors an occasion to learn about new business opportunities. Most quarterly luncheons also feature expert speakers on investing or entrepreneurism.

## MID-ATLANTIC CAPITAL RESOURCES
Bob Marik
4001 North Ninth Street, Suite 1426
Arlington, VA 22203
703-276-0136
fax: 703-812-8054
www.investorconnection.com

Mid-Atlantic Capital Resources provides access to one of the largest angel databases in the country. It is a regional office and affiliate of International Capital Resources.

## NATIONAL ASSOCIATION OF INVESTMENT COMPANIES (NAIC)
733 15th Street, Suite 700
Washington, DC 20005
202-289-4336
fax: 202-289-4329

The National Association of Investment Companies is an industry trade association for venture capital firms that dedicate their financial resources to investing in minority businesses. Besides offering technical assistance to member companies who need detailed information about sources of funding, managing investment operations, and legislation and regulations that affect their operation, NAIC is a catalyst for networking information among members, entrepreneurs, and other public and private partners.

## NATIONAL VENTURE CAPITAL ASSOCIATION (NVCA)
1655 North Fort Myer Drive, Suite 700
Arlington, VA 22209
703-351-5269
fax: 703-351-5268

The National Venture Capital Association is comprised of more than 200 professional venture capital organizations. It is designed to foster a broader understanding of the importance of venture capital to the vitality of the United States economy. The association is also interested in stimulating the free flow of capital to young companies. NVCA publishes a membership directory of 179 venture capital firms. The directory lists the company names, addresses, telephone and fax numbers, and the contact persons.

## NORTH FLORIDA VENTURE CAPITAL NETWORK (NFVCN)
7400 Baymeadows Way, Suite 201
Jacksonville, FL 32256
904-730-4700
fax: 904-730-4711

Managed by Enterprise North Florida Corporation, the not-for-profit NFVCN is designed for private investors, angels, and institutional investment companies seeking information on companies in need of financing. It is likewise designed for business and investment service providers and not-for-profit entrepreneurial support organizations throughout northern Florida.

## OKLAHOMA INVESTMENT FORUM
616 South Boston, Suite 100
Tulsa, OK 74119-1298
918-560-0207
fax: 918-594-0386
www.ok.investmentforum.org

The Oklahoma Investment Forum reviews approximately 30 high-growth companies and hosts an Innovation Expo that provides a look at new products, technology, and ideas being developed in Oklahoma. Attendees include business executives and high-risk investors from around the country.

## PENNSYLVANIA PRIVATE INVESTORS GROUP (PPIG)
Technology Council of Southeastern Pennsylvania
435 Devon Park Drive
Wayne, PA 19087-1991
215-382-0300
fax: 215-382-0366
www.techcouncil.org

A nonprofit corporation administered by the Ben Franklin Technology Center of Southeastern Pennsylvania and Wharton Small Business Development Committee, providing a forum for entrepreneurs to present business plans to potential investors. The group, however, is not an investor pool, and its members make their own investor decisions.

## PRIVATE INVESTORS NETWORK (PIN)
The Baltimore-Washington Venture Group
c/o Dingman Center for Entrepreneurship
The Maryland Business School
University of Maryland
College Park, MD 20742
301-405-2144
fax: 301-314-9152

The Private Investors Network, an angel network whose parent organization is the Mid-Atlantic Venture Association, brings together accredited investors and growth companies in Maryland, Virginia, and the District of Columbia.

## ROCKIES VENTURE CLUB (RVC)
190 East 9th Avenue, Suite 440
Denver, CO 80203
303-831-4174
fax: 303-832-4920
www.rockiesventureclub.org

The Rockies Venture Club is a nonprofit organization serving as a catalyst for entrepreneurism in the mountain region, connecting entrepreneurs, investors, corporate executives, service professionals, and consultants, among others. The club hosts regular meetings that feature networking time before and after the meeting, dinner, a keynote speaker, 12-minute presentations by the CEOs of emerging growth companies, and 5-minute presentations by anyone who falls into one of the following categories:

entrepreneurs seeking capital, deal makers, and members with an idea. All members are welcome to distribute literature at the dinner meeting.

## SANDLES CAPITAL RESOURCES
Ellen Sandles
145 East 16th Street
New York, NY 10003
212-677-8739
fax: 212-995-0788
www.investorconnection.com

Sandles Capital Resources provides access to one of the largest angel databases in the country. It is a regional office and affiliate of International Capital Resources.

## SMALL BUSINESS INVESTMENT COMPANIES (SBICs)
c/o Associate Administration for Investment
U.S. Small Business Administration
409 3rd Street, S.W.
Washington, DC 20416
202-205-7589
www.SBA.GOV./INV

Licensed by the U.S. Small Business Administration (SBA), small business investment companies are private investment firms that independently make their own investment decisions. These companies are participants in a vital partnership between the federal government and the private sector. Utilizing their own private capital plus funds obtained on favorable terms through assistance from the federal government, SBICs provide financing to small businesses for growth, modernization, and expansion. A free directory is available that lists nearly 200 SBA-licensed firms that supply equity and venture capital to qualifying businesses.

## SOUTHWEST CAPITAL RESOURCES, INC.
George Matthews
P.O. Box 571620
Salt Lake City, UT 84157-1620
801-293-8966
fax: 801-293-8976
www.investorconnection.com

Southwest Capital Resources provides access to one of the largest angel databases in the country. It is a regional office and affiliate of International Capital Resources.

## TECH COAST VENTURE NETWORK (TCVN)
195 South C Street, Suite 250
Tustin, CA 92780
714-505-6493
fax: 714-669-9341

The Orange County Venture Forum brings together users and providers of resources for new and emerging businesses. Such resources include public accounting, banking, legal, intellectual property protection, funding, marketing, sales, strategic planning, administrative, sources of professional information, and government resources. The OCVF, a nonprofit corporation, is actively involved in the Orange County/Southern California business community. Through its major program, the OCVF has entrepreneurs and other presenters tell their stories and share their professional business experiences. It has been directly or indirectly responsible for a number of new businesses and for assisting established firms to grow.

## TECHNOLOGY CAPITAL NETWORK, INC. (TCN)
P.O. Box 425936
Cambridge, MA 02142
617-253-7163
fax: 617-258-7395
www.TCNMIT.org

Technology Capital Network is a not-for-profit organization that introduces start-up and high-growth companies to potential investors through a confidential, computerized matching process and venture capital forums. The majority of the participating investors are individual "accredited investors" with a special interest in early-stage situations. Professional investors representing venture capital firms and corporations seeking business partners are also active participants in the network.

## VENTURE CLUB OF INDIANA
P.O. Box 40872
Indianapolis, IN 46240
317-253-1244
fax: 317-253-1211

Since 1984 the Venture Club of Indiana has facilitated the expansion of business and commercial investment activities. Opportunities exist for investors and entrepreneurs, investors with an ongoing source of contacts, and entrepreneurs with sources of capital and business expertise.

## WHITE-KNIGHT GROUP, INC.

Jerry White
26431 Quail Hollow Rd.
Pewaukee, WI 53072
414-798-5426
fax: 414-798-5427
www.investorconnection.com

The White-Knight Group provides access to one of the largest angel databases in the country. It is a regional office and affiliate of International Capital Resources.

## WHITNEY FINANCIAL CORP.

Victor Rogers
P.O. Box 26158
Austin, TX 78755
512-323-9669
fax: 512-323-0011
www.investorconnection.com

The Whitney Financial Corporation provides access to one of the largest angel databases in the country. It is a regional office and affiliate of International Capital Resources.

# 9

# Building Your Own Database
# of Angel Investors

## INTRODUCTION

New technology comes bundled with steep learning curves. As one story goes, during the 12th-century reign of Henry II, forks made their first appearance in England, much to the bewilderment of all the nobles at court. Unsure of what forks were and how to use them, those gathered at dinner that first night pondered the matter a good while, then finally figured it out—or so they thought. No longer hesitant, England's nobility vigorously proceeded to poke each other in the eyes.

Thus we have *in extremis* the consequences of unleashing the latest technology on the uninitiated. To be sure, setting up a highly sophisticated computer program is far less painful than the jab of a fork in the eye; still, the irritation and torment of the former can be sizable. In truth, there remains hardly anything more mystifying than using a computerized relational database. Even with the help of experts, pitfalls await. In particular, entrepreneurs going it alone need to understand what they are in for. What skills will they need to master to build a database? What technical expertise will ensure that information so painstakingly gained is not lost—information gathered from a placement agent, an alternative funding network, or an individual search effort?

But first, the question: What is a relational database? A relational database consists of data from which relationships among various pieces of information can be established, allowing the user of the database to look for specific *fields*, either individually or in combination. These fields—names, addresses, telephone numbers, and so on—make up individual *records*; multiple records make up a database *file*. A relational database connects these fields—pieces of data—from the various records to target particular markets the user wishes to reach. The user might want to assemble all individuals within a specific income level living in a particular zip code area. In a relational database, the end user can pluck any combination of fields from any combination of records, enabling him or her to *relate* only the desired information.

Relational databases replace old-fashioned databases, those composed of so-called flat files, tediously rigid sets of information. Similar to relational databases, traditional databases offer only whole records, but the various fields within those records cannot be isolated and then joined with matching fields from other records in the database. The *whole* record is pulled, or nothing is pulled at all. The telephone book is a nonrelational database. In using it, the address cannot be pulled separately from the name and then related electronically to its counterpart in other areas of the telephone book. This example illustrates the value of a relational database.

The strengths of a relational database, as we have indicated, lie in the ease of accessing data. A relational database allows the user to better target a specific audience. The user can pick out with a keystroke or two only those fields desired. People can be selected by income level or by last name. In a relational database, all information is incorporated within one big file and all fields or records can be related within that file, indexed or grouped in any number of ways—depending again on the target market.

## HURDLES

Database expert Don Siebert, who built ICR's relational database, warns of the problems even experienced database managers face in establishing a database for the end user. Setting up fields in each record is only the first among the tasks awaiting someone about to embark on the murky electronics of database development. There is no margin for error. Even very sophisticated relational database programs are unforgiving. For example, a field containing "Smith, Jr." can precipitate problems. No comma is allowed, for example, in a program that uses the comma to "delimit" fields (that is, to tell the database program where one field ends and the next field begins); thus, the comma cannot be used as it is used in normal punctuation. Even where there is no information in a particular field, the comma must still appear so that the program can determine that a field is blank. The program "looks" at a comma and "reads" a new field. Otherwise, all fields move forward: A city appears in a state field; a state field appears in a zip code field, and so on. Missing commas furnish scrambled information. Missing only one such technicality makes the entire database useless.

Another hurdle to leap may involve the database application itself. Siebert spent 100 to 150 hours becoming familiar with Access, one of the better-known computer-generated relational database programs, a program that sports "Wizards," a feature that purports to help the user set up the database more easily. The Wizards are supposed to lead the user through the steps necessary to create a query. (A query enables the user to search repeatedly for designated categories of information among all the records.) By setting up queries, the user can search the database, automatically accessing the desired information. And if the same set of information is likely to be required often, template queries can be established within the program. The user normally would not want all the fields of all the records for every mailing but may consistently want the same fields from different records for separate mailings. Also, there are additional types of queries, such as ICR's ability to copy records from one table to another table, a feature essential for exporting information to its mailing list. Fine and necessary though they are, queries take some study.

Using one of these more sophisticated packages can become extremely difficult. Without computer experience and database experience, an individual can get swamped quickly. Often the user has to reach beyond the manuals provided in the database package. Even finding the right third-party manual is a challenge. Each of the best-selling database application programs has generated dozens of manuals written to explain what is often impossible to decipher in the database company's user manual. The best way to shop for third-party manuals is to enter a bookstore with a few questions in mind. If you find the answer in one of the choices on the bookshelves—and understand what it says—odds are you have a decent book to work with. The quest for clarity has spawned an entire industry of third-party manuals, most notably the "For Dummies" series.

Too often, however, third-party books themselves offer little relief. Many are written by techies or programmers in a language that does not translate well into layperson's terms—repeating one of the problems the user faced in the first place. In addition, the reader may have to catch on to proprietary terminology: One company's nomenclature may not match another's, so the same thing is called by two different names. It becomes the reader's task to match the different terminology.

Once a person has selected a program, he or she still faces the formidable task of designing a database that fits specific needs. These programs supply designs that may turn out to be either too generic or, in some cases, too narrow. It is left to the user to map out a working design. And for the novice, trying to map a snug fit gets tough.

Cardinal rule number one, claims Siebert, is having patience and foresight: patience in setting up a database, foresight in knowing what you want your end result to be. "You have to know precisely what you want to do with your database," he cautions. "Having to *redesign* fields within the structure of a database creates even greater problems than creating the original design. You really have to give your design some forethought—setting up fields, setting up how things relate. And then you have to take a step back."

The better-known programs provide ways to change things, such as a field name. But if a user follows the program's method of changing the field name, all references to it must also change. When a field name changes, nothing refers to that field anymore, so all queries and all tables must reflect that change. If a user just dives in, he or she will get only so far, and then . . . trouble. Thus, only a full understanding of the program's potential precludes a setup that needs revamping.

This problem arises in particular in a business setting. "When I first sat down with the people at ICR," recalls Siebert, "and we talked about what they wanted, they didn't realize everything they could get out of it. They wanted to change their emphasis halfway through the project. Fair enough. It was just a matter of not knowing fully what a relational database can do. When I installed the program, they began to appreciate its potential. I was able to go back and make it do what they wanted it to do. Now they're really set. Any decent mail house is going to be able to take their disk and give them just what they want. The point is that you can't be afraid to try things, whether it's filtering for a particular piece of information or whatever. You have to be able to just go for it. But you can go for it *only* when you understand fully what the program can do."

For example, with its custom-made program, ICR can designate in what order the cursor will move, allowing the user to avoid stepping through the fields according to the program's original design. This enables the user to jump from selected field to selected field because certain fields are used more than others. The cursor can jump in the order selected by the user. It is possible, of course, to buy a preset package, basically a sales-contact kit, but it is likely not to fit well. The whole purpose of a relational database is to make sure it fits the user's needs. Otherwise, why bother?

Another cardinal rule is understanding that a relational database is designed to *save* time, not *cost* time. If you have the time and the inclination, you can do it yourself. If you do not, either suffer through with a packaged program or hire someone who can design it specifically for your needs. After all, people rooted to the database are supposed to be in the field collecting names. The big weakness in setting up a relational database is that unless you know what you are doing—that is, in designing anything beyond a basic mailing list—a database really is simply not worth your time. People trying to get the attention of private investors had better have more than a list for putting on labels and sending out Christmas cards. So stick with your forte. Stick with what you are supposed to be doing. Remember why you are in business.

Finally, a person setting up things on his or her own may not only invite problems but become overwhelmed. Nowadays the user has to be familiar with both the computer's operating system and the fine points of the application program. He or she has to know which is doing what—for example, which functions Windows is handling and which functions are performed by the database application. Exhibit 9.1 pinpoints what is involved in the setup of a computerized relational database.

## DATA ENTRY

One such overwhelming task is data entry, the ongoing, *accurate* collection of information. Again, everything has to be just so: using only the standard abbreviations for states, for example. In gathering data entry information, the source must be readable; names from napkins dampened at lunch by the bottom of a wet glass are of little use. With legible sources of information, the user can hire data entry personnel. Without readable sources, the user loses valuable time—time that could be used in getting on with the real task of furthering the venture.

However, "garbage in, garbage out" is the watchword in data entry. With each inaccurate entry—the wrong state, the wrong name, the wrong title, or simply spelling something incorrectly—the database's effectiveness is diminished. Without absolute accuracy in the information entered into the database, all is for naught.

It is also important to understand that if you go it alone, data entry is a never ending, time-consuming process. Keeping a database updated is easiest when done constantly, even daily, even if it means gathering information from someone during a telephone conversation. Getting the information at that time eliminates having to have other

Exhibit 9.1 **SETUP OF A COMPUTERIZED RELATIONAL DATABASE**

Managing the database
development budget

    Networking considerations

       Installing a backup system

         Data entry
         —Initial input, maintenance, and updates

           Decide on export formats

             Create relational queries and templates

               Design database to fit specific criteria
               —Fields, records, files

                  Select your database application

Source: International Capital Resources

people do it, or having to write the information in longhand and then entering it into the database. It should become a daily routine, but it takes time, discipline, accuracy, and patience. Waiting, say, until the end of the month makes for a weekend-consuming task.

The question arises about when a company keeping track of such information should switch to a computerized system. The answer, we suggest, comes when the company is spending more time doing things manually than it is in making contacts to sell its product or service—the real reasons the business was started in the first place. Another signal comes when the company has had to hire one or two people to manually keep up with the influx of information.

Siebert recalls watching one company pay a typist to input all the names and addresses in WordPerfect files, a different file for each group. When a mailing address was needed, the typist would print out on laser labels all the names and addresses, then sit for hours, typing things in, formatting the labels, and printing the whole file. But if the mailing did not require the whole file, the typist had to peel only certain labels. That meant manually placing labels on hundreds of newsletters, a job that consumed entire weekends. Once a company has reached that point, only a relational database makes sense.

## BACKUP

Another cautionary note seems worth sounding: the possibility of losing an entire database of information. It happens, although rarely. A database needs to be backed up, a feat accomplished with relatively little effort. If the system does crash, eliminating everything, the information can always be restored from the backup.

For safety's sake, the user can simply copy the entire file over to another area of the hard disk, although this is not the best way to back up such valuable information. If the disk crashes, the user loses both the backup and the master file. The safest way is to copy the data onto floppy disks or tape, storing the tape off-site. Fire, a natural disaster of some sort, and even a break-in are all good reasons to keep a disk or tape at home. Even if someone burglarizes the office and makes off with the computer, the backup tape is safe. A computer can be replaced by the insurance company, plugged in, and the information restored by tape. Barely skipping a beat, the company is back in business.

## COST

Finally, in going it alone, one has to consider the expense of setting up a relational database. First comes the expense of the software, the application program itself, costing a few hundred dollars. Cost continues to decrease for database software and Pentium-based computer hardware. Additional hardware—a good printer is necessary—would add several hundred dollars, unless everything would go on a disk to the mailing house. Still, with any word processing, a printer becomes essential. A basic laser printer, which does six pages per minute, costs about $600—fast enough for a small operation.

But those are just opening costs.

Another expense involves training, depending on how computer literate the user is to begin with. Windows is very user-friendly; going from square one should not take too much time. The tasks are repetitive, which speeds the learning curve.

Help from a consultant, however, is a different matter; at an average rate of $90 an hour, the user had better be able to catch on quickly. The same rate usually applies for a phone call to a consultant sitting at home or for an on-site visit.

For the database to be up and running and the project customized, 15 hours seems reasonable. There is hardly any point in slaving over something that does not quite work for you. It makes little sense to spend time and money, only to come up with something that could have been pulled off the shelf.

The most expensive component, however, will be data entry, that ongoing, tiresome task we discussed at length earlier. Data entry is not a onetime expense. In time, it could very well dwarf all other expenses combined.

We agree with Siebert's final piece of advice: "Don't try to reinvent the wheel, and since ICR has the wheel, why take on chunks of problems when you should be conducting business?"

Earlier we presented different ways of securing financial resources: by renting them, that is, renting the names from other databases; by growing them, that is, getting the names of people you know, then asking them for the names of people they know; or by buying them, that is, hiring a placement agent to obtain investors for your venture. In this chapter we have plotted the task the individual faces in attempting to engineer a proprietary relational database. We hope we have made that decision easier by suggesting instead that entrepreneurs tend to business, and, at the same time, grab the spoke of a wheel already in motion, a wheel being spun by the capable placement agent—as you will see in the next chapter.

# 10

# The Role of the Placement
# Agent in Raising Capital:
# A Marketing Partner
# for Your Deal

## INTRODUCTION

The great English Renaissance figure Francis Bacon bemoaned the truth that "In all things no man can be exquisite." We simply cannot do all things, much less do them well. It is no weakness, then, to admit that you need help in raising capital. Managing your business leaves little time to raise money. When neglected, businesses suffer. Worse, the principal who ignores the company's operating responsibilities while building capital will neglect the unwelcome blips certain to appear on the company's radar screen, problems that can quickly mushroom into dire circumstances.

The best institutions readily admit their need for help by placing their money with venture capitalists. In turn, some venture capitalists will use a placement agent to help them raise money. And much like those who run venture capital funds, entrepreneurs use placement agents—intermediaries who help raise money. In this chapter we discuss what is involved in retaining a placement agent to help you raise funds for your venture. Good help in marketing requires money. A placement agent is like a marketer, increasing your efficiency in raising money.

## THE PLACEMENT AGENT: A MARKETING PARTNER

Years ago, the industry looked down on placement agents; today, however, agents are appreciated for the services they provide. Using a placement agent enables you to spend more time on your venture, less on raising money. In a word, using a placement agent is simply more efficient.

Perhaps you believe you do not need help from an agent because you have raised money in the past. But think about how much the market has changed: You are competing with tens of thousands of money managers and perhaps hundreds of thousands of deals. Many alternative asset classes besides venture capital and private equity are competing for the same money. Six hundred fifty venture capital funds and 16,000 registered investment advisers are all after the same high-net-worth investors. Moreover, many ventures are vying for the attention of private investors. Thus, while you have been immersed in growing your business, several major changes have occurred: Start-ups need more money; external capital and financing have diminished; and more competition exists for start-up capital.

In some cases, entrepreneurs have been away from the fund-raising market for one to three years. During that time the investor roster will have changed, as will the amounts investors are willing to part with. It is easy to lose touch with the market. It is not uncommon to meet an entrepreneur who raised millions in the early 1990s, yet suddenly cannot seem to raise a penny beyond family and friends. He or she may no longer know today's investors—and much depends on knowing investors well. The good placement agent knows investors well.

In fact, the placement agent's stock-in-trade is knowing about the people being asked for money. An agent can tell you who is in the market and what they want. Agents can offer you far more than an impersonal mailing list. For instance, do you know what deals your competition is offering? Do you know who the investors are, where they are located, what they are looking for, and, most important, how to reach them and get them to notice your deal? The competent, trustworthy agent can help you in all these things. And beyond these important considerations, a good placement agent adds value by helping you determine if your deal is right for the private market. Furthermore, the good placement agent helps you understand the individual venture that investors seek.

A placement agent helps you accomplish things quickly—a special benefit for start-ups, development firms, or expansion ventures lacking stellar performance records. In their up-to-date databases agents keep detailed records of those private investors who have responded to introductions; they can link you to qualified investors, casting a wider net for prospective investors, helping you win appointments. The role of the placement agent is, after all, to match legitimate buyers (investors) to legitimate sellers (entrepreneurs) and to introduce entrepreneurs only to investors who have expressed a strong interest in their deal.

Investors and entrepreneurs alike see the competent placement agent as value-added, as a marketing partner, not as a retail salesperson peddling stocks and bonds. The competent placement agent retained at a reasonable price will save you time and improve your chances of success with information and follow-ups of qualified leads. He or she can help you meet your fund-raising goal, thus reducing your risk of falling short. Meanwhile, by spending more time building your company, you can make money for your other investors. Remember, your business is to *make* money, not *raise* it.

What exactly do placement agents do? During interviews the agent assesses the chemistry among the partners. He or she becomes involved in what normally turns into a full-time relationship. The agent will help with the business plan and offering memoranda—all amounting to a financing proposal package. The good agent will also help prepare sales material and put together a marketing road map. The professional agent is a competent, full-time person with whom you will share a positive relationship.

The agent commonly prospects 20 to 25 contacts per day for three to four days to set up appointments with qualified prospects for telephone or in-person conferences. Placement agents telephone selected investors they know—people whose investment criteria they understand—and introduce your deal to them without leading or selling them.

These prospects are difficult to reach, and busy. They open their own mail, have special projects, manage professional and personal crises, attend board meetings, and meet with current investors and intermediaries. But a good placement agent can get through to those investors and earn consideration for your deal. Respecting a good placement agent, busy investors carve out the necessary time, knowing that this agent matches the right deals to the right investors and does not waste anyone's time.

Remember, the task of an agent in a private placement of an angel investor is to match the investor with the deal, not sell *you* or your deal. *Selling* yourself and your deal is *your* responsibility, not the placement agent's. Placement agents may have sent questionnaires to investors requesting biographical information to determine in what form the investor wants to carry on due diligence. The agents also help prepare your financial proposal and venture documents and provide feedback, sometimes delivering criticism that others would feel uncomfortable mentioning. They can change the way you market yourself. Last, well-organized agents document their activities, providing call reports of contacts, leads qualified, and schedules of presentations. Placement agents can coach you in your presentation skills and can alert you to what investors are looking for.

The following list details the services a good placement agent will and will not perform.

## The Good Placement Agent's Commitment to Quality Service

A good placement agent

- Will not represent any deal
- Will not place the burden of screening on the investor and will prescreen deals to meet investor requirements
- Will not make an introduction to an entrepreneur without knowing the investor's capability and criteria
- Will understand a deal before introducing it to investors
- Will not waste an investor's time with inappropriate or poorly prepared deals
- Will assist entrepreneurs and investors with the increasing administrative workload associated with introducing investors in private placements
- Will not "sell" a deal to investors, nor undersell an introduction
- Will create multiple opportunities for entrepreneurs to tell their story
- Will follow up introductions, but only when there is reason for doing so
- Will not use pressure in introductory activities

The question remains: How do you find a competent, trustworthy placement agent? Intermediaries abound. But you must select an agent who can get the job done. Most seem charming, articulate, persuasive, and assertive. But to find the best, look below the surface. Ask your attorney, your accountant, and intermediaries whom they respect and why. But also gain firsthand knowledge of placement agents: Read their books; attend their speeches; visit their offices; speak to their partners and associates. Speak to them yourself. Ask whom they represent, how they work with clients, what they charge, and what results they have achieved.

The fees paid to a good placement agent become a modest investment when you consider the scale of the transaction and the stakes involved. Typically, a top placement agent will require a front-end retainer equal to about half the percentage expected from the first $500,000—nonrefundable against success fees—and a percentage of capital raised. Common success fees amount to 5 percent of the first million, 4 percent of the second million, 3 percent of the third million, 2 percent of the fourth million, and 1 percent of the balance. While the structures of expense reimbursement will vary, the company always pays the costs associated with distributing its offering memorandum. The investor rarely pays "success" fees directly; generally, the entrepreneur pays such fees.

Finally, ensure that your company fits the placement agent's profile. Also ensure that no conflict exists between your venture and any other of the agent's current or prospective clients. Then talk with some of the agent's clients, both entrepreneurs and investors. Last, select the most qualified agent based on price. A good agent will help you raise money and finish the job quickly.

The time and the money saved by good placement agents will more than cover the cost of their fees.

# Part 4

## The Investor Perspective

# 11

# The Venture Process

## INTRODUCTION

Private equity investing in venture capital is a relatively small but growing sector in the capital markets. International Capital Resources research suggests that of the $30 billion invested in the private equity asset class by private investors in 1998, approximately $4 billion was directly invested into early-stage ventures, that is, into seed and start-ups. Investors are attracted by the well-publicized financial and personal rewards associated with these more active investments. However, such rewards are associated with high risk and have unique requirements, requirements quite different from passive investing, such as the kind characteristic of mutual funds.

As an asset class, private equity and venture capital increasingly appeal to private investors. We will explain some of the reasons why, but the primary objective of this chapter is to provide information about the various steps involved in direct equity/debt investing to help determine if this type of investment fits into an investor's strategy.

## DRIVING FORCES CREATING DIRECT INVESTMENT OPPORTUNITIES

Venture capital is a proactive investment, not passive, as we have said. And the successful active investor requires a complex set of technical and interpersonal skills. We will cover the fundamentals necessary to launch a successful campaign: identify a flow of attractive investment opportunities, navigate the due diligence process, cultivate relations with coinvestors, value and select the terms of investment, define participation and assistance level in the venture, and plan alternative exit strategies. All of these fundamentals, however, will have little value without realistic expectations for potential returns and information about the availability of promising opportunities and prospects.

Daniel H. Case III, of the Hambrecht & Quist Group, defines venture capital as "the search for significantly above-average, long-term investment returns through equity ownership in, and involvement with, risky start-up and emerging companies, managed by experienced executives, providing rapidly growing markets with innovative products or services based on proprietary technology or possessing other significant barriers to entry." Popularly defined, venture capital investing is "the business of building business." Implicit in this definition is the commitment to contributing more than money to the company-building process. Venture investing involves the process of building and financing successful, self-sustaining companies—often from scratch. A successful company, by definition, will become a rewarding investment. This form of investing also requires a disciplined, focused, long-term orientation; an abnormally high tolerance for risk, ambiguity, and illiquidity; patience; and, of course, good luck.

## HISTORY OF EARLY-STAGE INVESTING

Venture capital is hardly a new concept. Consider Queen Isabella's financing of Columbus's voyage to the New World; the financing of Saugus, Massachusetts, Ironworks in 1645 (fueled by John Winthrop Jr.'s entrepreneurial skill in raising £1,000 in England to buy the necessary equipment); the Middlesex Canal in 1803, connecting the Merrimack River with Boston Harbor; the Scottish law firms' pooling of surplus funds of local industrialists in the late 19th century and making a "bonny" bundle investing in New York railroads and Texas ranches. Familiar names pop up. In 1880 an obscure bank clerk managed to obtain $5,000 from a private investor. Eight years later George Eastman debuted his $25 Kodak camera. In 1901 an employee at the local drugstore borrowed money from his father to buy the place. The employee's name: Charles R. Walgreen Jr.

Or consider modern institutional venture capital, beginning with American Research & Development in 1946 and its later investment in Digital Equipment Corporation, or the Small Business Investment Companies started in the 1950s or the individual family-held funds of the 1960s and the 1970s, or the private pension funds of the 1980s, or public funds of the 1990s. Venture capital (or high-risk, early-stage investing) has been around for a long time.

The driving forces that have created direct investment opportunities are numerous. For one thing, as we have pointed out earlier, capital is scarce for rapidly growing companies. For another, the IPO market remains vigorous, although the number of IPO issues has decreased, as we mentioned in Chapter 4. In addition, an expanding array of alternative financing methods has emerged, including joint ventures and strategic partnering, management buyouts, lease financing, R&D arrangements, venture capital, cash management and tax strategies, private placement (exempt offerings), government financing in the form of loans and grants, traditional sources of capital, Employee Stock Ownership Plans (ESOPs), bartering, incubator-based financing, and asset-based loans and factoring.

## OVERVIEW OF THE OMNIBUS BUDGET RECONCILIATION ACT OF 1993 AND ITS IMPLICATIONS FOR PRIVATE INVESTING IN HIGH-RISK DEALS

Other driving forces behind direct investment opportunities concern private capital market inefficiencies, the rise of the manager-investor, and the government Tax Incentive Bill (with its top marginal income tax rate set at 39.6 percent and its ceiling on capital gains rate retained at 28 percent). Known as the Omnibus Reconciliation Act of 1993, this bill allows investors who hold qualified small business stock for at least five years to exclude 50 percent of the gains realized on disposition of their stock. This reduces the tax burden on many investment dollars to about 14 percent. This reform should markedly stimulate the flow of investment dollars controlled by wealthy individuals or taxable institutions to the venture capital investment area.

Still other forces at work on direct investment opportunities are the *re*equitizing of the economy, a reequitizing that compensates for the *de*-equitizing of buyouts and mergers of the 1980s.

While there are great social benefits from private equity investing—such as capital for cash-strapped business, enhanced corporate/personal income tax bases, job creation, and increased worldwide competitiveness for U.S. products—individuals have invested in venture capital because, as an asset class, it has provided a high return on investment.

Depending on whom you believe, studies show rates of return for the venture capital industry ranging from 15.3 percent over the last 30 years, to a compounded rate of return of 35 to 40 percent over shorter periods of time. Total capital under management currently is more than $31 billion, according to Venture Economics, a respected firm that tracks the venture capital industry.

(For more information on the '33 Act, the '34 Act, the '40 Act, and other Federal Rules and Regulations, see Appendix A.)

## DISADVANTAGES OF HIGH-RISK INVESTING

While venture capital investments involve high potential for return, they are likewise characterized by high risk. Disadvantages of direct venture capital investment include illiquidity, high mortality rate, a high level of anxiety, no diversity, and a large consumption of time. Moreover, getting into private venture investments is easy; getting out is not. In this regard, disadvantages may include severe restrictions on the liquidity or transferability of registered securities (exempt offerings).

Start-ups and young companies have a high mortality rate. In a study by VentureOne of 383 venture investments by professional venture capitalists, only 6.8 percent returned ten times the capital invested, while the balance lost money or failed to exceed the returns of a standard bank account. An SBA study confirms that 50 percent of all start-ups survive the first year; by the fifth year, only 10 percent of these remain in business. Characteristic risks may involve a product that cannot be made to work, a market that will not accept the product, or an operation incapable of producing a quality item in volume. Finally, if management fails to get the company up and running quickly, a no-growth crisis looms.

Additional risks may emerge at any time; expect Murphy's Law to prevail. Consider that most investments fail to return their targeted multiples and that financial projections are rarely met. Projected revenues exceed actual revenues, which arrive later than expected; projected expenses lag behind actual expenses, which occur sooner than expected. Further, the need for more capital comes sooner than expected, and more rounds of financing than had been forecast become necessary.

## RISK CHARACTERISTICS

Risk can vary significantly, depending on different dimensions of an investment—for example, the category of the private equity class and the company's stage of development. The private equity class of investments has broadened to encompass a range of different transactions: preseed, seed, start-up, growth, mezzanine, LBO, buyout, spinout, postventure, turnaround, special investment situations, and distressed security investing. The life cycle of potential portfolio companies evolves from start-up to expansion to mezzanine. Of course, risk stands significantly higher in the earlier stages of the development of the venture, a stage in which founders attempt to comprehend the concept, the company's reason for existence. At this stage, management capability remains limited as they struggle to clarify strategic advantage, develop a business plan, and commence to prove practicability. Exhibit 11.1 outlines the different risk types.

In addition to considering the stage-of-development risks inherent in early-stage transactions, investors must study five other risks. First, management risk does not center on the more obvious question of qualification of the individuals; this aspect of due diligence is taken for

Exhibit 11.1 **TYPES OF RISK**

1. Management risk (Can a cohesive team be formed?)
2. Product risk (Can it be made to work?)
3. Market risk (Will the market accept the product?)
4. Operations risk (Can the product be produced in volume and with quality?)
5. Financial risk (Can the venture survive with the amount of capital projected?)
6. Business strategy risk (Can the venture survive changes in the targeted market?)

granted. The real management risk is whether the principals involved can perform as a team and carry the venture through.

Another risk involves the product. If we are dealing with a start-up or early-stage company, with the product in development, the investors are being asked to put up money before a prototype has been developed. Whether the product can be made to work becomes a critical risk.

A third risk of these types of ventures centers on the market. Will the market accept the product? Such a consideration involves the push-pull of market forces. Having to push a product onto the market makes missionary selling necessary—an expensive proposition tied to considerable risk. However, a product being pulled by market demand means less risk.

Operations, another area of risk, depends on a company's ability to meet its sales projections. Can the company produce with quality the projected volume to meet customer expectations, keep them happy, and maintain their loyalty (and the company's reputation)?

Still another risk associated with early-stage ventures is financial risk, an assessment of how much money will be needed beyond the investor's investment. If a venture needs $10 million in the next round, and the investor's contribution is only $50,000, a major financial risk looms. The entrepreneur will not likely be able to raise such a sum. So financial risk has to do with raising money for the balance of the present round and future rounds necessary to move the company into becoming a profitable venture.

Expansion companies, meanwhile, immerse themselves in analyzing competition, trying to get "real" customer feedback, meeting the needs of customers, and developing both management team and market acceptance.

The last type of risk is a business strategy risk, the assessment of the potential that the company's targeted market could change during the venture's beginning. Can anything occur that might have an impact on the acceptance of the company and its strategy in the market? Carefully assess the answer to this question.

For many private equity investors, the "venture" in venture capital has been a misnomer. Venture capitalists in many instances have avoided investing in start-ups because they believed that the risk/reward ratio was unattractive compared with the opportunities to enact mezzanine transactions with shorter time horizons. This perception has spread, attracting a disproportionate amount of money over the past several years to the later-stage segment of the financial spectrum. Inevitably, the market has responded at the seed end of the spectrum with lower entry level pricing and an improving risk/reward ratio.

In the end, the private investors must decide to select private equity categories with which they have experience and that offer opportunities for them to consistently apply their strengths.

## HEDGING STRATEGIES—HOW ANGELS MANAGE RISK IN DIRECT INVESTING

In the face of the foregoing caveats, if investors remain interested in investing directly in early-stage deals, they will consider a few of the advantages: No middleman exists; the upside potential is unlimited; the experience is satisfying; and such investments involve investors in one of the few areas in which they can influence the outcome of the investment.

Of course, no one minds having advantages. However, as we have noted, investments do have their risks.

In direct investing, there invariably comes the intricate decision concerning how to manage risk, a consideration that has to do with "hedging strategies." One way the investor can begin to manage the risk associated with this type of investing is to require a business plan.

Other advice for managing venture investment risk involves high selectivity, extreme discipline, and personal responsibility, such as allocating assets to different elements in the private equity class or different regions, industries, technologies, or stages of development; diversifying investment and monitoring financial performance of the portfolio companies; and monitoring investments through tight controls and strict financial reporting requirements of the investor's own design.

Consideration must be given to structuring transactions with any collateral available, using cash or cash equivalents. Moreover, deals must be thoroughly analyzed prior to *every* investment. Also essential is aggressively structuring terms and conditions as much as possible early in negotiations to protect against loss. Controlling risk through staged infusion of capital based on performance is likewise essential, as is taking responsibility for due diligence by using experts and advisors. Remember, for investors to achieve attractive rates of return, avoiding the bad ones is more important than hitting a home run. To avoid the bad ones, investors rely on an investment plan.

Investors do not let that portion of their capital earmarked for the high-stakes, higher-risk investments burn a hole in their pocket. While their expertise should drive development of their investment—since so much depends on the value they can add to the venture—they need to clarify the answers to some critical questions: "How much can I make?" "How much can I lose?" "Who else is involved in the deal?"

When considering ROI, investors calculate not only the amount of return but the time they deem acceptable in realizing that return. For example, a ten-times multiple may be possible but may require hanging in for seven years or more. Investors must determine what is acceptable to them.

So take some bits of advice from some of the savvy investors in ICR's private investor network. Note their hedging strategies (Exhibit 11.2) in direct venture investing offered freely to the uninitiated: Negotiate steep discounts; never invest at the price/valuation suggested by the entrepreneur; search for coinvestors early to share due diligence and financial risk; use other people's money as soon as possible; expect the unexpected; and learn to live with the disadvantages inherent in developmental-stage investing.

## THE SYNDICATION BIAS

The syndication bias—the major hedging strategy—involves the investors' understating how much they can invest. Our experience tells us that an investor with $100,000 in capital will declare an investment capability of only $50,000, preferring to have that judgment confirmed by finding another investor willing to invest a like amount. The syndication bias (see Exhibit 11.3) is a factor constantly at work in these types of investments.

Investors also need to be certain that their personal "syndicate" agrees that the deal is worthwhile *before* they invest in it. It pays to syndicate early. Syndication helps ameliorate financial risk, pulls together

---

Exhibit 11.2 **HEDGING STRATEGIES IN DIRECT VENTURE INVESTING**

Negotiate steep discounts
Never invest at the price/valuation suggested by the entrepreneur
Search for coinvestors early to share due diligence and financial risk
Use other people's money as soon as possible
Expect the unexpected
Learn to live with the disadvantages

---

Exhibit 11.3 **REASONS FOR SYNDICATING EARLY**

---

Helps to mediate financial risk
Pulls potential management resources together with similar interests/commitment
    before problems occur
Broadens available technical expertise to evaluate deals

---

potential management resources with similar interests and commitment before problems occur, and broadens available technical expertise to evaluate the venture.

## HOW INVESTORS GENERATE DEAL FLOW

Take note also of the requisite skills necessary to the successful direct venture investor in developmental-stage deals, skills we have covered throughout the book: generating deal flow; conducting due diligence; structuring and negotiating terms and conditions; attracting coinvestors; monitoring portfolio companies; adding value; harvesting returns; and managing portfolios.

Many novice investors in direct investing attempt to initiate their deal flow by responding to classified advertisements such as those in the *Wall Street Journal* or in the Business Opportunities section of their local newspaper, or by networking with friends, colleagues, and through local organizations and events. Since ICR's research suggests that fewer than 2 percent of all deals currently looking for capital will be financed by investors other than family, friends, and the founders, investors must review hundreds of deals in this fashion before "stumbling" on a venture that merits a more time-consuming, and possibly costly, due diligence.

Generating deal flow amounts to much more: offering services for free; serving as mentors to entrepreneurs; convincing colleagues to offer services free; publishing newsletters; contributing articles; volunteering to speak—either alone or on a panel; joining venture capital clubs; helping to place senior executive job seekers; referring accountants and attorneys to entrepreneurs; sponsoring or hosting seminars; teaching evening courses at a university; volunteering for advisory boards; publishing a book or audiocassette on the subject of raising capital; sharing good deals with coinvestors; attending meetings of private investor networking groups; listing yourself in capital resources directories read by entrepreneurs; and subscribing to publications and networks that list investment opportunities.

A particularly interesting way in which deals are generated occurs when someone really finds a deal attractive and brings it to the attention of associates and colleagues, grandfathering those other individuals into looking it over. But entrepreneurs commonly say, "Hey, you're interested in the deal, and we have another party over here who's interested. Can I introduce the two of you? Perhaps you can discuss the venture together." So generating deals flows both ways. This harkens back to the syndication bias, except that oftentimes it is the entrepreneurs who initiate the branching out from a single investor.

## FINANCIAL AND NONFINANCIAL RETURN ON INVESTMENT: ANGELS' EXPECTATIONS

Returns on investment are the result of various combinations of good judgment, skill, and luck (although we should remember that the harder we work, the luckier we seem to get). Since 1988 investors in venture capital have seen returns of around 20 percent on investments made as limited partners in venture capital funds. Nonfinancial returns sought by investors include creating jobs in areas of high unemployment, developing socially useful technology in medicine or energy, contributing to urban revitalization, and deriving personal satisfaction from assisting entrepreneurs in building successful ventures in a free enterprise economy.

A look at Exhibit 11.4 shows how well the professional venture capital industry has fared regarding return on investment. According to Venture Economics, important in considering ROI is the time that passes before harvesting returns. Three times investment in three years yields a 44 percent ROI, whereas three times investment in five years yields a 38 percent ROI.

Exhibit 11.5 shows the stages of venture capital annualized targeted rates of return.

---

Exhibit 11.4  **PROFESSIONAL VENTURE CAPITAL RETURNS\* ON INVESTMENT**

| | |
|---|---|
| Total loss | 11.5% |
| Partial loss | 23% |
| Break even | 30% |
| 2–5 times investment | 19.8% |
| 5–10 times investment | 8.9% |
| 10 or more times investment | 6.8% |

---

\*Cash on cash + capital gains.

Exhibit 11.5  **ANNUALIZED TARGETED RATES OF RETURN**

| Description | Internal Rate of Return* |
|---|---|
| Seed/start-up | 60%–100% |
| Development+ | 50%–60% |
| Management team revenues/expansion | 40%–50% |
| Profitable/cash poor | 30%–40% |
| Rapid growth | 25%–35% |
| Bridge to cash out | 20%+ |

*Before applying subjective factors.

## ELEMENTS IN STRUCTURING THE PRIVATE PLACEMENT

Although a range of appropriate deal-structuring methods exists, the private placement seems to be the preferred investment vehicle for private investors. It essentially amounts to placing treasury securities with a small number of individuals. The private placement presents a range of different structures, debt and equity, or a combination of the two. But more important, the private placement is flexible because it involves anything that is not a public offering.

However, there are primarily three practicable structures, with equity fundamental to each. First is preferred or common stock. The second is convertible subordinated debt, a structure much more common to the institutional transactions, typically involving some type of interest payment arrangement. And third is some form of long-term debt with warrants, a debt situation applicable only to later-stage ventures.

In almost all cases, the only way that investors in these types of transactions can benefit from the risk that they have assumed is to share in the upside potential if the venture proves to be successful. And the only way they can do that is through equity. So, at bottom, all structures relate to equity. And what we see is a reliance on preferred stock, for a couple of reasons. One, it is senior to common stock; therefore, it provides leverage to influence management when things go askew. Also, preferred stock requires the entrepreneur to remain in contact with the investor. This provision creates warning mechanisms that permit the investor to change management or set time frames and conditions for making changes when they become necessary.

Preferred stock can also provide some income through dividends, although this is not a circumstance typically arising in early-stage ventures. However, preferred stock is redeemable by the corporation, which may set up a sinking fund and establish compulsory payment.

And preferred stock is convertible to common stock, so if, in fact, the company is purchased or does go public, or experiences some other liquidation event, the holder shares in the success.

Another type of deal structuring involves the comingling of funds in order to create an investment that would be suitable for the entrepreneur. Basically, individual investors will interact with the entrepreneurs who supply them with equity in the venture commensurate with the amount of money each has invested. They do not invest as a pool, as would a venture capital partnership; rather, they conduct individual transactions. Individual transactions, of course, must be in accord with the valuation and with the amount of the individual's share of equity; otherwise—count on it—issues among the parties will arise.

## APPROACHES ANGELS USE TO MONITOR INVESTMENTS

As we discussed earlier, investors implement hedging strategies to manage risk *before* investing. To manage risk *after* the investment is made, however, investors implement monitoring strategies to track the performance of the venture. Monitoring strategies are designed to identify problems before they require drastic action to rectify them.

Think of the instrument panel a pilot uses to monitor a flight, particularly a flight imperiled by low visibility. Like pilots in fog, investors find themselves flying in bad weather because projections fuel most of what has lifted their investments off the ground. Little is based on historical financial fact or current reality. Fueling an investment's gas tank are conjectures based on assumptions.

Given these circumstances, investors need to create their own instrument panel. By doing so, they put in place an early warning system capable of alerting them to dangers so they can take corrective action. Investors, then, have to know how to set up an instrument panel whose dials they can read. This ability to read the panel means that investors establish their own instruments—ones appropriate to the venture, ones they are familiar with.

Instruments familiar to many investors include tracking monthly financial statements through tight controls and strict financial reporting requirements, daily contact with management, and attending regular meetings; comparing performance against business plan objectives; and maintaining vigilance relative to terms and conditions of the investment contract. Individually and collectively, these monitoring devices amount to being able to help when help is needed, instead of waiting past the time when adversity can be reversed.

As one investor put it in Chapter 6, "What also gets my attention is . . . an action plan from someone who demonstrates that over the next 90 to 180 days, from the time the company receives the money, he or she can enumerate what exactly has to be done to make this business go. The more specific those kinds of milestones are, the more comfortable I am in knowing that I can measure progress after I've made the investment and calibrate how I should react—that is, whether I've made a mistake, or whether I should put money in if I'm asked. This is a very good way both to monitor the investment and to assess how management is doing and what you can do to help them."

## HARVESTING RETURNS: REALISTIC EXIT STRATEGIES

Venture capital is "patient" money. Returns to investors take the form of long-term capital gains realized after an extended period during which an investment provides little or no liquidity or marketability. The method and timing of liquidation expectations are important variables in a venture capital investment decision.

Patience and shared exit expectations are particularly critical for ventures with limited prospects for a public offering or acquisition by a larger firm within the typical five- to ten-year exit horizons of venture capital investors. Alternative exit strategies include an IPO offering, selling stock back to the founders, an LBO (recapitalizing company), selling to a public company for stock, transferring to other investors, or merger/acquisition.

If an investor expects to cash out by selling securities back to founders, he or she should be sure that the terms and conditions of the sale are tied to the operating performance and cash flow of the venture. Legal and financial advisers can be helpful in designing appropriate arrangements.

Regardless of the anticipated liquidation method, it is important to make clear early the investor's interest in achieving liquidity at the highest price within a specified time frame, for example, seven years. This interest in achieving liquidity needs to be more than a verbal agreement; terms should be clearly specified in writing and on solid legal ground. In developing a strong set of terms and conditions during negotiations, do not underestimate the importance of auditing, monitoring, and engaging good legal counsel.

# 12

# The Valuation Process
# in Private Transactions

## INTRODUCTION

If any term receives reverential treatment in the business of financing a venture, it is surely *valuation*. And such distinction is well earned. Valuation haunts every aspect of a venture; in its very scope, valuation becomes the entire process writ small. No deal gets very far without it; no deal can be torpedoed more quickly if it is off the mark. The best test of a deal's practicability and pricing is whether it can attract, and be sold to, another private investor at the same price, in other words, its valuation. However, investors must rely on their own judgment in evaluating a deal, a judgment requiring comprehensive investigation and analysis.

John Cadle, International Capital Resource's valuation expert, has sage advice about valuing a venture. To begin with, explains Cadle, unlike buying an existing business with lots of assets—an event possessing formulated definitions of what value is—for the early-stage company, no recognized definition of valuation exists. Cadle warns entrepreneurs to realize that in an early-stage venture, the value is in the future. Therefore, definitions are limited. Determining value in early-stage investing is highly subjective, because such determination depends on something that has not yet happened.

Thus, into the valuation mix go many subjective elements: the experience and cohesion of the management team; the size and growth rate of the market; whether the business is in manufacturing, service, or retail; whether the business is in manufacturing, service, or retail; whether the product or service has a competitive edge; whether the venture is a product or business; the degree of market development (missionary selling) required; the likelihood of additional financing, planned or not; whether the exit strategy is realistic; whether the deal has been shopped; and how persuasive and committed the founders and management team are.

With so subjective a mix, valuation is best deferred until later on in the process, after you have that investor believing firmly in you as an entrepreneur, after he or she is sold on the dream. It is a big mistake, cautions Cadle, to bring up valuation too early; better that valuation be considered later on in the relationship.

## SWEAT EQUITY

Valuation is an emotional issue with entrepreneurs because their egos are involved. They want value for their sweat equity, the time and effort they have previously invested in the venture. A highly charged issue, valuation needs to be prodded to the rear until the entrepreneur can reach the point where he or she can approach investors. Understandably, the entrepreneur wants the highest value for the hard work already done.

Sweat equity, however, carries different emotional messages to entrepreneurs than it does to investors, a difference that entrepreneurs especially need to understand. As an entrepreneur, you consider only the two years or so you have slaved away, the mortgage you have taken out on your house, and the salary you have not paid yourself. This is sweat equity—obviously an issue for you. Perhaps you used to work for IBM and commanded a $200,000 yearly salary. Therefore, you wish to declare to your potential investor that he or she should pay your back salary, a hefty $400,000 for a starter. From your point of view, what could be simpler? From your point of view, those are the facts, facts that speak for themselves.

But those are *your* facts. The investor's "facts" differ markedly. The investor appreciates that you have chosen to do what you have done, that you have chosen two years of sweat equity instead of a salary, that you have mortgaged your home, and so forth, but the investor judges that sweat equity only on what he or she will realize from this point on. What is on the investor's mind is how far along you are in the process and what he or she can get for this thing in the future. Failing to get inside the investor's perspective on this issue can quickly derail the valuation process.

These are different perceptions, different starting points. The task falls, of course, on the entrepreneur because *it is the entrepreneur who must try on the investor's shoes, not the other way around.*

## THE "LIVING DEAD"

So if the entrepreneur is concentrating on sweat equity, what is the investor mulling over? We have an idea of what sweat equity means to the entrepreneur. But in valuation, different starting points are generated by the cavity between the entrepreneur's sweat equity and the investor's fear of gaining membership among the "living dead." Who are the "living dead" and what does the term mean to investors?

If you have a business and an investor invests in you, he or she becomes your partner. You are your own boss, having a wonderful time manufacturing your widgets—as any entrepreneur would. You love to make these widgets; you love being your own boss. Things are fine with you. But if the investor can never obtain liquidity from the investment a problem emerges. The business is doing well, and you are enjoying what you are doing because it is what you do for a living. But to the investor, the investment is a failure because he or she cannot get money out at an appropriate multiple of the investment. The investor needs what Cadle calls a "liquidity event." He explains, "If I'm looking at a deal, and I think I can get liquid in two years, I'll probably accept a lower rate of return, rather than accept a long-range development project that is not going to be liquid for seven years."

Liquidity can be achieved through a number of different mechanisms, for example—as we discussed in Chapter 2—through a sale back to the entrepreneur, a merger, an acquisition by a public company, a trading of illiquid stock for publicly traded securities, the sale of the company to other entrepreneurs, or an initial public offering. The investor has to keep in mind that fewer than 8 percent of all ventures in the last several years have reached liquidity through IPO. Either the entrepreneur has to buy the investor out or some other situation has to occur that turns the investment into a return for the investor. In other words, the investor has to get money out of the investment sometime. If none of these alternatives works, we have an investor who has become a member of the living dead.

And while IPO is only one way—and not the typical way—to obtain liquidity, people are often fooled by the publicity generated by an IPO. A headline on the front page of the August 8, 1995, issue of the San Francisco *Chronicle* shouted in typical fashion: "Investors in Frenzy as Hot Software Firm Goes Public." And in case anybody missed the news, the next day this banner was splashed above the front-page headline: "STUNNING DEBUT FOR NETSCAPE." The fact is many more businesses are acquired than experience an initial public offering. Perhaps this is the reason entrepreneurs often fail to realize how important it is to impress on the investor what liquidity options are available on an investment.

No investor wants to suffer in financial purgatory by being left in a venture without liquidity. For many investors, being a member of the living dead has been a dreadful financial experience—hanging in limbo, not wanting to slip backward, but unable to move forward. The money is in, but the investor has no way to get it out.

## RISK

In valuation, then, everything centers on the degree of risk. When investors look at an investment prospect, they hope to determine the amount of work the entrepreneur has already done in developing a product, developing the market, or selling the product—all things that reduce risk in the deal. Again, such determination remains subjective.

Further, risk is layered in terms of the stages of the deal. Obviously, if only a concept exists, if we have no more than an idea, we place ourselves at great risk. In fact, the investor may feel that despite the talent and trustworthiness of the entrepreneur, the risk simply remains too great.

On the other hand, if the entrepreneur is already selling a product, and the market has already validated its willingness to buy it, the risk is substantially less. The valuation depends largely on how investors perceive the risk. Different investors will perceive risks differently. Investors will not measure risk in the same way nor to the same degree. Investors want answers to some specific questions: How much risk remains in the deal? How far along is the entrepreneur in the process? Has validation through other investors occurred? Is the market already buying these products or services? These are the questions that connect directly to risk.

Thus, as an entrepreneur you must defend your valuation in terms of risk/reward. You have to understand the process that the investor is going to go through. You should have in mind a range of valuations. Valuation, after all, is a negotiation, probably one of the more subjective negotiations an entrepreneur will endure because of so many nonfinancial factors—nothing pat, nothing to map the area. No set value at one percent of revenue, or one times revenue, or a Price Earnings multiple. In valuation, where there is no E, there cannot be any P.

The question becomes one of why an investor should invest in you. What makes you a decent soul? What is right about the deal? How might it be structured to lower the perceived risk? You should have all this in mind—for both your benefit and the investor's. If the business is high in cash return, perhaps it is not high growth but will throw off some cash. Maybe a structure is in order in which the investor receives some of that cash in terms of a royalty stream or dividend on stock. Sometimes—not often—the investor may receive a royalty stream on those revenues. So the investor receives money off the top rather than off the bottom. Royalties on sales reward the investor with immediate cash as opposed to a wait of five years for a return.

One structure in particular works well: funding in smaller increments. Suppose an entrepreneur and investor agree to a $2-million plan, but the $2 million is not given all at once. In fact, giving the entrepreneur all the money at once may prove imprudent because it tempts the entrepreneur to do other things with it. In a smaller deal involving smaller increments, only $1 million is offered up front. The entrepreneur gives the investor an option on the second million at the same price. But if the entrepreneur fails to meet specified targets—volume milestones, perhaps, or product development milestones—the investor is absolved from putting in that second million. If milestones are met, the investor *is* required to put in the second million. This lowers the investor's risk because he or she is off the hook for $1 million if the venture flops. If the venture succeeds, the investor has a fixed price—today's price a year later—on the second million.

Critical to this transaction, of course, are understandable, simple milestones that people can agree on. Fuzzy milestones—perhaps different interpretations of a cash flow formula, for example—later become serious hindrances to the company's progress. In structuring a deal in this way, the entrepreneur is declaring that if he or she fails to perform, the investor has the option—but not the obligation—to put in further money, perhaps negotiating a lower deal.

But before all other considerations comes the importance for the entrepreneur in selling the dream to the investor, best accomplished by bringing that investor into your vision of the future early on. Make sure that you and the investor have the appropriate chemistry, a vital aspect of any venture.

The part such chemistry plays in valuation is hard to overestimate. Because these types of investment are such precarious things, because so much operates beyond our control, good chemistry among the active parties is paramount. Compatible chemistry with sophisticated investors who understand the risks is far more important than a high initial valuation.

And without investors who understand the risk, who understand that private investing is a long-term process, who are willing to sail with you for the long run, frankly, a high initial valuation is a shallow, short-term victory, often a negative rather than a positive. Entrepreneurs should trade a lower initial valuation for helpful, smart partners with the right chemistry and the willingness to stand by them.

Valuation, after all, boils down to what percentage of ownership of the business the entrepreneur is giving to the investor. In effect, the entrepreneur is bringing in a partner, somebody the entrepreneur will virtually be living with. Valuation is not a sale, after which the buyer strolls away. This is partnership, a partnership built on compatibility. Moreover, the smart entrepreneur will be hoping to get more from that partner than just money. In fact, the chances are better than not that the entrepreneur will be returning to that same partner for additional infusions of capital. So valuation is far more complex and selective than simply selling a business to the highest bidder and then cartwheeling away.

Valuation, then, can certainly occur prematurely. It can dampen a relationship like nothing else. It can badly influence a deal, especially if it occurs before the entrepreneur sells the dream. Make no mistake; early valuation has killed many early-stage deals.

Valuation is not guided by something as unchanging as a Euclidian formula. The best that valuation can offer are rules of thumb. And again, all investors may view such "rules" differently. How investors perceive risk, or stage of the venture, relates to value. In other words, the higher the risk investors perceive, the higher the return they will require; the higher the return they require, the lower the valuation is likely to be. The farther along you are, the less risk investors perceive. Put another way, investors are willing to pay more for what you already have.

## NEGOTIATING VALUATION

The pricing of venture investments is part art, part science, and part old-fashioned Yankee horse trading. Old-fashioned Yankee horse trading, of course, means negotiating. And few things, it seems, escape negotiation. "Every desire that demands satisfaction—and every need to be met—is at least potentially an occasion for people to initiate the negotiation process," noted Gerard I. Nierenberg 30 years ago in *The Art of Negotiating.*

Negotiating means dickering over *fair market value,* a term defined by the American Society of Appraisers as "the price at which a property would change hands between a willing buyer and willing seller when neither is acting under compulsion and both have equal access to all relevant information about the business." However, in early-stage companies, as we have said, value lies in the future, infusing valuation with its subjectivity. Such subjectivity renders established definitions useless. Cadle offers, instead, this expanded, real-world definition of value for the small early-stage business: that "point at which an investor's fear (risk profile) is in equilibrium with his greed (return requirements)."

In the real world, then, an equity ownership position should produce an expected annualized rate of return over a reasonable time period proportional to the investor's tolerance for risk. Valuation in this context does not depend on hard assets, prior sweat equity, intellectual property, book value, or similar items. These factors enter into the equation only to the extent that they can generate future value. Valuation depends on the creation or expansion of a going concern into a marketable commodity through an event that provides liquidity for the investor, such as by acquisition or IPO. Valuation also depends on the amount of risk that has already been mitigated by the company in product development, marketing, customer franchise, and cohesion of the management team.

In sum, entrepreneurs need to alert themselves to certain existing conditions. Leverage in establishing value normally operates in favor of the investor for the following reasons: Approach to value is primarily subjective, not objective; there exists a limited, inefficient market; the seller (entrepreneur) needs capital while the buyer (investor) does not have to invest; and the investor may not believe he or she has all the relevant information about the business.

## VALUATION AND STAGE OF DEVELOPMENT

Potential risks and rewards vary substantially during the different stages of development in a new venture. (See Exhibit 12.1.) Despite every entrepreneur's confidence in this "sure thing," more new ventures fail than succeed. However, investors need only a few big winners to offset the losers. Depending on the risks involved, compound rates of return from 25 to 50 percent or more constitute reasonable expectations.

The stages of development (seed, research and development, start-up, first stage, expansion stage, mezzanine, bridge, acquisition/merger, turnaround—all defined in Chapter 4) of venture capital targeted rates of return (noted in Chapter 5) run from 60 to 100 percent for seed or start-up, to 20 percent for a bridge to cash out.

Using projected revenues, profits, and growth rates, entrepreneurs and investors should arrive at a shared vision of the venture's value for

Exhibit 12.1  **VALUING THE VENTURE OVER TIME**

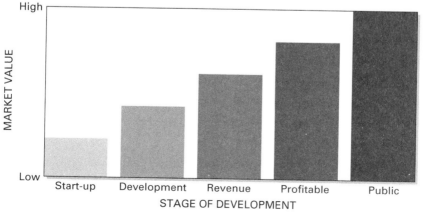

A stylized but accurate reflection of the direct relationship between market value and stage of development.

the five to ten years that follow financing. A business plan built on realistic assumptions is an entrepreneur's best friend at this point in the negotiations. At least four basic principles are involved in arriving at a pricing decision: (1) the division of equity determined by future value and equity required to compensate investors at competitive rates; (2) the greater the "expected" worth of the venture at some future time, the lower the share of equity required to "purchase" any given amount of capital; (3) the longer the track record of a new venture, the lower the investment risk, and, therefore, the lower the share of equity required to purchase any given amount of capital; and (4) the shorter the waiting period to liquidation, the lower the risk and, thus, the lower the share of equity required to purchase any given amount of capital.

In addition, investors could do worse than seek opinions from their network of coinvestors in order to obtain the bids of other respected, experienced investors. Estimates from others that reasonably approximate an investor's own appraisal can increase confidence in a valuation assessment.

Note, however, that pricing is not a function of relative dollar investment between the founders and outside investors.

As we have indicated, subjective factors do figure prominently in the valuation mix. But other items can swing the pendulum toward more objectivity. For example, a Term Sheet would delineate other issues as the entrepreneur attempts to gain financing for a venture. Detailed issues for consideration would include the value of the company, the amount of the investment and its timing, the form of the vesting of stock owned by the founders, guidelines for increasing the number of members on the management team, possible employment agreements with the founders (regarding matters such as compensation and benefits), proprietary rights of the company, and, certainly, exit strategies for the investors.

Does the private investors' added value lessen their risk? Investors will tell you the answer to this question is no. Investors will not trade money to the company for their expertise because their added value, they feel, is what they are contributing to the process and they will want to be compensated for that contribution. Moreover, the extent to which they are familiar with your business will lower their perceived risk. If you are going into the software business, for example, and the investor used to work for Microsoft, such familiarity will redound to the entrepreneur's favor because the investor knows the risks and knows the people.

Obviously, to the extent that investors are familiar with the business, they might give the entrepreneur a higher valuation because they perceive their risk as being lower, whereas the investor who is investing in a business about which he knows nothing will not. This investor can probably add little to the building of such a business.

Different types of investors have different risk profiles, as we have outlined in Chapters 6 and 7. Things will be different for private investors, amateur investors, and professional investors. And things will also be different within each group. Risk profiles of investors seem hardwired, that is, tough to readjust. The only way to mollify their perception of risk is to work on the subjective factors that will make them feel more comfortable with the deal. In other words, you must convince them that you are the world's greatest manager, convince them of the vision, sell the dream. Rather than sell investors on the subjective elements of the venture, some entrepreneurs mistakenly try to convince investors that they don't understand their own risk profiles.

## TRUISMS IN THE VALUATION PROCESS

Entrepreneurs must grasp some truisms regarding their position with investors. Be convinced of the merits of the opportunity before discussing valuation. Also recognize that demand for capital greatly exceeds supply; embrace this leverage in favor of investors during valuation negotiations. Further, understand that investors always discount projections, so run your own cash-flow forecasts, paying particular attention to unforeseen follow-up financing requirements. And remember, in the last five years, fewer than 10 percent of exit transactions have been through IPOs.

It is worth taking a closer look at some of these truisms.

First, prospective investors do not necessarily share the entrepreneurs' enthusiasm for the project. Investors must be thoroughly convinced of the merits of the opportunity before any discussion of valuation or terms. Entrepreneurs have to understand that sophisticated investors are besieged with projects. Investors could look at business plans seven days a week. A project may soak up 100 percent of an entrepreneur's life, but it constitutes only one more business plan on an already prodigious stack of business plans as far as the investor is concerned. So entrepreneurs have to adjust their mind-sets; they have to concentrate on selling the investor on why this venture is a great deal. Also, entrepreneurs sometimes become upset because an investor fails to jump at a project; they fail to realize that the investor may have invested in three similar projects, each of which turned sour. As we mentioned earlier, for most early-stage enterprises, the demand for equity capital largely exceeds supply. Consequently, investors have substantial leverage in valuation negotiations.

Second, entrepreneurs must allow for the high degree to which investors are risk-averse. Some entrepreneurs think that venture capitalists love risk. But investors who do are not investors for long. No investor, especially no professional venture capitalist, is in the business of jauntily taking a flyer. No investor is interested in floating out there on gossamer wings. To the wise investor, a venture must be built on tresses and struts. The way investors stay alive is by minimizing their mistakes. So entrepreneurs, along with everyone else, need to cast off the misconception that early-stage investors love taking risks. Investors try to manage risk against return. But the popular notion of investors lovingly embracing risk is hogwash.

A third truism is that investors will always discount projections in reviewing a proposal. The management principals of early-stage enterprises rarely forecast cash requirements accurately, not because they are bad managers but because the situation is fraught with circumstances beyond their control. As we have suggested, nearly all new deals need more money than their management team had thought. Such discrepancies between hope and reality are woven into the fabric of building dreams. The fictional Willie Loman, Arthur Miller's failed salesman in *Death of a Salesman,* is eulogized this way by Charley, his sympathetic next-door neighbor: "A man is got to dream, boy; it comes with the territory." But Willie failed to realize that some dreams must come to earth. Unforeseen follow-on financings are a fact of life in early-stage investing. Follow-on financing weighs heavily in the valuation process. When entrepreneurs say $1 million and no more will do the job, sophisticated investors are thinking otherwise—and with good reason. The sophisticated investor's mental cash register is clicking away as it adds numbers to the entrepreneur's modest valuation appraisal.

Another truism: Acquisition or buyout is the predominant method for achieving liquidity for small company shareholders. We have already pointed out that the primary method of achieving liquidity is not IPO—far from it. But the misconception remains. Too often, entrepreneurs and their business plans say they will take their company public in five years. The odds are that such an event will not occur. So entrepreneurs need to consider how that investor is going to achieve liquidity.

Axiomatic is the truism that any valuation becomes irrelevant if the venture does not survive. Survival, survival, survival—in private investing the word rings like a Buddhist mantra. As we have reiterated, smart investors are risk-averse. The foremost thing they want to know is *not* what their return on investment will be in five years, but whether the company will survive at all. Entrepreneurs can talk glory, displaying the infamous hockey-stick projection extending through the next five years, but if they cannot survive the first 18 months, further talk becomes immaterial. So before investors even look at anything else, the entrepreneur has to convince them that the company will survive.

# CAVEATS—FOR ENTREPRENEUR AND INVESTOR ALIKE

There is, however, a caveat attached to selling investors on the survival of your company. It is this: Watch the fine line between a straightforward sales job and overselling, because you are not walking away from this transaction. You are going to be partners with this individual. The critical thing in obtaining the fairest price for both of you is to emphasize your strong areas—without hoopla, without hype. Then you must justify, not hide, the weak areas of the venture. Concede—to yourself as well as to others—that every deal has weak areas; otherwise, it would not become a high-return opportunity.

Many entrepreneurs do not want to confess weaknesses. They will claim that everything is great. "There is no competition; people are grabbing this thing off the shelves." This attitude is not only unrealistic; it is unfair, not only to the investor, but to the entrepreneur as well. You are dealing with smart people who want you for a partner. They understand conditions that surround the process; they understand that the opportunity presents itself because there are holes in the deal, and because unknowns lurk everywhere.

So talk about the holes; talk about the unknowns. Do it up front. Maybe your investor can see something he or she can help you with. But if you gloss over them rather than reveal them, the investor will question your ability and whether your feet hover anywhere near the ground. Of course, such common sense should pervade the whole process, not just valuation.

Part of having your feet on the ground involves a realistic view of the market size and growth rate, two things entrepreneurs seem to have, understandably, an inveterate desire to inflate. With no intention of fooling anyone, they talk about huge markets, entering the worldwide telephone business, perhaps, instead of focusing on the narrow market they will serve. Entrepreneurs must realize the market segment they are after.

Because many entrepreneurs have heard that investors want to invest only in areas containing huge markets, many entrepreneurs express themselves globally, or in billions of dollars. But the "global" nature of the venture depends on the deal. Recall the diversity among investors. Not every investor—perhaps not even many—is globally motivated. Again, when talking about your project, be realistic. To the sensible investor, realistic assessment has a circumference narrower than the globe yet worth more than a billion fantasy dollars.

Not all caveats, however, are offered to entrepreneurs. We offer this one to investors: Do not lose your objectivity. As practicing venture capitalist Lucien Ruby wisely admonishes, "Don't get swept away." Entrepreneurs, he warns, are persuasive—and well they should be if they believe in the venture. It is easy to get fired up by one with fervor.

Other, but no less important, subjective factors enter into the valuation mix, the sales cycle, for example: It always takes longer than you think to bring a product to market. You may have great customer market research that proclaims how much people are going to love the product, but nobody has written a check yet. Distributors may rave, but no one is talking floor space.

So you have to understand what point of the cycle your product is in, an understanding that results in having to walk a fine line: You do not want to be too early and have to spend all your money educating the market on why it needs your product. Nor can you afford to be too late, behind everybody else. This is why you have to understand the length of time the sell cycle for the product is going to take. Entrepreneurs can become dazzled by their vision, overlooking this aspect of the process.

Another pitfall awaits even the best product. In three years, the company may be producing the world's greatest product, but not selling it. If educating the marketplace and educating prospective competitors soak up too much time and energy, the venture will die. This scenario captures a company exhausting its capital in educating the market without being able to sell the product. Three years later that company is out of business. Survivability dries up, vividly clarifying the critical nature of the sell cycle.

Although no hard figures have been tracked, a reasonable guess would suggest that 90 percent of the deals worked out will need more money than had been originally thought. Then what you have is dilution, best explained this way: If a deal calls for $1 million, 12 months later it will need more money. An investor with a 40 percent ownership for his or her first million dollars is faced with two options if, say, another $500,000 is necessary. The investor can put in $500,000 or only a portion of it. Or that investor can choose not to put the money in at all, in which case, in order to survive, the company has to raise the $500,000 from somewhere else.

Either way the investor will be *diluted*. He or she has to put more money in to maintain 40 percent ownership, or that 40 percent ownership will shrink. Comes liquidity, how much of the company will the investor own? The answer is that the investor will own less than when he or she started out. This illustrates the problem created by needing more money than was originally thought. This constitutes dilution—something else to seriously consider in the valuation process.

All these considerations influence perceived risk. So to the extent that you can convince an investor that less risk is involved in the deal, he or she will raise the valuation. To the degree the investor cannot be convinced of low risk, one of two things will happen: The investor will walk away because of too much risk for the desired rate of return, or the investor will write a check but the valuation will sink because the need for a higher rate of return rises.

The fact is an entrepreneur may be able to find some investors who are unsophisticated, or who are willing to take a flyer, or who just do not care about their money, and thereby gain an unrealistically high valuation. But an initial ego gratification of a $5-million valuation on sweat equity belies the essentials of a long-term partnership, a partnership built with investors who understand the business and the process, who will be there to smooth the bumps in the road, who understand that there will doubtless be a need for further infusion of money.

# 13

# Due Diligence

## INTRODUCTION

Due diligence forms a vital aspect of the investment mating process. And due diligence should be reciprocal. From the investor's point of view, one of the best tests of a deal's practicability and pricing is whether it can attract and be sold to another private investor at the same price. However, an investor must rely on solid judgment in evaluating a deal. The entrepreneur must do the same when considering investors. To do so requires comprehensive research and analysis—and sometimes the help of a private investigator.

If summoning a private investigator sounds extreme, think again. According to investigator Jay Mahcan, due diligence is no more than what any prudent person would exercise with his or her own money. The need for due diligence depends largely on the industry to which the venture belongs. In some situations in which investment is not a factor, no due diligence is required. For example, in the temporary help industry, none is needed. Since temps are placed for a short time, the risk to the health of the agency or the company to which the temp is sent is minimal. But where financial transactions are involved, a business marriage is taking place, so extensive due diligence is the order of the day. Once the papers are signed, no escape is possible for a minimum of three to five years—if ever.

Too often entrepreneurs and investors alike assume that a few phone calls will suffice, perhaps a call to ensure that a college degree has been earned from the school the person claims to have attended. Perhaps a credit check is in order and a call corroborating work or past investment experience. But is this enough? When Mahcan does his work, he thoroughly investigates academic background and asserted achievements. Mahcan also checks with employers to determine salary and then cross-checks with the Social Security Administration to corroborate the person's checking and savings accounts, stocks, bonds, and money funds to make sure everything is in order and to find out how often the accounts have been moved.

Detailed investigation of this kind may seem elaborate, but you should be at least as cautious as a bank or financial institution. With such potential risk, why do less? Mahcan cites case after case of partnerships built on trust where, on one side or the other, trust was not warranted: A business partner enters into a transaction, then takes off with $95,000 plus all the trade secrets. Only through the culprit's love of "Jennifer," his chronically ailing collie in need of quarterly injections at the veterinarian's, was he apprehended.

In another case, two people formed a genetic engineering firm, only to have one of them take off after nine months with six tightly packed cardboard cartons containing all of the personnel records, financial records, and intellectual property. These cases should give both entrepreneur and investor a long pause, long enough at least to exercise an ounce of prevention.

Far better it is to be able to trust a partner than trust blind luck. Is it not better to know that Mr. X "appears weak financially" and "may be a risky addition" to the entrepreneurial team? Or that "the work record from some employers listed is missing" and that "his educational record cannot be taken at face value"? Is it not better to know that Mr. X neither graduated nor even attended MIT or Columbia, as he indicated on his resume?; that Mr. X has a criminal record for investment fraud, which, at the very least, casts doubt on his moral character?

There are such people out there. In addition to painstaking investigation, many investors will ask an entrepreneur "country-boy questions," questions to which the investor knows the answer and by which the entrepreneur is being "tested" to determine what he or she knows.

But nothing takes the place of full legal and financial audits, assessment of the market potential, and investigation of the founders and entrepreneurs themselves, including comprehensive background checks and reference interviews with former superiors, peers, subordinates, and business associates. Judging the practicability of a prospective early-stage, direct investment will require numerous in-person meetings between the parties involved; a thorough review of the business plan; interviews with management, customers, suppliers, and competitors; and counsel from relevant industry experts.

International Capital Resource's due diligence expert Jeff Ferries defines his vital aspect of the process as the means by which "investors investigate and determine a company's strengths and weaknesses" by assessing its "realistic future profit potential," particularly the investor's profit potential. Particularly, Ferries explains, investors want to know the potential and identifiable risks in the venture.

The basic concepts of the due diligence process, performed by professional advisers such as CPAs and attorneys, apply regardless of a company's stage of development. Due diligence becomes the "final exam" which the company passes (by getting the money) or fails. Many of the questions raised by investors in the due diligence process are those addressed in creating a business plan. The questions for a start-up or seed company will begin by focusing on the quality of the management team. If your company has an operating history, questions will focus on your performance to date and how you have addressed and overcome business hurdles as they have arisen. Next will come questions on your effort to identify and quantify the potential market for your product or service, and questions on existing or potential competition, particularly from financially stronger companies.

Ferries urges entrepreneurs to project a positive attitude in order to promote the venture's strengths and competitive advantage, but cautions against being less than candid in terms of risk factors and weaknesses in the management team, for example, or in the technology, or in production delays. In fact, the entrepreneur should preclude the investor's detection of such risks and weaknesses by being ready with proposals to remedy them. It is preferable by far to be up front on such issues; being so adds to your credibility.

Concerning financial projections, the entrepreneur should provide thoughtful assumptions regarding growth about adequate capital and the management team. How reasonable your financial assumptions seem will also reflect on your credibility, because, as we have warned, there will be problems. Count on it.

Following is a sampling of the questions that arise in due diligence.

1. Why did you start your company?
2. What is your vision for your business?
3. What are the primary obstacles to achieving success in your business?
4. What do you plan to do to overcome those identified obstacles?
5. What is the company's primary market and how will you capitalize on that market?
6. What is your marketing strategy to capture market share?
7. Who is your current competition? Who could potentially enter your market?
8. How do you plan to deal with these competitors?
9. How much money and time have you and other members of management invested to date?
10. Are there outside investors? Will they be making an additional investment in this round of financing?
11. Are you obtaining credit terms from your suppliers? If so, what are they?
12. What is the value of your company?

13. Do you currently have, or have access to, debt financing?
14. How do you plan to use the proceeds of our investment?
15. How much dilution in management ownership is acceptable to you?
16. What are the key assumptions behind your financial projections?
17. When will you next require financing, and how much will you need?
18. What are your company's short- and long-term business goals?
19. Who are the key management personnel?
20. What is your exit strategy for investors? When can we expect to recover our original investment?

In addition to answering these and many more questions, you will be expected to add certain documents, including but not limited to articles of incorporation, federal and state tax returns, business plan, resumes of management personnel, and financial statements. And, of course, the entrepreneur must be emotionally able to handle rejection, an aspect of the private placement discussed in Chapter 2.

What follows is a complete due diligence questionnaire, which reflects the rigors of this essential part of the investment process.

## DUE DILIGENCE QUESTIONNAIRE

   I. **Overall industry assessment**
   II. **Products and services**
   III. **Sales and marketing**
   IV. **Competition**
   V. **Production**
   VI. **Suppliers**
   VII. **Management**
   VIII. **Employees**
   IX. **Corporate finance**
   X. **Investment parameters**
   XI. **Miscellaneous**

Please include the following items with this packet: a business plan, a financial plan highlighting best- and worst-case five-year pro forma projections, a capitalization table disclosing pre- and postfinancing ownership, a chart describing corporate structure, a marketing plan with product samples, biographies of key management personnel (with at least five references), and copies of purchase orders, contracts, or letters of intent from current customers.

## I. OVERALL INDUSTRY ASSESSMENT

1. What industry (or industries) is the company involved in (energy, high tech, etc.)?

2. How would you categorize your company (service, manufacturing, etc.)?

3. How would you define the competitive structure of the industry (fragmented, oligopoly, monopoly, etc.)?

4. Currently, how large is the industry?

5. What has been the five-year industrial sales growth rate, and what is it expected to be over the next five years?

6. What has been the five-year earnings growth of the industry?

7. How volatile are industrial sales and earnings during economic cycles? Please indicate a best- and worst-case outline.

8. What are the significant barriers to entry into the industry?

9. What is the success rate for new entrants into the industry?

10. What is the history of the industry, and have there been any recent events affecting it?

11. What regulatory agencies supervise the industry, and do you expect any changes in their authority in the future?

12. Are there any unspoken rules in this industry of which an outsider would be unaware?

13. What sources were consulted to obtain the above information?

## II. PRODUCTS AND SERVICES—IF YOUR COMPANY IS SERVICE-ORIENTED, PLEASE ANSWER THE FOLLOWING QUESTIONS ACCORDINGLY.

1. What is your current product line?

2. Which product is most important to the success of the company?

3. Which product is a "weak link"?

4. What makes your product unique?

5. Has all R&D been completed on products?

6. How long did it take to develop the products (R&D time cycle)?

7. What research has been conducted on competitive products?

8. If applicable, what is the current status of the patent (process/product)?

9. What is the timetable for new product introductions?

10. Estimate revenues and market share for all products over the next 12 months.

11. At what rate will the company capture market share over the next five years, and what is the ultimate share goal for the company?

12. What are the margins for each product, and how will they change as market share increases?

## III. SALES AND MARKETING

1. What is the basic marketing strategy?

2. How does this vary from that of your competitors?

3. Does the company currently have purchase orders or letters of intent from potential customers to purchase products?

4. Is there a sales force currently assembled?

5. Does the sales force have relevant industry experience?

6. Please discuss separately: the dollar amount, duration, and restrictions of customer contracts (if any).

7. How fiscally sound are the company's largest customers?

8. What percentage of sales is expected to be repeat business?

9. What types of warranties, guarantees, or service contracts are offered to customers?

10. How are customer relations handled?

11. Are customers provided with credit?

12. Does the company have any distribution, joint venture, or technology transfer agreements established?

## IV.  COMPETITION

1. Ranked by sales, who are your five largest competitors?

2. Are they fiscally sound (well capitalized and profitable)?

3. What is their focus: Are they expanding niches in the industry; are they expanding into new markets or diversifying into other industries?

4. How do you differentiate yourself from the competition?

5. Are your competitors aware that you exist?

6. What do you perceive to be your competitors' greatest weakness?

7. Has the number of your competitors increased or decreased in the last two years, and do you expect this to change?

8. How do your competitors usually deal with small competitors (push out of market, buy out)?

9. At what sales level do you consider yourself to be a competitive threat, and what portion of market shares does that level encompass?

10. How do you plan to combat the competition and vice versa?

11. Has the company identified any of its competitors in the international marketplace? If so, who are the three largest and what are their geographic market shares?

## V. PRODUCTION

1. How can production be characterized (automated, labor-intensive, etc.)?

2. Does the company manufacture products or subcontract to another manufacturer?

3. Where is the plant located?

4. How long is the production cycle from raw components to the customer?

5. Does the company currently have the capacity to meet expected future demand for the product? How long before capital expenditures will be needed to meet excess demand?

6. Is the production process capable of changing quickly to meet with changes in demand?

7. What is the rate of product defects?

8. How old is the equipment you are currently using?

9. Is the manufacturing process considered hazardous to the environment?

10. Where are problems encountered in the manufacturing process?

11. Are there any alternative sources of production if there is an interruption in the current assembly line?

12. What means of transportation does the company use to ship finished products (rail, barge, truck)?

## VI. SUPPLIERS

1. Who are the company's major suppliers?

2. Are they fiscally sound?

3. Do they work with your competitors?

4. Are they unionized?

5. How did you elect them?

6. Have they caused any problems (bottlenecks)?

7. Will they provide you with credit?

8. Who are your secondary suppliers?

9. How do you receive your raw materials?

### VII. MANAGEMENT

1. How many top- and mid-level managers are with the company?

2. What is the management team's background?

3. Have team members been involved in any other start-ups?

4. What is their level of experience with publicly traded companies?

5. Are they members of the board of directors?

6. How are they being compensated (salary, equity, etc.)?

7. What is their % ownership, and how much, if any, of their own capital has been invested in the company?

8. How long are their equity holdings restricted?

9. How would the overall style of management be characterized?

10. Are any of the managers part-time?

11. Do the managers all reside within the same geographic area?

12. How were they selected?

13. Did any come from the competition?

14. Has an employee/management evaluation system been installed?

15. Have members of management worked together before, or are they related?

16. Are there any vacancies in management positions, or is any member of management temporarily filling a position until a permanent professional is located?

17. Does any member of the management team have international experience or language capabilities?

18. Has any member of the management team sued or been sued within the last five years?

19. Has any member of the management team ever been convicted of a felony?

20. Are there any civil or criminal charges pending against any member of management?

21. Has any member of the management team ever been terminated from a management position?

22. Has any member of the management team personally filed for bankruptcy within the last five years?

23. Has any member of the management team ever been the officer of a company that has filed for bankruptcy?

24. Has any member of the management team been disciplined by a regulatory agency or professional association within the last five years?

25. Does any member of the management team have any serious health problems?

26. Has any member of the management team been through any serious difficulties in his or her private life (divorce, deaths, etc.)?

27. Is any member of management not expendable? If yes, why?

28. Does the company hold key-man insurance?

29. Have members of the management team signed employment contracts, and do the contracts include "noncompete" clauses?

30. Have there been any problems with previous management, and, if so, have those problems been resolved?

31. Is there anything that has not been specifically covered in this section that you feel we should know about any member of the management team?

## VIII. EMPLOYEES

1. What is the number of nonmanagement employees?

2. How many employees do you expect to have over the next 12 months?

3. Over the next five years, how many employees does the company expect to hire?

4. Does the company employ any independent contractors?

5. How are employees selected (hiring criteria)?

6. Have they worked for competitors?

7. How are employees compensated (salary, stock, etc.)?

8. How is employee performance evaluated?

9. Are any employees members of labor unions?

10. How high is employee turnover, and in what areas?

11. Are any employees or former employees involved in litigation with the company?

12. Could any steps of the manufacturing process be considered hazardous to the employees?

13. How would you categorize your employees?

    Highly skilled labor _____%
    Semiskilled labor _____%
    Nonskilled labor _____%

14. How are the employees trained?

15. Characterize the perfect employee for the company.

### IX.  CORPORATE FINANCE

1. At what rate are revenues projected to increase over the next five years?

2. At what rate are earnings projected to increase over the next five years?

3. Will you report sales on a monthly basis?

4. What is the monthly cash burn rate, and how will it fluctuate pre- and postfunding?

5. How much cash does the company have?

6. Does the company have access to working capital and lines of credit?

7. When will cash flow be positive?

8. What expenses are critical to keep under control?

9. At what rate is tangible net book value of the company projected to grow over the next five years?

10. At what point will the company be able to internally finance future growth?

11. What percentage of stock is restricted, and when does it become unrestricted?

12. Do you intend to use debt for start-up costs?

13. What is management's view of expense accounts?

14. Who is the accountant/auditor?

15. Who is the primary banking institution?

16. Have in-house accounting systems been installed?

## X.  INVESTMENT PARAMETERS

1. What is the company's fund-raising strategy?

2. What is the total amount needed in this round, and what percentage of that money is expected to be venture capital?

3. What will be accounted for in the use of proceeds once financing is complete?

4. What is the funding schedule (how much and when)?

5. How much has been raised to date?

6. What are the terms and conditions of the private placement?

7. What will the total dilution be at the end of funding?

8. Is all equity diluted equally?

9. List all categories of investment made by the company (common or preferred stock, convertible, debt, etc.).

10. What is the timetable for a public offering?

11. How much time is spent by management promoting the company's stock?

12. Is management experienced in raising capital?

13. Does the company have an investor/public relations firm? If so, what are the terms of its contract?

14. What is the budget for promotional (funding) activities?

15. Who is the securities attorney?

16. Has the company granted director status to investor groups?

## XI.  MISCELLANEOUS

1. Are there any other lawsuits, not previously mentioned, in which the company is a party?

2. What is the history of the company?

3. How have the directors been selected?

4. What is the overall goal of the company?

5. What is the biggest problem facing management?

6. Has the company established an advisory board?

7. Who is the corporate legal counsel?

8. What type of insurance is needed for this business? (Please disclose a summary of all insurance coverage.)

9. Who are the company's insurers?

10. Has the company completed all appropriate corporate filings?

11. Does the company have all necessary licenses, building, and operating permits?

12. Does the company have all essential contracts and joint venture agreements fully executed?

13. Is the company currently, or in the past, in arrears regarding federal, state, or local franchise and income taxes? Payroll taxes? Real estate taxes? Personal property taxes? Sales taxes?

14. Have there ever been inquiries or reviews by a taxing authority?

15. Disclose all real estate currently owned, leased or otherwise used by the company.

16. Is there any other topical area regarding the company, not covered by this questionnaire, that you feel would be important for us to consider during our evaluation process?

# 14

# On-Line Options: Entrepreneurs, Investors, and Web Sites

Of all of nature's groups of honeybees, none is busier than the group pollinating business contacts on the Internet's World Wide Web. In its November 1998 article "Resizing On-line Business Trade," *Business Trade & Technology Strategies Report* estimated that by 2003, business commerce over the Internet will reach an astounding $1.3 trillion—9 percent of all U.S. business trade. Web sites of electronic data hoping to match entrepreneurs and investors are indeed flourishing—and indications persist that they will continue to do so.

Meanwhile, the number of on-line links lengthens rapidly. Before we get to that list, however, we will be well served by looking at the respected and reliable Forrester Report (Forrester Research, Inc., Cambridge, Mass.) and what it foresees as "A Capital Democracy" emerging on the Internet, a capital democracy that by the year 2005 will bring an active and efficient capital market serving savvy buyers and sellers in low-cost transactions.

Amid genuine fears by those surveyed by the report—particularly regarding poor-quality offerings, fraud, and regulatory and technology hurdles—Forrester studied the on-line formation of capital. An evolving capital democracy, explains the 1998 report, will manifest itself in three phases: the first, from 1998 to 2000; the second, from 2001 to 2004; and the third, from 2005 and beyond.

Specifically, the report envisions venture capital being raised in the future on-line from individual investors rising from 2 percent in the first ("broader access to information") phase, to 3 percent in the second ("diffusion of placement power") phase, to 5 percent in the third ("a capital democracy") phase. In those same categories, direct public offerings and private placements on-line would climb to $2 billion by 2005. And angel financing matched on-line would swell from approximately $50 million in the first phase, to $200 million in the second phase, to $750 million in the third phase. In addition, says the report, by the year 2005 and beyond, the SEC will loosen on the Internet those documents that today inhibit funding.

For a discussion of legal matters and the Internet, see Appendix A.

## ON-LINE LINKS

### ADVENTURE CAPITAL REGISTER
www.adventurecapital.com

This monthly print publication serving investors, entrepreneurs, and inventors, is capable of making direct investments up to $10 million. The AdVenture Capital Register serves entrepreneurs looking to expand their existing business or for a new venture, invention, or idea. Investors can get in on the ground floor of "the next better mousetrap."

### AMERICA'S BUSINESS FUNDING DIRECTORY
www.businessfinance.com

Targeted to entrepreneurs, the America's Business Funding Directory is designed to get capital for business and real estate projects. Its research engine leads to funding sources by industry, size, stage, and amount. Clients access potential funding sources for commercial finance, equipment leasing, government funds, investment funds, real estate finance, and venture capital.

### CAPITAL MATCHMAKER
www.matchmaker.org/capital

Focusing on entrepreneurs and angel investors, the Capital Matchmaker joins investors with investment opportunities in a variety of industries worldwide. All listed ventures seek a minimum of $25,000.

### COMMERCIAL FINANCE ONLINE
www.cfol.com

Focusing on entrepreneurs and angel investors, Commercial Finance Online boasts the largest business finance search engine in the world. The CFOL works in deal flow and new referral partners through a variety of searches, partnering sites, web pages, and links.

### DEALFLOW
www.dealflow.com

DealFlow is strictly an information service, not a venture capital firm or a broker-dealer. It offers a free listing to an entrepreneur or a venture in need of capital and the expertise of private investors; it also offers a free search of ventures by private investors or venture capitalists. In DealFlow, an entrepreneur can search by keyword to find investors interested in particular products and markets before submitting his or her name to the list. Meanwhile, private investors can download venture listings immediately. In addition, DealFlow contains a Strategic Partner database.

## DPO CENTRAL
www.dpocental.com

Through direct public offerings, dpo Central brings investors and small businesses together over the Internet. Companies are allowed to sell stock directly to the public, avoiding expenses associated with IPOs. To avoid conflicts of interest, dpo Central remains neutral in the process.

## EDIE-ONLINE
www.edie-online.com

Edie-Online (Electronic Data for Investors and Entrepreneurs) specifically offers early-stage through mezzanine-stage private emerging-growth companies to accredited professional investors. The link allows for custom searches of companies with business plans, financials, and other data. Through an intermediary, entrepreneurs and investors carry on confidential communication.

## ENTERPRISE ONLINE
www.enterprise.org

Enterprise Online dedicates itself to the needs of entrepreneurs; its intention is to provide information to help entrepreneurs start and expand high-growth potential companies.

## ENTREPRENEUR RESOURCES
www.v1.com

Entrepreneur Resources is VentureOne's resource for entrepreneurs seeking to identify interested venture capital firms, track venture-backed companies, and seek further rounds of financing. It also delivers this information to investors through the database service. Its clients include "the nation's leading venture capitalists, who manage over $50 billion in funds."

## ENVIRONMENTAL CAPITAL NETWORK
www.bizserve.com/environmental.capital.network

The Environmental Capital Network offers services to both environmental companies and to individual, professional, corporate, and institutional investors. These groups of investors are provided with access to early-stage and expansion companies commercializing "green" technologies, products, and services. Environmental companies are assisted in raising capital.

## FINANCEHUB
www.FinanceHub.com

A nonprofit organization, Financehub serves as a resource for small business owners, other entrepreneurs, and professionals, providing information on many aspects of business credit, including help in gaining credit, writing a business plan, and otherwise educating entrepreneurs.

## FINANCING SOURCES
www.financingsources.com

Financing Sources offers contacts and how-to advice on obtaining business financing, including money from venture capital, loans, mortgages, and IPOs. A tap on the keyboard allows the viewer a look at its Venture Capital Database. In addition, its various departments include financing sources, business valuation, commercial mortgage resources, and careers among others.

## GARAGE.COM
www.garage.com

Garage.com's mission is to "start up startups" by helping entrepreneurs seeking seed-level financing with advice, research, an investor network, and a speeded-up "time to money." On the investor side, high-technology ventures are prescreened and matched to investor criteria.

## IDEA CAFE
www.ideacafe.com

Idea Cafe serves up a thick booklet's worth of information on getting ready to get money and sources of money, including debt, equity, and creative financing. Information includes how much money the entrepreneur will need, the right kind of financing for the individual entrepreneur, how long it may take to get it, and the like.

## MONEYHUNTER
www.moneyhunter.com

MoneyHunter, with its on-line companion, MoneyHunt TV, attempts to educate and empower entrepreneurs seeking capital for starting a business or growing a business. Searchers can download a Business Plan Template, contact a Mentor, and use the Golden Rolodex. MoneyHunter has developed for investors a separate "How to Use" section.

## MONEYSEARCH
www.moneysearch.com

MoneySearch has segmented itself toward investors and does not intend on becoming a general search site. Although MoneySearch does not provide evaluation or reliability of each of its postings, it does attempt to preview and visit each site before posting it for viewing. MoneySearch also works to upgrade sites.

## MORINO INSTITUTE
www.morino.org

The Morino Institute's mission is to attain systemic change in education, economics, and society. Its focus on netpreneurship fosters new models for the improvement and learning empowered by the Internet.

## NETPRENEUR EXCHANGE
www.netpreneur.org

Netpreneur helps "netpreneurs" seek financing and investors seeking greater Washington investment opportunities. Netpreneurs are told how to find money; investors, how to find companies. Netpreneur Search (database) contains more than 900 regional businesses; Funder Search contains names of funders. The Morino Institute is one of Netpreneur's charter sponsors.

## NVST.COM
www.nvst.com

NVST.com proclaims itself as the world's largest network for private equity, venture capital, merger and acquisition professionals, offering the most current investment information available. It is in the business of helping both the expert and novice in making informed business decisions. The categories of NVST.Com include a contact base, professional publications, on-line education, investment opportunities products and resources, and custom service.

## PRIVATEFINANCING
www.privatefinancing.com

PrivateFinancing.com publishes investment opportunities for accredited and non-U.S. investors. For the accredited investor, PrivateFinancing offers current investment opportunities in public and private companies, reviews of on-line corporate information, investment terms and conditions, downloads of documents and subscription forms, and communication with company representatives. Issuers receive international exposure, convenient information exchange, reduced time and cost in printing and distribution, and a simple listing format.

## SCOR-NET

www.scor-net.com

SCOR-Net offers links to companies that already have gone or are going public by using the Small Corporate Offering Registration Form U-7 Regulation A, SB-2, or similar method. SCOR-Net enables users to reach service and other information providers knowledgeable about raising funds for small businesses.

## SOURCE CAPITAL NETWORK

www.sourcecapitalnet.com

The members only Source Capital Network, targeting entrepreneurs and angel investors looking for fast-growth venture opportunities, has entrepreneurs present business plans to angels through a video-audio format.

## VENTURE CAPITAL ONLINE

www.vcapital.com

Venture Capital Online targets entrepreneurs and investors, referring plans from companies seeking capital to its network of professional venture capitalists.

## VENTURE CAPITAL RESOURCE LIBRARY

www.vfinance.com

Focusing on entrepreneurs, advisers, and investors, the Venture Capital Resource Library's investment opportunities section is fashioned to attract venture capital firms and investors looking for venture capital opportunities.

## VENTURESCAPE

www.venturescape.com

Focusing on investors, advisers and entrepreneurs, Venturescape's purpose is to attract hi-tech entrepreneurs or those involved with promising start-ups with help in venture financing and strategic business development. It likewise wants to interest accredited investors, business angels, and successful entrepreneurs to invest in hi-tech start-ups and entrepreneurs.

## WIT CAPITAL

www.witcapital.com

For investors, and offering its members access to investment opportunities and services such as IPOs, investment research, venture capital, and institutional-style electronic trading, Wit Capital seeks to become the premier Internet investment banking firm focused on offering and selling securities to on-line individual investors.

# PROMISES AND PITFALLS

As the number of on-line sources grows, even the government has become involved through its ACE-*Net*.

## ACE-*NET*
www.ace-net.org

ACE-*Net* (Angel Capital Electronic Network, also known as the Access to Capital Electronic Network), the government's attempt to link entrepreneurs with angel investors, was born out of the suggestions from delegates to the 1995 White House Conference on Small Business and announced by the President of the United States in October 1996. Expected to pay for itself through fees, this nationwide Internet-based network (www.ace-net.org) service is sponsored by the SBA's Office of Advocacy and is maintained by the Center for Venture Research at the University of New Hampshire. The ACE-*Net* system is managed by 38 local network operators that are nonprofit, often university- or state-based entrepreneurial development centers. The current list of network operators is maintained on the ACE-*Net* Web site. (The ACE-*Net* Web site can also be reached through the SBA's Office of Advocacy at www.sba.gov/advo.)

ACE-*Net* hopes to attract entrepreneurs who seek $250,000 to $5 million in equity capital, a range of funding needs well below the average $10 million professional venture capital deal, deals that total fewer than 5,000 annually (1997 SBA data). On the investor side, ACE-*Net* hopes to "net" accredited investors (who must certify on their Investor Subscription Form that they satisfy the SEC's definition of "accredited," that is, generally, those possessing a net worth of more than $1 million or an annual income of more than $200,000). However, participation in ACE-*Net* is open not only to accredited investors but to Small Business Investment Companies (SBICs) as well as other venture funds. In fact, many of the participants are institutional rather than individual investors. As of early 1999, there are approximately 800 investors enrolled in the ACE-*Net* system. The hope is that once ACE-*Net* is in full swing, it will become a private, independent, not-for-profit organization.

Initially, posting an offering on ACE-*Net* was no small order. In addition to meeting relevant state securities requirements, small companies were to have a registered or qualified federal securities offering (under Regulation A, to raise up to $5 million; or under Regulation D, Rule 504, to raise up to $1 million). Companies were required to complete a Small Corporate Offering Registration (SCOR) form, known as Form U-7, which, although abbreviated compared to a full-blown prospectus, requires much of the information included in a comprehensive business plan. In summary, as a securities offering, the process was lengthier and more costly than most entrepreneurs anticipated. A SCOR offering—in California, for example—can cost anywhere from $10,000 to $15,000, and it is estimated that nationally, average SCOR offerings expenses approach $30,000. Additionally, ACE-*Net* network operators are permitted to charge individual companies up to $450 to list their business.

Partly because of the daunting registration requirements and related expenses, ACE-*Net* got off to a slow start. Recognizing that the system was not meeting the needs of small business, federal and state securities officials streamlined the registration process and created the ACE-*Net* "Short Form" for companies seeking to raise up to $1 million. By limiting the offering exclusively to accredited investors in the 33 states that currently allow the "Short Form" option, small business listings on ACE-*Net* can bypass the need to register their offering in those states and with the SEC.

Under the "Short Form" requirements, companies provide a summary business plan in a four-page format. Not surprisingly, 85 percent of ACE-*Net* registrants now use that option. However, most observers note that the "Short Form" does not provide sufficient information to support an investment decision and strongly encourage "Short Form" users to attach a complete business plan to the electronic documents. As of early 1999, approximately 100 deals are listed nationally on the ACE-*Net* system.

Several of the network operators maintain matching networks, in addition to offering local access to ACE-*Net*. However, these networks operate independently, and there is no guarantee that investors who sign up for the matching networks are also enrolled in ACE-*Net*. Investors who are in the MIT Network, for example, are not necessarily signed up for ACE-*Net*. In any case, the matching networks rely on investor motivation to seek out and review posted deals. With an ACE-*Net* listing, the entrepreneur has to sit back and hope that potential investors will proactively use the Internet to begin a search for a private equity investment. Consider the likelihood of success using this approach compared to a program based on a uniform nationwide database—shared and updated, personal assistance to the entrepreneurs, active marketing of the entrepreneurs' ventures through various introduction programs, and regularly scheduled presentation of selected investment opportunities to prescreened investors in a familiar format.

From the investors' perspective, ACE-*Net* does not facilitate a quick, "first-cut" review of listed deals. An investor is required to key in his or her industry preference, deal size, and stage of development. The deals with matching criteria are then extracted from the database. If someone's deal does not *exactly* match the selected criteria, the investor will not be exposed to it.

Fundamentally, ACE-*Net* offers a passive rather than proactive system of entrepreneur/investor matchmaking service. ACE-*Net* is not designed to support a custom search for investors, which could identify investors who have expressed interest in a certain type of investment and might welcome a targeted mailing describing an interesting deal; likewise, it lacks a direct referral program in which self-selected investors could learn by phone about investment opportunities that fit their criteria.

Confidentiality and privacy concerns also may inhibit the growth of ACE-*Net*. On-line security is still likely to be an issue for investors and entrepreneurs. While the reality is that data prudently maintained within well-constructed on-line systems are quite secure, investors may be hesitant to permit private information to be potentially accessible on-line. Similarly, entrepreneurs may be reluctant to publish detailed business plans when they have no control over who might view the information.

Perhaps most problematic is ACE-*Net*'s inability to screen entrepreneurs; as long as they have submitted the minimal required listing information and the listing fee (if any), they are entitled to list. No entrepreneur is selected for introduction; thus, the quality of deals posted is likely to be highly variable. Without quality deals, investor interest is hard to attract and impossible to sustain. Finally, ACE-*Net* is not equipped to track the results of its listings. Prospective investors contact the entrepreneurs directly. Introductions cannot be properly tracked without knowing which investors respond to which deals.

Thus, despite the groundswell of interest in the Internet and the spectacular growth of other types of on-line investing, words of caution seem in order. (For a full discussion of cautionary matters, see the Internet section of Appendix B.) To the entrepreneur, we advise extreme caution in advertising private equity investment on-line. For one thing, in many states, advertising a private placement investment is illegal. For another, even where it is legal, the entrepreneur must be cautious. An advertisement for a private placement investment that reaches inappropriate or unqualified investors could lead to legal problems related to the way investors were initially identified and solicited.

The Internet may well provide the most efficient means to present investment opportunities to a wide audience, but for the moment, the tail is wagging the dog. Internet technology is developing so fast and people are jumping on it so quickly that in many ways, people are indiscriminately flinging deals out there on the Net without thinking about the implications of using it, particularly as such behavior is related to existing securities regulation.

The Internet offers dynamic, but as yet unrealized, potential for bringing together private equity investors and entrepreneurs. However, because of the many legal issues associated with it and uncertainty about federal and state regulatory responses at this time, we advise stepping gingerly, and only with the advice of competent legal counsel. Meanwhile, be assured that these issues are being addressed on a national and state level. The SEC's orientation to the Internet seems positive but understandably cautious. Within the regulatory community, there appears to be clear recognition of the potential of the Internet to facilitate capital formation. However, it is important to keep in mind that the SEC's primary duty is investor protection. Even from that perspective, though, the Internet may provide the SEC with a useful tool to monitor private security transactions, which is exceedingly difficult when transactions are conducted by telephone and mail. Still, it takes time for the bureaucratic structure and legislative process to catch up with the technology. Technology easily outruns legislative capability.

Therefore, as long as the existing gap between the available technology and the legal and regulatory community's ability to fill its traditional role in the on-line marketplace remains, and as long as the laws remain in flux, we recommend using these sites for information and education rather than as sources of capital or investment opportunities. (ACE-*Net* may yet prove to be an exception to this general statement, but at present our concerns relate to ACE-*Net*'s effectiveness rather than its legal compliance.) Just as a sophisticated investor researches the Net looking not for deals but for information on companies, so should you use it as a tool to inform, educate, and sensitize yourself to the capital raising process. We hope our own Web site, www.icrnet.com, is valuable in that regard. But haphazardly listing your offering on the Internet, being exposed to investors in states where you are not registered and to investors who are not accredited, or even to competitors who would be happy to stumble upon information about you, is a poor idea.

You need not be cynical, but being wary is just plain smart.

# 15

# Answers to Common Business Angel Investor Questions

Assembled here are often-asked questions related to direct investment into early-stage, private transactions.

What is angel investing?

What is a good working definition of venture capital?

Don't venture capital firms fund start-ups?

How much do entrepreneurs usually seek from angels?

Who is the typical angel and how would you characterize them?

Where is the line drawn between the function of a venture capitalist and that of a banker?

Is there anyone else other than the SBA, the banks, and venture capitalists to fund ventures?

What do private investors find attractive in a company?

What are the three things an entrepreneur should ask before he or she seeks angel investment?

What is considered "significant participation" on the part of the investor?

How did ICR get into this type of business?

What are some of the primary industries of interest to your ICR pool of private investors?

Why such an interest in manufacturing?

What have you found to be the best financing method or structure?

An investment suitable to entrepreneurs sometimes involves commingling of funds. How do these commingling deals usually work?

Is commingling organized by the entrepreneur?

Do guidelines exist on how to assess risk, or the risk-reward ratio?

What is the typical return on investment?

What is the typical time frame for return on investment?

It seems as if the average investor can do pretty well by investing money passively in highly liquid markets and have almost as good of a shot, maybe better, at a return without the degree of risk. So why not just avoid the risk?

What hedging strategies do these investors use to limit their downside risk?

Do private investors spend more time in evaluating a deal *before* investing or in adding value *after* the investment has been made?

How does this type of investor generate and expand deal flow?

Is it difficult trying to educate entrepreneurs about how to find angels and educate wealthy people on how to invest in entrepreneurs? Is there a disconnect between the two groups?

A number of Web sites try to match entrepreneurs and angels. Is the Internet a useful approach?

### Q: *What is angel investing?*

A: The angel investor market is very large, around $30 billion a year (more than double the size of the venture capital market). Many individuals in start-ups have used up their own money, spent money from family and friends, and cannot qualify for bank loans or funds from venture capital. They need funding from private individuals—angels—to keep going.

### Q: *What is a good working definition of venture capital?*

A: First, let us offer a classic definition, then develop that with our personal perspective on venture capital, particularly on private investors. Basically, venture capital is a search for significantly above-average, long-term investment returns, returns accomplished primarily through equity ownership, that is, ownership in or involvement with risky start-up or emerging companies.

Typically, those companies are managed by experienced executives. Deals involving these companies tend to be focused on rapidly growing markets. These companies provide innovative products or services; they need not be just products, and they have a proprietary technology or proprietary edge. In part, this represents the institutional investor perspective, the professional venture capitalist who is managing money primarily for institutions.

A wide range of alternative asset investments are available to investors. One of those alternative asset classes is the private equity investment, or venture capital. Within the venture asset classes, a number of different types of investment opportunities open up to the investor, ranging from seed, R&D, and start-ups at the riskier end, through to bridge, acquisition/merger, and turnaround investments at the less risky end. Those at the riskier end provide higher return when they are successful; those at the less risky end provide less return on investment since they involve more established companies.

Definitions of these stages help: "Seed" means that a company is in the idea stage when the process is being organized; "R&D" is typical of the financing of product development for early-stage or more developed companies; "start-up" designates a venture completing its product development and initial marketing. At the safer end, "bridge" designates a venture requiring short-term capital to reach stability; "acquisition/merger" refers to a company in need of capital to finance an acquisition or merger; "turnaround" denotes a venture in need of capital to change from unprofitability to profitability.

But our research reflects a change in the source of this capital. Part of that change has come from the professional venture capital industry. In 1994 the venture capital industry invested about $4 billion to $5 billion. It invested $1 billion into approximately 300 early-stage deals. If we compare that pool of capital and that level of investment with what private angel investors have contributed, we see an interesting phenomenon. Private investors in 1994 invested approximately $55 billion to $56 billion into 700,000 companies and approximately $3 billion to $4 billion into early-stage transactions, that is, seed, R&D, and start-up.

So entrepreneurs have a substantially higher probability of being funded by private investors, particularly if their company is not one of the "darling" industries. These private investors are high-net-worth investors, typically possessing a net worth between $1 and $10 million; 90 percent are self-made, and own their own businesses. They represent a pool, together with the richest families in the United States, of about $8.2 trillion in net worth derived from approximately 3.4 million households. However, when we correct for only those who make these aggressive investments, the numbers drop significantly. Still, this is a major pool of capital, growing at a rate of about 14 percent to 20 percent per year. And when compared to pension fund growth, currently at about 8 percent per year, we see an immense source of capital.

## Q: Don't venture capital firms fund start-ups?

A: Venture capital firms have become more like money management firms. Fewer of them exist, and they tend to gather larger and larger pools of money. As a result, the size of their investments have increased, often into the range of a few million dollars. This tendency leaves seed-stage companies behind.

*Q: How much do entrepreneurs usually seek from angels?*

*A:* Anywhere from $150,000 to $1.5 million, which is all they need when they start up. If an entrepreneur seeks early-stage venture capital, he or she is going to raise more money than needed and will give up a bigger stake at a lower valuation. That's the attraction of dealing with angels: An entrepreneur raises less money but they keep more equity.

A lot of entrepreneurs do not like to raise money. They like to write software code or work on a product but view raising money, selling themselves, as an undesirable activity. But the most significant difference between a successful start-up and a failure is that the successful company learned how to raise money.

*Q: Who is the typical angel and how would you characterize him or her?*

*A:* There is no typical angel. Angels vary in background and what they want out of an investment. Right now there are about 300,000 active angel investors, but the potential pool is much larger. About 2 million individuals possess the discretionary net worth to make angel investments.

The age of the private investors is typically around 48 to 59 years old. They have postgraduate education and extensive previous management experience. They probably owned their own company. They are very interested in earlier-stage deals because they can aggressively negotiate strong discounts, and they find the potential for high returns through capital appreciation is best realized through these kinds of deals.

Within the bimodal distribution we have already described—the one between $10,000 and $50,000 and the other between $100,000 to about $250,000—private investors typically pool their money or invest with a syndicate of co-investors, the motivation for which concerns hedging strategies and managing risk. But there is a strong preference for manufacturing ventures, particularly those that overlap with their previous industrial experience and expertise. There is a myth that angel investors only invest close to home. The fact is, in our study, we found that about 50 to 55 percent do want to invest geographically proximate to home. But fully up to 48 percent said location was not a major criterion.

*Q: Where is the line drawn between the function of a venture capitalist and that of a banker?*

*A:* Primarily the difference between a venture capitalist and a banker is in the stage of development of the venture. Banks are not investors, they are creditors. Therefore, bankers do not make investments, particularly in early-stage deals that have no assets that could be offered as collateral, nor do they lend to companies without cash flow with which to service debt. So it is unreasonable to expect to find resources for earlier-stage or developmental-stage deals from bankers. Last year the SBA served as a very effective source of guaranteed funding for small businesses, about $15.8 billion invested through its 7(a) guaranteed loan program. But those funds went into operating businesses. When we deal with early-stage ventures that have no assets and no cash flow, we have no alternative but to turn to someone willing to put up money for an equity share of the business. These are risk-takers, investors looking for substantial growth in capital appreciation on their investment.

**Q: Is there anyone else other than the SBA, the banks, and the venture capitalists?**

**A.** Actually, a range of players appears in the picture. If we look at the creativity of entrepreneurs finding capital in the tight, competitive capital markets, we see a diversity of options. We see many people trying initially to fund their deals through family and friends and on credit cards. And we see individuals looking beyond these immediate sources toward private placements with strangers who are themselves professional investors. We see individuals using banks, SBIC (Small Business Investment Corporations), or MESBICs (Minority Enterprise Small Business Investment Corporations). They turn to venture leasing firms, factoring firms, and asset-based lenders. They use such structures as partnering or strategic partnering with a corporate investor. So there are different financing sources out there. The issue becomes one of deciding which capital source is appropriate for your venture at its particular stage of development.

**Q: What do private investors find attractive in a company?**

**A:** The entrepreneur needs to be aware of the things an investor is looking for in considering an investment. A study of approximately 600 investors listed in our proprietary database of investors tells us that they are looking for something they can identify with. They are looking for something that provides fun. Everyone seems to imagine that these investors are looking only at a return on investment. Return on investment is important, but these investors are looking for much more. Having already displayed their ability to make money—which has positioned them to be able to invest again—they are looking for something they can get involved in, something that excites them, something they can embrace, understand, and identify with. And, as we have said, it is fun to make money.

Real excitement occurs with what we call the pre-IPO (pre–initial public offering of stock). The only way to make $1 million to $5 million with $100,000 is to get involved in a pre-IPO. A lot of people do not because they worry about the risk, but there are ways to manage and hedge against the risk to 25 percent. And if you hit a home run two out of ten times, the returns can be significant and more than enough to make up for those risks.

In addition, investors are looking for deals that have a proprietary advantage or unique technology that positions that venture ahead of any competition. Investors are looking at recipients of capital who can articulate that competitive advantage in their documentation. The financial statements must spell out the potential and promise for ROI and must offer multiple scenarios supporting the figures. The argument and potential for return on investment must be strong. And where there is no history of profitability, entrepreneurs need to have a track record elsewhere in the industry.

It is a truism that business plans do not get funded, people get funded. So entrepreneurs need to have demonstrated within the context of the venture that they can make money for investors; they need a track record of having made money and having been able to raise capital. Another thing investors look for is not a promotion or even an invention but a plan for a profitable business enterprise. They are looking for people with perseverance, people who can survive rigorous background checks, people who are competent and successful, who exude a burning desire to succeed. Finally, the people investors are scrutinizing must have made a personal financial commitment of a significant portion of their own net worth to the venture.

*Q: What are the three things an entrepreneur should ask before he or she seeks angel investment?*

*A:* First, ask whether your company is financeable in terms of its business plan, its valuation, its competition, and a host of other factors. Second, ask yourself if *you* are financeable. That is, do you have a history of legal problems or other issues capable of raising red flags? Do you have the skills to make the company work? And third, is the risk financeable? If the deal is too risky, an angel will not want it. Investors have told us that they lost money when they got caught up in the entrepreneur's enthusiasm without really evaluating the investment.

*Q: What is considered "significant participation" on the part of the investor?*

*A:* Basically, these investors separate largely into two categories. Within our database of over 8,000 investors, for example, a bimodal distribution occurs concerning their preferred investment size. One segment of the database invests between $10,000 and $50,000. A second segment invest from $50,000 or $100,000 through $200,000 to $250,000. Small percentages invest more than $250,000 or less than $10,000 in each transaction; individuals are always looking for an opportunity to put a few thousand dollars in, just as there are individuals able to invest from $500,000 to $1.5 million directly in a venture. But these two extremes comprise less than 10 percent of our database. The two central distributions encompass the vast majority of individuals.

## Q: How did ICR get into this type of business?

A: International Capital Resources started as a venture capital club. After approximately 12 years as a corporate finance consultant, I saw a need for assisting clients whom I was helping with venture documentation to raise capital because they were not successful doing it on their own. I saw an opportunity when I relocated to California. My partners and I assessed that market. And as the chairman of the Northern California Venture Forum—the name of that venture capital club—I was able to interview hundreds of investors and meet with entrepreneurs, some of whom had failed to raise money and some of whom were successful. My partners and I saw an opportunity to provide a service to that group. That served as the impetus to get involved.

Secondarily, we discovered after a year and a half of Venture Forum meetings that while the forum was great idea for networking and education and introducing entrepreneurs and investors, we needed a larger pool of capital to influence those deals. That is when I started the Nationwide Private Investor Network, the first nationwide network of private angel investors. Such networks had been primarily regional. This network provided us with a wider pool of capital and also with access to sister networks with whom we soon affiliated. In 1998 we were among the top five networks out of some 44 operating networks in the United States. To date the top 20 alternative introduction networks in the United States have raised more than $2,554,000,000, not including deals in due diligence or deals in the pipeline—not bad in an industry that, in effect, is only about four or five years old.

From our experience with the Venture Forum, we realized that many people did not have information about how these private, very secretive investors were conducting these transactions. So we initiated the *Private Equity Review,* an effort to analyze and report on private transaction activity, particularly within our geographic locale. The review has been an outstanding success. We currently have a controlled circulation of approximately 8,900 investors who read the bimonthly review. In each issue we examine 15 to 20 different private transactions in process, deals that do not include institutional investors.

These are all private placement transactions occurring between private investors and the entrepreneurs, founders, and owners themselves. From this activity, we have substantial data on nearly all of those investors in terms of the size of their investment capability, the investments they have made in the past, the kind of industries they are interested in, the stage of development they are looking at, and the geographical locales they want to conduct business in. We have placed all that information on an interactive relational-database platform, an activity that has helped us identify individuals suited for specific deals. So that is where we are now. Within the next year or so, we hope to raise our own fund to work exclusively on private placement investments.

*Q: What are some of the primary industries of interest to your ICR pool of private investors?*

*A:* The hottest industries number five or six, but manufacturing commands the greatest interest. It make no difference if it is a consumer product, such as a new personal flotation device, or an industrial product or commercial product, or a high-technology product. There is big interest in manufacturing.

*Q: Why such an interest in manufacturing?*

*A:* Many of the successful individuals involved in this kind of investing have a background in the manufacturing and industrial areas. Investors stay close to what they know. These investors do not invest just money; they invest knowledge and experience, two assets central to hedging strategies and managing the risk associated with this kind of investing. Secondarily, however, computers remain highly interesting, particularly in networking hardware and also in multimedia and database development software, and the Internet. These areas foment a great deal of excitement. Information technologies, telecommunications, wireless technologies—these too stir interest. And despite the FDA's turtle-paced approval process, medical devices—particularly those that will command a substantial market—remain very appealing to more astute, technical investors, as well as to some of the professional classes.

Other tantalizing areas include any kind of health care ventures that assist in cost containment, automation, assistance in interfacing with the insurance industry or managing paperwork, such as billing. These are always big pulls with private investors. Electronic equipment, analysis equipment, measuring equipment, sophisticated, subtle, highly sensitive measuring equipment—these are emerging areas of investment interest. And at the end of 1994, two businesses in the entertainment field were also coming on strong: casino gaming and, secondarily, New Age amusements, that is, either the virtual-reality amusements or amusements combining hydraulics, electronics and computers—all designed to entertain individuals and create simulation. As one highly successful businessman puts it, "Entertainment is where America is going."

These are the areas in our database that generate the most interest.

*Q: What have you found to be the best financing method or structure?*

*A:* There is really no single best method or structure because a range of appropriate methods or structures exists. A deal structure becomes appropriate when the entrepreneur properly targets the investor. Too often entrepreneurs, convinced that they have an extraordinary deal—the next Apple Computer, for instance—approach venture capitalists, failing to grasp how slim the possibility is that they will be interested. Venture capitalists need to invest in national companies, companies with the potential to be very large businesses that will eventually go public. Professional venture capitalists are essentially portfolio managers, with a unique set of pressures. They have to raise their next fund; they *have* to invest the money under their management; they are responsible to overseers. None of this operates with the private investor.

However, once the entrepreneur is on target, the private placement—the placement of treasury securities with a small number of private investors—has certainly become the preferred investment vehicle. The private placement is important to understand. It allows for different structures: debt and equity, or a combination of the two. It is a more flexible vehicle because a private placement is anything that is not a public offering. The main advantage of a private placement is its flexibility.

But in looking at the structures used most, three stand out, and underlying each is equity. First is preferred or common stock. The second is convertible subordinated debt, which is much more common to the institutional transactions involving as it does some type of an interest payment arrangement. Third comes some kind of long-term debt with warrants. Long-term debt applies only to later-stage ventures. In almost all cases, the only way that these investors can really benefit from the risk they have taken is to share in the upside potential if the venture becomes successful. And the only way that they can do that is through equity. So, at bottom, all structures relate to equity.

What you see is a reliance on preferred stock for a couple of reasons. One, it is senior to common; it provides leverage to influence management when things go sideways. It requires the entrepreneur to remain in contact with the investor. The provisions can create warning mechanisms that permit the investor to make changes in management or establish time frames and conditions for making changes. Preferred stock structures can provide some income through dividends, although such an action, especially in the early-stage deals, is not exercised. Also, preferred stock is redeemable by the corporation.

The corporation can set up a sinking fund and establish compulsory containment. In addition, preferred stock is convertible to common stock, so if, in fact, the company is purchased or does go public or otherwise liquidates, there is the option for the holder to share in that.

*Q: An investment suitable to entrepreneurs sometimes involves commingling of funds. How do these commingling deals usually work?*

*A:* Basically, each participant is an individual investor. Those individual investors will interact with the entrepreneurs, and each investor will be supplied equity in the venture proportional to the money each invested. The investors do not invest as a pool, as a venture capital partnership does. They do conduct individual transactions. But each investor's share of equity has to be measured against the venture's valuation. Of consequence is the share of equity each receives among all the parties, because any instance of inequality could spell trouble later on.

*Q: Is commingling organized by the entrepreneur?*

*A:* Well, typically, the establishing of coinvestors can go either way. It is our experience that when someone finds a deal attractive, he or she will bring it to the attention of associates and colleagues and will grandfather in other individuals to look it over. However, it is not uncommon for an entrepreneur to foment excitement in a deal. So it runs both ways.

*Q: Do guidelines exist on how to assess risk, or the risk-reward ratio?*

*A:* There are a couple of things you can do to assess risk. Risk in these ventures takes different forms. This kind of risk differs from quantifying the risk in an investment in the public market. A private placement is more qualitative in nature. First of all, you have management risk. Can the management carry out the plan they are so passionately presenting? Do they have the ability, the experience, the background, and the track record to accomplish the forecasted sales and/or manage the internal operations? More important, are they going to be able to form a team within the ranks, or will they succumb to resentment as a result of negotiating founder stock shares? Has discord been struck among the members?

Another type of risk you have to evaluate is product and technology risk. If this is a technology that has not yet been developed, significant risk emerges. If it is the assembly of existing technologies that have been well tested and molded into a new technology, the risk is substantially less. So you have to assess product and technology risk.

Market risk is another consideration. The need for missionary selling creates a horrible situation. It becomes expensive to grab the minds of the American public. If no market exists, will the market accept that product? And if the market has not demonstrated its desire to purchase the product through purchase orders or through sales in terms of the company's performance, substantial risk arises in having to market the product. You then have operations risk that emerges regarding the company's ability to produce in the volume and quality the company has projected. Unanticipated problems, such as those experienced with Pentium in 1995, can strike a company at any time. If such a problem arises, can the company deliver the product in such a way that it will achieve its projections?

There also exists financial risk if—more likely "when"—the company will need more money than it claims, or if your investment is a very small percentage of the amount claimed to be needed. You're investing $25,000 in this round, but the next round asks for $25 million. So you have a very substantial risk that the company will not be able to raise the rest of the money. Suddenly your small investment does not amount to anything. Ways to quantify risk come through the pro forma financial statements. But remember: Most investments fail to return targeted multiples. Talk to any investor; rarely have deals returned the multiple that entrepreneurs had claimed.

## Q: What is a typical return on investment?

A: From the point of view of private investors—not from the institutional venture capital perspective—angels seek a number of nonfinancial returns. Angel investors have a broader palette of motivations than just return on investment. However, that is not to deny a strong interest in a return on investment. First of all, we have seen great interest in job creation and urban revitalization. So we see a number of matching networks, venture forums, venture capital clubs, and other types of relatively loosely structured organizations trying to pool investors and make the market more efficient for investing in ventures that will create jobs within a proximate geographic locale. Also, a major increase has occurred in the number of organizations facilitating investor and entrepreneur introductions for socially responsible investments.

And although more inherited wealth participates in technology for medicine or for energy, many angel investors also are interested in investing in these useful areas. In addition, we see some entrepreneurs funding women and minority entrepreneurs. So a different dimension drives these investors over and above making money, a dimension that includes the personal satisfaction they derive from assisting entrepreneurs to build successful ventures.

To answer the question in terms of venture capital returns, let us be realistic about what someone can expect. On the average, 60 to 65 percent of these investments break even, do not break even, or represent a partial or total loss. So a substantial portion—six out of ten—even after meticulous due diligence, result in no financial return or in returns below a bank deposit account. Approximately 20 percent of these investments, based on our research, provide a two to five times multiple on the investment. About 8 to 9 percent provide about five to ten times the investment, and about seven times out of 100, about 6.9 percent, we see a return of ten times or more the investment made. As venture capitalist Lucien Ruby shrewdly notes, venture capital investors do not have to get their desired return. In fact, they usually do not. But they want to see the desired return as a possibility. Now, when we calculate the targeted rates of return for a typical direct investment, the multiple is a major consideration, but so is the time within which the investor wants to receive that multiple.

*Q: What is a typical time frame for return on investment?*

*A:* What we see is a range in the acceptable time frame. If we look at the activities from the 1970s and the 1980s, we see the time for holding investments ranging from five to ten years. Although for the institutional investor the goal is always to liquidate within three to five years, reality sets in, making the wait much longer before achieving fruition and creating a substantial liquidation event. On average, the holding time to liquidation for successful direct, private investments reaches eight years.

*Q: It seems as if the average investor can do pretty well by investing money passively in highly liquid markets and have almost as good of a shot, maybe better, at a return without the degree of risk. So why not just avoid the risk?*

*A:* We cannot underestimate how astute many of these investors are. They are multimillionaires. Over and above their house and car, they have net worth between $1 and $10 million. They have been successful investors. They are banking on their sound judgment to once again select a venture like the one that put them where they are today.

We find it sobering to examine the targeted rates of return that these individuals bring to these ventures. With a seed and start-up, we see individuals seeking strong indications that they will realize an annualized international rate of return around 60 to 100 percent. In expansion, the company is generating revenues but might not yet be profitable or in the black. Here we see targeted returns of around 40 percent to 50 percent. In a profitable situation—the company is making a profit but is cash poor—we think 30 percent to 40 percent is the typical target. In mezzanine, a company is bridging to cash out. Here we commonly see a targeted internal rate of return of 20 percent per year. So, although very substantial returns are targeted for early-stage deals, within the private equity class called venture capital, more developed situations offer much more security and provide the potential for lesser rates of return, for example, a 20, 25, or 30 percent return, such as in a mezzanine transaction.

*Q: What hedging strategies do these investors use to limit their down-side risk?*

*A:* Hedging strategies begin by conducting thorough due diligence and by being thorough in all investigation related to due diligence. It is much more important to avoid a bad investment than to try to hit a home run. After all, these investors are making an average of between one and three investments per year. So their ability to diversify risk becomes limited. They can manage only so many value-added invest-ments, which take huge chunks of time to administer.

Hedging strategies begin with due diligence, but they continue by negotiating steep discounts very early on in the negotiating process for the risk being taken by these early-stage investors. These investors rarely invest at the price valuation suggested by the entrepreneur.

Another way to hedge is by syndicating as early as possible. Bring other investors into the deal, backing off what you might have planned as your investment amount. Say an investor plans to put in $250,000. The investor backs off to $125,000 and attracts other investors who come in and do a couple of things. One, they carry on due diligence. Two, they confirm—or fail to confirm—the original investor's opinion. And three, if the additional investors do confirm, they share the financial risk.

Another strategy involves individuals using other people's money as soon as possible in the transaction. For example, rather than directly investing in the venture, an individual may provide a guaranteed line of credit as a part of the transaction. This saves the investor from touching current cash flow but guarantees his or her participation while using other financial capabilities that he or she possesses.

Also, rather than waiting until the venture goes "south," or discov-ering that milestones have been missed, many investors hedge on the risk associated with these highly illiquid investments not only by taking a seat on the board but by looking for increased involvement. Whether as an informal consultant, counselor, or adviser, or as a part-time indi-vidual or full-time manager in the firm, their involvement keeps them close to the action.

*Q: Do private investors spend more time in evaluating a deal* **before** *investing or in adding value* **after** *the investment has been made?*

*A:* The answer is both. Remember that the essence of venture investing is value added. So each investment is time-consuming. These investors bring their own contact network. They provide technical and marketing guidance and expertise to less-experienced entrepreneurs. They pro-vide recruitment support and assistance in developing strategy and business plans. They also provide introductions to customers and ven-dors. They assist in joint venturing, identifying joint-venture partners, and so forth. Venture capital investing and value-added investing involves a commitment over and above the capital that is committed to the deal.

*Q: How does this type of investor generate and expand deal flow?*

*A:* Let us use International Capital Resources as a case study. These are the procedures that worked for us in developing substantial deal flow. We see about 200 deals a month. Granted, only about 1 or 2 percent are financeable, and will be financed by other than family, friends, or the entrepreneurs themselves. But, because we have a large and diverse deal flow, we can be selective about the deals we want to work on or introduce.

When we first started, we gave up the desire for short-term returns. We offered our services free, no fee on a very selective basis to companies we wanted to work with. By so doing, we were able to find operating companies looking for capital. We built some critical relationships and generated referrals. Another area that we have found very fruitful is mentoring. We conduct monthly seminars. It takes only about two hours of our time, and we arrange for them at the office. Typically 10 or 20 entrepreneurs contact us after we place a brief advertisement in the local business press. In this way, we find out about one or two additional deals per month.

Today, with the availability of desktop publishing software and the reduced cost of computer hardware, it is easy to obtain a system with which to produce a newsletter. And with the extensive directories and lists available on incubators, venture capital forums, venture capital conferences, entrepreneurial associations, and growth-company professional associations, it is easier than ever to obtain lists of likely targets, that is, companies that have an operating history and that are searching for capital. By publishing a newsletter and providing advice and information on due diligence, valuation, and raising capital, we generate inquiries. Also, giving a major speech each month typically generates three to four telephone calls to us after the presentation, an action that usually leads to personal meetings with the entire management team and/or investors involved in the venture.

By the way, it is impossible to overemphasize the importance of the new generation of venture capital clubs, investment forums, and matching services—all of which are ideal ways to contact other investors interested in this esoteric area of direct investing. And one of the most successful methods of generating deal flow is to volunteer in a venture as an adviser or as a technical board member. As an investor becomes immersed in the interlocking network of board members, the quality of the deal flow improves. Developing relationships with other individuals who make the investments is indeed a worthwhile endeavor.

Last, a number of publications concentrate on private placements. ICR's *Private Equity Review* focuses on angel transactions, but a number of newsletters focus on institutional transactions, another resource to find out about deals and about the people working on them. Many organizations have their own directories and investors, listing themselves, thereby stimulating inquiries.

Of course, a downside exists to any of these strategies. As soon as someone finds out that people have money to invest in these kinds of deals, they are inundated with inquiries. They will be ferreted out. At a party, a meeting, a professional event—it does not matter. Someone will approach them, slide out the old guitar, and start singing the song. In short, the investor who surfaces has to be ready for what follows. ICR's investor database buffers these investors from this intrusion into their privacy, a major reason for the rapid growth of the database. The database ensures that investors receive information about only those transactions that match their investment criteria.

*Q: Is it difficult trying to educate entrepreneurs about how to find angels and to educate wealthy people on how to invest in entrepreneurs? Is there a disconnect between the two groups?*

*A:* There is—and therein lies a marvelous opportunity. The entire economic structure of the country is changing as we move from a labor-based manufacturing economy to a knowledge-based entrepreneurial economy. Ten years ago everybody was working on resumes in the quest to get ahead. Now everyone seems to have a business plan in the top drawer. What these people need most is financing. The key is to bring these two groups together and feed this hungry economic movement.

*Q: A number of Web sites try to match entrepreneurs and angels: Is the Internet a useful approach?*

*A:* We found the amount raised on the Internet matching services last year totaled $44 million—barely a drop in the bucket. We are finding that investors are not using the Internet to find deals but to research companies instead. This condition could change; the Internet could become more important, but right now entrepreneurs can end up wasting time that could be better used to develop a plan to get money in a more realistic way.

# Conclusion

*We want all pleasant ends. We don't do what we ought to do and what we*
*ought to do, we don't, hoping somehow that "chance" will bring us through.*

Matthew Arnold

We feel that enough chance is already mixed into our lives. Wherever
and whenever we can eliminate it, we should. This book is our attempt
to eliminate some of it. We think that chance in deal making, for
instance, is financially dangerous, that it accommodates too many traps.
This book represents an attempt on our part to minimize the element of
chance that lurks in the opportunity and practice of raising capital and
investing in early-stage ventures.

With this challenge in mind, we have tried to smooth the way that
awaits entrepreneurs and inventors in their struggle to raise the funds
needed to fulfill their dreams. Likewise, we have tried to put faces on
seemingly disparate investors, reminding everyone that however many
designs, colors, and beads a rotating kaleidoscope may display, the
entire show is reflected off only three mirrors. Just so, individual private
investors may appear to reflect innumerable patterns of investment
behavior but share at the core far more likenesses than differences. In
short, we have tried to animate and humanize the two groups, one to
the other.

Further, we assert that there need not exist any antagonism between
the private market and institutional market. In fact, a close reading of
our book suggests that many private investors will not get involved in a
deal unless institutional investors can help them in the future. Thus,
whether the individual personalities wish to acknowledge it or not, a
mutually helpful, healthy symbiotic relationship is germinating. The
two markets need to begin working together in earnest toward their
mutual goals.

Three areas remain ripe for cooperation. The first is in deal flow. With no shortage of private investors, the real challenge is in finding good deals. Perhaps institutional investors will come across particularly promising deals but, for any one of a number of reasons, are unable to complete the transaction. Referral of these deals to private investors and networks will provide a place to park and improve the deal's condition, while simultaneously helping the network to offer a product of greater quality to the investors in its circle of contacts.

Second, we have inferred from our experience that investors are best identified by observing them while they are actually involved in the transaction process, particularly with regard to (1) their approach to due diligence, (2) their interaction with principals and intermediaries, and (3) their rationale for investing in or rejecting a venture. Another way to improve cooperation is to access the investors through informal or matching networks, inviting them to "piggyback" on deals in which the institutional investors have done due diligence. Listing a venture with a network, inviting some of the astute, sophisticated, accredited investors to partner with institutional investors, offers private investors numerous insights into the venturing process while supplying institutional investors with a fresh pool of potential coinvestors.

Finally, it will benefit institutional investors to support private investor networks in their regions. The most successful networks got their start with the financial and consultative support of the professional venture capital community. Institutional investors can sponsor, or at least participate in, network events and publications. Institutional investors may even consider investing in a network and supporting this "farm league" as an advisory board member, recognizing that the for-profit networks can be profitable businesses in their own right. It is worth reiterating that for early-stage ventures attempting to raise from $150,000 to $1,500,000, few options for capital exist, yet these ventures hold the potential for pulling even states as large as California out of a recession.

Finally, we are reminded of the statement of James Watson, codiscoverer with Francis Crick of DNA and author of *The Double Helix*. He declares in the opening lines of that seminal work, "science seldom proceeds in [a] straightforward logical manner." His statement prompts this question: What does? The cinder path to success is long and twisted.

In writing this book, we have tried to brush the cinders from that path; if we have not thoroughly straightened its numberless turns, perhaps we have shortened its distance.

# Appendix A

EVERS & HENDRICKSON, LLP
PRIMER SERIES

LEGAL PRIMER ON
SECURITIES LAW ISSUES
FOR NONLAWYERS

(Emphasis on Small Business and California)

William D. Evers, Esq.

# CONTENTS

Foreword                                                           249

1. OVERVIEW                                                        249
   1.1 Federal Acts                                               249
       1.1.1  General—Full Disclosure                             249
       1.1.2  Securities Act of 1933                              249
       1.1.3  Securities Exchange Act of 1934                     250
       1.1.4  Investment Company Act of 1940                      250
   1.2 Federal Rules and Regulations—Exemptions
       from Registration                                          251
       1.2.1  Regulation D                                        251
       1.2.2  Regulation A: Public, Limit $5 Million              251
       1.2.3  Rule 504, SCOR: Public or Private, Limit $1 Million 251
       1.2.4  Rule 505: Private, Limit $5 Million                 252
       1.2.5  Rule 506: Unlimited Private, Preemption             252
       1.2.6  Regulation S                                        253
   1.3 The States                                                 253
   1.4 California Laws                                            254
       1.4.1  General: Merit Review, Suitability                  254
       1.4.2  Section 25113(b)(i): Qualification, Public          254
       1.4.3  Section 25113(b)(ii): Qualification, Public         254
       1.4.4  Section 25102(f): Private, No Review                254
       1.4.5  Section 25102(n): Private with Announcement         254
   1.5 Accredited and Excluded Investors                         255

2. PRIVATE OFFERINGS—THE FIRST STEP                               255
   2.1 Introduction                                               255
   2.2 Multistate: Section 4(2) and Rule 506                      255
   2.3 California: Section 25102(f)                               256
   2.4 Mixture: 25102(n)                                          256

3. PUBLIC OFFERINGS                                               257
   3.1 Rule 504: $1 Million Maximum                               257
   3.2 SCOR Offerings                                             257
       3.2.1  California SCOR: Public Offering                    257
   3.3 Small Business Rules: Suitability                          258
   3.4 Regulation A: Public, $5 Million Maximum                   259
   3.5 SB-2: Public, No Maximum                                   259
   3.6 S-1: Public, No Maximum                                    260

4. DISCLOSURE DOCUMENTS                                           260

5. INTEGRATION RULES: TIMING                                      260
   5.1 Problem                                                    260

5.2 Five Tests                                        261
5.3 Safe Harbor—Reg. D                                261
5.4 California Rules                                   261

6. RESTRICTED SECURITIES AND TRADING                  261
   6.1 Rule 144                                        261
   6.2 Nonissuer "Secondary" Trading (by a Shareholder,
       Not the Issuer)                                 262

7. THE INTERNET                                        263
   7.1 In General                                      263
   7.2 The Offer                                       264
   7.3 Suitability                                     264
   7.4 The Sale                                        264

8. FEDERAL/STATE                                       264

9. THE '40 ACT                                         265

10. THE USUAL                                          266

11. SALES—"AGENTS" (CALIFORNIA)                        266

*Foreword: This primer is intended to assist our clients in thinking through what route to follow when embarking on a program to finance their business. It is not a complete guide, but we hope it will be of some help. It should not be considered legal advice.*

## 1. OVERVIEW

There is a jumble of terms, rules, and regulations in the securities regulatory area. This primer concentrates on a portion of the spectrum—the offering of equity (stock) by small and emerging companies.

There are three primary federal statues: the Securities Act of 1933 (the "'33 Act"), the Securities Exchange Act of 1934 (the "'34 Act") and the Investment Company Act of 1940 (the "'40 Act").

The Securities and Exchange Commission ("SEC") administers these laws at the federal level and issues rules, regulations, and orders pursuant to the terms of these laws.

The states also have jurisdiction. It's as if there were 50 countries to be dealt with. A minority of the states use "full disclosure" (also used by the SEC) and the rest use "merit review" (used by California). New York has a unique antifraud approach. Clearing with the states is called "blue skying." The higher up the scale one goes in being a reporting company (to the SEC), being listed on an exchange, and having substantial assets, the easier it is to be qualified to sell securities in the states. Small business, lacking these attributes, has an expensive and difficult time getting qualified.

### 1.1 FEDERAL ACTS

#### 1.1.1 General—Full Disclosure

The SEC administers the '33 Act based on the policy of requiring "full disclosure." The idea is: "Let the facts be told, precisely and accurately, and then, caveat emptor—let the buyers beware." The SEC usually reviews the filing of an application very thoroughly. Regulation A and SB-2 offerings are reviewed in Washington. The initial response is usually received in one month. One then responds to the SEC comments and gets the second round of comments in two to three weeks. Each response cycle is usually shorter than the initial response time. Finally, if and when the SEC finds that their comments have been responded to adequately, the SEC will declare the filing "effective." Only when a filing is effective can the actual sale of securities begin.

#### 1.1.2 Securities Act of 1933

The '33 Act deals with the offer, sale, and issuance of securities. Transactions that involve more than one state are under the SEC's jurisdiction: Both public and private transactions are covered.

Under the '33 Act, all companies wishing to sell their stock or other securities must go through a registration process unless the transaction is one which by law or regulation is exempt from registration. Section 3(b) of the '33 Act allows the SEC to exempt from registration small offerings under $5 million. Thus we have the Small Corporate Offering Registration or "SCOR" for up to $1 million under Rule 504 and Reg. A offerings for up to $5 million. Section 4(2) of the '33 Act covers those offerings not involving a public offering and provides the authority for Rule 506 of Reg. D (see below). Section 4(6) of the '33 Act exempt from registration up to $5 million of sales to certain high-income or net-worth individuals or institutions ("Accredited Investors"). All these sections are in the '33 Act.

### 1.1.3 Securities Exchange Act of 1934

As its name implies, this act deals with trading and regulation of the Exchanges. The primary method of regulating broker-dealers is through a self-regulating organization ("SRO"), the National Association of Securities Dealers ("NASD").

The impact of this act on issuers (companies selling securities) relates to the reporting requirements and to trading in the company's securities.

When one files for registration of a public offering, as in an SB-2 filing (but not in a Reg. A offering, which, though public, is anomalously an exemption from registration), one becomes a "reporting company." Reporting companies are required to file annual, quarterly, and other periodic reports (on Forms 10-K, 10-Q, and 8-K) with the SEC, submit shareholder proxy statements to the SEC, and follow various other reporting requirements.

Companies also can become reporting companies voluntarily by filing with the SEC. A company must become a reporting company if it has at least 500 shareholders and $10 million in assets.

A small company can have a broker-dealer file information akin to that in a prospectus by complying with the requirements of Rule 15(c)(2)(11) under the '34 Act. This then allows the company to have a market maker and to be posted on the Bulletin Board maintained by the NASD. The NASD has proposed to limit Bulletin Board stocks to reporting companies only. This would knock off about half of the Bulletin Boards stocks. Presumably the knock-offs would either become reporting or go to the "Pink Sheets." Any stock that is traded and has a market maker can be listed on the "Pink Sheets," maintained by the National Quotation Bureau.

### 1.1.4 Investment Company Act of 1940

The '40 Act controls mutual funds and numerous other activities including investment advisers (advising as to funds over $25 million).

This act comes into play when a fund has over 100 investors. It is very restrictive and is the reason venture capitalists have less than 100 partners. Quite simply, it inhibits our country from having any "peoples" or "public" venture capital activity. A pity, in that the venture capitalists are no longer very venturesome and do not offer finance in the "chasm" or "gap" area of $250,000 to $5 million.

## 1.2 Federal Rules and Regulations—Exemptions from Registration

The SEC has promulgated certain key rules and regulations that define those offerings that are exempt from the SEC's registration process. The most widely known are:

### 1.2.1 Regulation D

Reg. D contains Rules 501–508. Rules 504 and 505 are based on Section 3(b) of the '33 Act; Rule 506 is based on Section 4(2) of that act.

### 1.2.2 Regulation A: Public, Limit $5 Million

Regulation A allows for a public offering as an "exemption from registration" in the form of an Application for Exemption for offers and sales of securities up to $5 million (under Section 3(b) of the '33 Act). There is an anomaly involved: Even though not registered, the securities are not "Restricted" and can be traded (with the same possible limitations as in a SCOR offering, see below). Using a Reg. A does not cause the issuer to be a "reporting company", an important distinction from the use of an SB-2.

### 1.2.3 Rule 504, SCOR: Public or Private, Limit $1 million

This is a "safe harbor" for public (or private) offerings not exceeding $1 million. The federal government asserts no jurisdiction in a 504 offering. It is under Section 3(b) of the '33 Act (small offerings). This means that if a company follows the requirements of Rule 504, its public or private offering (Rule 504 and SCOR) will be exempt from the registration requirements of the SEC.

Rule 504 provides the basis for SCOR offerings. (See below.) All 504 small public offerings, including SCOR, must be cleared with the state regulators. Stock issued pursuant to Rule 504 is not "restricted"; however, in California it frequently is not freely tradeable through brokers.

Rule 504 is not usually used for a private offering as one frequently can offer in only one state or use Rule 506. In California, one would probably use Section 25102(f) of the California Corporations Code, which provides for any number of accredited investors and allows up to 35 nonaccredited investors. If the offering is in more than one state, Rule 504 could be utilized with blue skying in each state. Remember that Rule

504 is nothing more than the SEC not asserting any regulatory jurisdiction. At the present time, stock issued pursuant to a 504 offering (public or private) is not, under federal rules, "restricted" except as to "affiliates" (officer, director and control persons). However, a state may impose restrictions. In California, under Section 25102(f), the stock is technically not restricted, though the investor must vouch that the stock is not being purchased with a view to further distribution and the stock is usually not tradeable through a broker, unless on an unsolicated basis.

The SEC has proposed a new rule that would require that a 504-issued stock be restricted in order to stop the abuse taking place, particularly in New York by brokers mishandling the aftermarket of 504 issues.

Rule 506 requires that a more relatively complex offering document (same as in a Reg. A offering) be given if stock is going to be sold to nonaccredited investors, whereas Rule 504 does not require that any specific form of offering document be used; however, each state may require a disclosure document, especially in the case of a public 504 (SCOR) offering. Regardless of whether a rule requires use of an offering document, proper disclosure of material information is absolutely necessary to be able to avoid and/or defend securities fraud claims from investors.

### 1.2.4  Rule 505: Private, Limit $5 Million

This rule comes under Section 3(b) of the '33 Act (small offerings) and provides a "safe harbor" for private offerings up to $5 million. It is contrasted to Regulation A (also under Section 3(b)) which provides for a public offering up to $5 million. Up to 35 nonaccredited investors are allowed. No general solicitation or advertising is allowed. Strictly prescribed information is required to be given to the nonaccredited investors, including audited financials (offerings of $5 million). Stock issued pursuant to Rule 505 is "restricted."

This rule is seldom used as the requirements for nonaccredited are stiff, and, if going for a private placement, one would use Rule 506 (unlimited amount) with its preemption of state review (below).

### 1.2.5  Rule 506: Unlimited Private, Preemption

A new opening was created by the National Securities Markets Improvement Act of 1996 in which Congress preempted from the states the authority to review securities exempted from registration by Rule 506, a rule adopted under Section 4(2) of the '33 Act (not involving a public offering). The states can not review a 506 offering; if to accredited investors only, no prescribed disclosure document is required. However, one would use a Private Placement Memorandum ("PPM") to avoid fraud charges. If nonaccredited investors (up to 35) are involved, a prescribed disclosure document is required. The "joker" is that

Congress allowed the states to require a notice filing and to assess filing fees just as if no preemption exists. Nonetheless, this is an attractive alternative for those who can find accredited investors. No advertising is permitted. The rule also allows a public offering to follow immediately after the termination of the 506 offering.

Stock issued pursuant to Rule 506 is "restricted."

### 1.2.6 Regulation S

Regulation S provides an exemption from registration of securities that are sold outside the United States by companies meeting certain criteria. Reg. S can be used for overseas sales, either public or private, and either in conjunction with or separate from a U.S. offering. The securities, generally, must not be sold to U.S. persons for one year (equity securities) or 40 days (debt securities). Note, also, that resale into the United States, if done quickly, must be done pursuant to an exemption from registration.

There was considerable abuse of Regulation S as a means of avoiding the SEC's registration requirements. As a result, the SEC has increased the period during which the equity securities may not be sold to U.S. persons from 40 days to one year.

### 1.3 The States

The states all regulate the offer and sale of securities (The District of Columbia, oddly, does not.) Clearing with the states is known as "blue skying." As noted above, some states use full disclosure (similar to the SEC) and some use merit review (such as California); however, in administration of the laws, the shades of difference tend to blend. Merit review requires a finding by the state that the offering is "fair, just, and equitable" to the purchaser. This test is frequently met by the administrators declaring the offering is fair, just, and equitable only if offered to persons of a certain level of wealth and/or sophistication. This is known as "suitability" and is used extensively in California under a "limited" (as compared to an "open") public offering permit.

The states belong to the North American Securities Administrators Association ("NASAA"), an organization that attempts to coordinate state regulation so as to lessen the burden on small issuers. The irony is that most listed (on stock exchanges) companies only need notify the state to be cleared. It is the small issuer that faces the task of clearing in each jurisdiction in which offers (see "Internet" below) and sales are to be made.

Certain states are cooperating on a regional basis for review. The New England and certain western states are examples. Generally, California is not participating. However, most states, including California, are now (October 1997) participating in "Coordinated Equity Review" wherein the state of Arizona assigns one full disclosure state and one merit review state to review for the states in which offerings are to be made. Unfortunately, this very good step forward is limited to SB-1 and SB-2 offerings (and S-1's).

New York state is unique in that it has an antifraud statute (the Martin Act) administered by the New York Attorney General.

Washington, D.C., is even more unique in that it has no securities regulation scheme.

### 1.4 California Laws

#### 1.4.1 General: Merit Review, Suitability

As noted above, California is a merit review state using "suitability" in public offerings. In a private offering (no advertising, no general solicitation), one is allowed to sell to any number of accredited (California uses the term "excluded," which includes accredited) investors and up to 35 nonaccredited ones. Only a one-page filing is required in the private offering. (See "25102(f)" below.)

#### 1.4.2 Section 25113(b)(i)*: Qualification, Public
*(All sections refer to the Corporations Code of California)*

This is the general qualification section for a public offering; usable if one cannot use SCOR, for example, a foreign (Nevada or other state) corporation not qualifying under Section 25115.

#### 1.4.3 Section 25113(b)(ii): Qualification, Public

Provides for California corporations and foreign (out-of-state) corporations that meet certain tests to use the special rule of SCOR ("Small Corporate Offering Registration") offerings.

#### 1.4.4 Section 25102(f): Private, No Review

This is the great escape valve allowing one to raise any amount from excluded investors and not more than 35 nonexcluded on a private basis (no ads, no general solicitation). There is no state review of the offering materials. There are limitations on who can buy securities in an offering under Section 25102(f). Purchasers must have a preexisting business relationship with the company or have demonstrated investor sophistication. The stock is not "restricted"; however, finding buyers without the intervention of brokers (who usually are not able to handle) is most difficult.

#### 1.4.5 Section 25102(n): Private with Announcement

This section allows one to advertise in a private placement with sale to "qualified investors" only. The ad, a "general announcement," is strictly prescribed. It is in the form of a "tombstone ad." Many states are now adopting similar laws. The California act is very complex and, because of this, is the subject of a separate paper. So far, "n" has not proven to be very useful, despite early high hopes.

### 1.5 Accredited and Excluded Investors

"Accredited" investor is defined in Rule 501(a) of Reg. D. There are several categories, the most important of which is a "natural person" with a single income of $200,000 (or joint income with that person's spouse of $300,000) in the past two years and reasonable expectation of that rate of income continuing for the current year, OR having $1 million of net worth, including home equity.

California uses the term "excluded" to indicate exclusion from the count of 35 nonexcluded that are allowed under Section 25102(f). Thus, in a private offering, one can have any number of "excluded" investors because they are excluded from the count. There are many categories of "excluded." The primary ones are:

1. Partner, officer, director of the issuer together with their relatives sharing a residence.

2. Owners of more than 50 percent of the shares of the issuer.

3. Promoter.

4. A Purchaser who purchases $150,000 of the offering, has enough sophistication (or has an investment adviser with enough sophistication) to protect his/her interests, and whose investment does not exceed 10 percent of his/her net worth.

5. An individual who alone has an income exceeding $200,000 or, with spouse, has income exceeding $300,000 in the two most recent years and expects continuation of this income, OR has a net worth exceeding $1 million. Home equity is included, so the definition is the same as the federal for "accredited."

## 2. PRIVATE OFFERINGS—THE FIRST STEP

### 2.1 Introduction

Normally, one raises the first funds on a private basis, especially if the need is modest, say, under $1.5 million. The cost is considerably less and the time involved is frequently less, depending on one's ability to raise funds from wealthy sources. These are two basic criteria: amount and contacts.

This section reviews various approaches.

### 2.2 MultiState: Section 4(2) and Rule 506

If one knows wealthy sources in more than one state, there are two primary routes to follow: the "safe harbor" of Rule 506 or simply Section 4(2) of the '33 Act (not involving a public offering).

If Section 4(2) is used, each state must be bluesky'd. There are different requirements as to nonaccredited (California 35, Nevada 25, etc.) If only accredited are approached, some states require only a simple form and a fee.

Rule 506 has an obvious advantage; it preempts the states except as to fees and a simple filing. One is sure that all one has to do for each state is pay the filing fee and file a Form D report (a few pages showing sales in that state). The disadvantage is that, if nonaccredited investors are involved, the disclosure document is rather elaborate (like an Offering Circular in a Reg. A offering).

The legal costs of a 506 offering only to accredited investors can be as low as $4,000 (excluding filing fees) if the business plan has good disclosure in which case a "wrap-around" can be used: wrapping the legal requirements around the business plan to provide disclosure sufficient to protect against successful fraud claims in the future.

If nonaccrediteds are approached, the cost rises substantially to around $10,000 to $15,000 as the work is similar to a Reg. A offering, with the exception of not having federal review of the document.

### 2.3  California: Section 25102(f)

In the event one offers securities only in California, Section 25102(f) stands alone. It permits a private placement of any amount of money to be raised from "excluded" or "accredited" investors and up to 35 nonexcluded investors. The stock would not be "restricted" in the federal sense (no rule 144) but would be limited in trading. (See Section 6 below.) If more than one state is involved, either Rule 504 of Reg. D or Section 4(2) must be utilized and each state blue sky'd. Section 25102(f) would still be used in California.

Note that if Rule 506 is used, one wouldn't use Section 25102(f) as the state is preempted. When using Section 25102(f), there is no required disclosure document other than that necessary to avoid fraud charges: the classic use of a Private Placement Memorandum ("PPM") and a one-page reporting form must be filed with the commissioner with a modest (top $300) fee.

### 2.4  Mixture: 25102(n)

This Section allows a modest form of advertising (a "general announcement") for a private placement in California only. It is an innovative step in the right direction. Sales can be made to "qualified" investors only. It has not been very successful in attracting "angel" money.

This is an extremely complicated code section.

NASAA and the SEC are pushing all states to adopt laws similar to Section 25102(n) in order to allow advertising (the general announcement is like a tombstone ad) for accredited ("qualified") investors. Many other states have adopted "n"-like statutes with its use restricted to sales to accredited investors, rather than the California "qualified" allowance.

## 3.  PUBLIC OFFERINGS

### 3.1  Rule 504: $1 Million Maximum

Rule 504 is discussed above. It is a federal "safe harbor" for public and private offerings up to $1 million. Nothing is filed with the SEC other than a Reg. D form (a simple form showing sales). Rule 504 is much misunderstood: It is simply no federal jurisdiction. Note that the SEC is proposing to declare securities issued pursuant to Rule 504 to be "restricted" under Rule 144.

### 3.2  SCOR Offerings

SCOR represents an abdication by the SEC (pursuant to section 3(b) of the "33 Act and Rule 504), to the states of jurisdiction over public or private offerings of $1 million or less. California and 47 other states have SCOR statutes for public offerings. The Form U-7 adopted by NASAA is the required disclosure document. It has 50 questions that must be answered. The U-7 form is currently under revision by a committee of NASAA. This revision is long overdue as the U-7 form is not investor friendly. Its emphasis is "legal" rather than financial.

This is a public offering and advertising (approved) is permitted.

In addition, the federal rule provides that securities sold pursuant to SCOR are not "restricted." They may be traded. However, this is a serious trap as some states, particularly California, may well place restrictions on transfers (see Section 6.2 "Non-issuer Secondary Trading" below) and finding a "market" (buyers and sellers) may be difficult, if not almost impossible. There is a move to have Internet markets established so that sellers and buyers can "meet on the Internet." The Direct Stock Market of Santa Monica (Tel: 310-395-5213 or e-mail: www.dsm.com) is seeking SEC permission to establish such a third-party mechanism. Companies may establish their "matching" service for owners of the company's stock. That is, matching buyers and sellers.

In California, filing with the Commissioner of Corporations is required; there is "merit review." Process time varies from two weeks to six months depending on the reviewer and the quality of the applicant and the application.

### 3.2.1  California SCOR: Public Offering

Used up to $1 million. Suitability is usually imposed and so is a required minimum amount before funds can be used. Price of stock must be $2 or more. Use of U-7 as a part of the application and as the disclosure document is mandatory. Audited financials are usually required if over $500,000 being sold. "Reviewed" financials are OK up to $500,000. A majority of the board must sign off on the application.

SCOR is used for Direct Public Offerings ("DPOs") in many cases. The success rate of DPOs is limited. Only a minority of offerors have been able to raise the minimum requirement for funds. However, there is a trend toward greater success, especially with use of the Internet. Issuers with an "affinity group" have met with the most success, for example, catalog companies.

Stock issued pursuant to the SCOR offering is technically tradeable, but see Section 6.2 "Non-Issuer Secondary Trading" below.

The state filing fee is $2,500 (up to $3,500 if review has complications). SCOR is not available to out-of-state corporations (unless subject to state jurisdiction under Section 2115 of the Corporations Code), blind pools, oil and gas companies, investment companies, and companies reporting to the SEC.

Legal fees in a SCOR offering can vary from a low of $7,500 to up to $30,000 or more in a complex application. Average is probably around $15,000 to $20,000. Again, the legal fees depend on the quality of the client's answers to the 50 questions in the Form U-7. There is no review by the SEC, but California and the other states do review.

### 3.3 Small Business Rules: Suitability

In the public offering arena, the California Small Business Suitability Rules are important as they "give a break" to small businesses. By Rule 260.001(i) the commissioner defines a "Small Business Issuer" as an entity having annual revenues of less than $12.5 million and is a California corporation or a foreign (from another state) corporation subject to certain tests of "doing business" (average property factor, payroll factor and sales factor of 25 percent in California with payroll having to be 50 percent Californian, and have at least 25 percent of its shareholders in California).

If the entity is a small business and the sale of securities is $5 million or less, and the offering price is at least $2 per share, the suitability standards, subject to certain other criteria, for the investors are:

$50,000 income
$75,000 net worth (excluding home, auto and furnishings)
or
$150,000 net worth (same exclusions)

provided that $2,500 of stock can be sold to any investor. This rule and its $2,500 loophole are not available to companies reporting to the SEC (10K's, 10Q's, etc.)

The $2,500 exemption is important to SCOR offerings in particular. The average purchase in a SCOR offering is around $1,600, so the exemption fits.

### 3.4 Regulation A: Public, $5 Million Maximum

The Disclosure Document is either a U-7 or a conventional "offering circular." The latter is similar to a full prospectus. Some clients prefer the "offering circular," even though it is usually a bit more expensive (legal), as it is a decidedly better selling document than the U-7.

Reg. A itself (the federal rule) does not require audited financials. California requires audited financials for an offering without "suitability" standards, known as an "open permit." In some instances, as long as there is sufficiently high suitability, audited financials are not required. Audited financials are strongly recommended for two reasons: better reception by the regulators and better reception by investors. Filing with the SEC is now done in Washington. Paper filing is still permitted.

SEC filing fees for Reg. A's have been eliminated by Congress. California has a maximum fee of $2,500. Most states handle Reg. A's by coordination, that is, if OK with the feds, OK with the state. California's commissioner can handle by coordination but is not required to do so and usually does not.

A Reg. A, due to the SEC review and the required precision of offering detail for "full disclosure," involves legal fees of $25,000 to $60,000. Expect as much as twice that from large firms. This does not include filing fees and blue sky clearing. Blue sky work done by lawyers usually runs about $1,500 per state (includes filing fees).

### 3.5 SB-2: Public, No Maximum

SB-2 is the federal form for public offerings and sales of securities of any amount. It is available to companies that have no more than $25 million in sales or $25 million in publicly held stock float.

It is reviewed in Washington and must be filed electronically ("EDGAR").

The filing fee is $\frac{1}{33}$ of 1 percent of the aggregate offering amount.

This is a full-blown registration and involves a detailed prospectus. The issuer becomes a "reporting company" by use of the SB-2 qualification.

A registration using SB-2 usually involves an underwriter or investment banker as direct public offerings over $5 million are not easy to make successful. Because an underwriter has counsel (whose fees are paid by the issuing corporation), legal fees for the issuer range from $35,000 to $75,000, and the underwriter's counsel fees are about the same. It is clear then that, in the event there is no underwriter, an SB-2 makes sense only when the issuer wishes to be a reporting company or is assured of being able to raise the targeted amount of money.

Clearance in California and any state in which offers/sales are made is also required. (As noted, this is "blue skying.")

This stock is registered and therefore not "restricted."

### 3.6 S-1: Public, No Maximum

This is the granddaddy of all offerings. It is expensive and is usually used by listed companies or by emerging Silicon Valley IPO companies. Three years of audited financials are required.

## 4. DISCLOSURE DOCUMENTS

The disclosure document in a private placement is normally called a "Private Placement Memorandum" ("PPM"). The PPMs usually are not subject to review by the regulators. The offering document in a Reg. A offering is called an "offering circular." This is reviewed by the SEC in Washington, D.C. Most states accept the SEC review, but California normally does its own review. An SB-2 (or S-1) uses a "prospectus," which is also reviewed by the SEC in Washington and is reviewed by some states as well, particularly California.

## 5. INTEGRATION RULES: TIMING

### 5.1 Problem

This is a complex area. Integration is a curse on small business because it can delay sequential offerings. The problem is best explained by an example: One has a private placement under California Section 25102(f) followed by another private placement. Unless great care is taken to meet the five tests (below), the two private placements could be integrated, causing the offerings to lose their exempt status because more than 35 nonexcluded investors were involved. This would then require offers of recission to be made to all the private investors.

The "safe harbor" period under Regulation D is six months between offerings. California more or less follows this rule.

Regulation A, pursuant to Rule 251(c), can be used without the six-month period and also can be followed by a registered offering within six months.

A Section 4(2) and a Rule 506 offering (private) may be followed immediately by a public offering or an intrastate offering (Section 3(a)(11)) within the six-month period (Rule 502(a)). This is a most important exception.

Suffice it to say that "integration" is a thorny and dangerous area. See the rules below.

### 5.2 Five Tests

When no specific rule applies, such as Rule 506, there are five tests for integration (Rule 502(a)). The federal and California rules are similar. The five tests are:

1. Is the new issue part of a single plan of financing?
2. How much time has passed since the offering?
3. Is it the same type of security (common, preferred, notes)?
4. Is the sale for the same general purpose (use of proceeds)?
5. Is the same type of consideration given? Cash or property?

No particular weight is given to anyone of the tests by the federal regulators; however, the courts appear to give the difference in security type the most weight.

### 5.3 Safe Harbor: Reg. D

Regulation D (Rule 502(a)) provides a "safe harbor" of six months between issues. A Reg. A offering can follow another offering without a time span; however, the amount of $5 million is reduced by any offerings in the prior year (Rule 251(c)).

Rule 506 allows for a public offering right after the termination of a private or public offering. The prior offering under 506 must cease upon filing with the SEC of an application for a public permit.

### 5.4 California Rules

In the main, California follows the federal rules. The two factors given the most weight are:

1. Part of a single plan of financing, and
2. Proceeds used for the same general purpose.

The "safe harbor" in California is similar to the federal rule (Reg D) of six months after completion or before start of an offering (Rule 260.102.12(b)).

## 6. RESTRICTED SECURITIES AND TRADING

### 6.1 Rule 144

Rule 144 applies to resales by shareholders of stock required by means not involving a registration. The idea is to prevent issuers from selling stock on an exempt basis to a purchaser who then distributes the stock to others. This is held to be an underwriting unless Rule 144 is followed.

The rule prescribes holding periods for stock and makes a distinction between "affiliates" (those who, directly or indirectly, control, or are controlled by, the issuer) and noncontrol persons.

To use the rule, the issuer must either be a reporting company (10K's, 10Q's, etc.) that is current in its filings or a company that makes publicly available the information required by Rule 15c2-11 (Exchange Act Rules). This information covers the basic identity of the issuer, its products, management, financials, and so on.

The rule, if followed, provides a "safe harbor" for the selling shareholders; that is, the seller will not be an "underwriter" illegally selling securities.

The holding period under Rule 144, shortened in 1996, is now:

For Nonaffiliates:

(A) One year from acquisition from the issuer and/or affiliate one may "dribble" each three months the greater of: up to 1 percent of the amount of stock of the issuer as shown in its most recently published balance sheet; or the average weekly reported volume of trading in the security on all national exchanges and NASDAQ during the two calendar weeks preceding the sale.

(B) After two years one may sell without restriction (Rule 144(k)).

For Affiliates:
Same rule as A above; B does not hold.

Rule 144 is very complex—whole volumes are written about it. There are rules and rulings as to the measure of the time period, "tacking" the holding periods, affiliates, and so on. One should not act without consulting an attorney experienced in this field.

### 6.2 Nonissuer "Secondary" Trading (by a Shareholder, Not the Issuer)

A common assumption is that shares issued in a public offering (whether done via SCOR or Regulation A) will be freely tradeable under state and federal law. Although shares issued in these types of offerings are not "restricted" securities under federal law, blue sky laws of various states (most notably California) can limit the ability of shareholders to resell their shares.

When the California Department of Corporations imposes suitability requirements on the investors who buy shares in an offering, the Department almost invariably adds a restriction on the use of broker-dealers for secondary trading of those shares. Essentially, broker-dealers are not allowed to solicit customers to purchase these shares. Instead, these shares may be transferred only under certain limited circumstances, such as:

1. In a private sale to another person.

2. By a broker-dealer in an unsolicited transaction (where the purchaser initiates the contact, not vice versa).

3. Sales taking place in another state where the trade is permitted.

Under recent amendments to federal and California securities laws, many of these restrictions have been eliminated for reporting companies. However, because many companies that sell stock pursuant to public offerings under SCOR or Reg. A are not generally reporting companies (in fact, they cannot be reporting companies if they use SCOR or Reg. A), these restrictions will continue to apply for those companies.

In some cases, the Department of Corporations may place additional limitations on the transfer of shares issued in public offerings as well. Thus, in California, one must not assume that shares issued in a SCOR or Regulation A offering will be freely tradeable through the use of broker-dealers; oftentimes they are not.

## 7.  THE INTERNET

### 7.1  In General

Surprisingly, the regulators, federal and state, do not oppose (they actually encourage) the use of the Internet as a vehicle for the sale of securities.

The reason for their enthusiasm is rather obvious: It is easy to monitor the Internet, certainly easier than the telephone or the mails. This is enforcement made easy. In addition, the regulators appreciate that for the first time there is an inexpensive vehicle that can be used by small and emerging companies to raise capital. The capital "gap" between $250,000 and $5 million may be bridged for the first time by the use of the Internet.

The use of the Internet for selling securities is a cutting-edge issue. Those involved, both private and government, are feeling their way. Direct public offerings (without an underwriter) on the Internet promise to be a very good source of financing for small business.

A brief rundown on how it works would be:

1. The electronic prospectus (U-7, Reg. A Offering Circular, SB-2 Prospectus) must provide the same information as a written prospectus. The "electronic prospectus" is really an ordinary disclosure document usually sent by e-mail to the potential purchaser.

2. If there is a suitability issue, the issuer must question (Offeree Questionnaire) the potential investor to establish suitability prior to accepting any funds.

3. Electronic means (e-mail) may be used to transfer documents. (This saves considerable funds due to lower printing costs.)

4. The issuer must have qualified or have an exemption in the jurisdiction in which the purchaser resides.

In California the Internet can be used in a private placement, subject to strict rules. (See California's Section 25102(n) analysis.) In most states, if the Internet is used, a private placement is not possible.

## 7.2 The Offer

Traditionally one was not allowed to offer (let alone sell) in a jurisdiction without qualification or exemption. The Internet, of course, does not respect state or country lines; this means an offer in one state becomes a universal offer. To cope with this, the states are either ignoring the issue or considering the issue or adopting laws and regulations that permit offers without qualification as long as the offer is accompanied by "disclaimer" language that states, in effect, "This is not an offer in any jurisdiction where it has not been qualified. No sale may be made within any state unless pursuant to qualification or an exemption from Qualification." California has accepted the concept of allowing Internet offers that contain the legend or "disclaimer" just noted.

## 7.3 Suitability

In the event suitability is imposed by the commissioner, the offeror must obtain a completed offeree questionnaire establishing the investors suitability prior to accepting any investment funds. Again, this may be done using e-mail to send the questionnaire.

## 7.4 The Sale

A sale may not be made without qualifying or being exempt in the jurisdiction where the sale is being made.

The Internet, in effect, allows one to "test the waters" by seeing how many inquiries one gets from the Internet exposure. If 50 inquiries come from Texas, better qualify to sell in Texas.

Of interest, the purchaser may use a credit card to pay for the purchasers security.

## 8. FEDERAL/STATE

Subject to its abdication in SCOR offerings, the federal government has jurisdiction if any offers (usually ignored) or sales are made in more than one state. The use of the Internet is an example of ignoring offers as one simply says "This is not an offer in any state where not qualified" and the "offer" becomes a "nonoffer."

For small offerings one usually uses the private placement exemption provided by Section 25102(f) and offers in California (or one's resident state) only.

If more than one state and over $1 million, the federal government asserts jurisdiction. So does each state. One must "blue sky" (clear) both private and public offerings in each state. A new program, Coordinated Equity Review, promoted by NASAA, involves two "lead" states handling the clearance for all states. One state coordinates the merit review states and the other state coordinates the "full disclosure" states. Arizona has been appointed as the state that coordinates the routing to the two lead states. California has recently joined. Such review is limited to SB-2's and above. The process eliminates "suitability" in California. Blue skying is laborious and expensive.

## 9.  THE '40 ACT

The Investment Company Act of 1940 controls mutual funds. If a fund has over 100 owners, it comes under the '40 Act.

The '40 Act is infamous as being extremely restrictive and is one of the primary reasons venture capital is confined to relatively few very wealthy individuals and institutions: a "cartel of capital." The VC's wish to avoid the '40 Act and thus have few investors.

SBICs (small business investment companies) with more than 100 owners come under the '40 Act. That is the primary reason there are very few (less than ten) publicly owned SBICs in the United States.

Congress, in its last session, passed laws providing for two types of closed-end and single state funds that are exempt from the '40 Act.

The first category is that of economic, business, and industrial development companies. They must be regulated under state law. Eighty percent of the funds must come from persons residing in the state, and only accredited investors may invest (unless the SEC changes the rules, which Congress said it could.) Until September 19, 1998, California had a regulatory law that was extremely burdensome. Thanks to the efforts of attorney Lee Petillon with the backing of the California Capital Access Forum, a new law (SB2189) was enacted, which provides a more usable regulatory scheme in California. This new law should result in California spawning many new business development companies. It is hoped other states will also encourage such activity.

The second category that is exempt from the '40 Act is simply Congress authorizing the SEC to exempt by rule or order closed-end funds that are intrastate in their source of funds with a maximum of $10 million or "such other amount as the SEC may prescribe by rule, regulation or order." There are no prescribed standards as to investors or type of investments. One applies to the SEC for an exemption.

This is a promising opening for raising funds to finance small business. It should catch on.

Venture Capital funds have successfully dodged the Federal Investment Advisors Act; it appears they do not fall under the state's rules regarding investment advisers. The "blind pool" prohibition rule applies only to public offerings and to Section 25102(n) solicitations.

## 10. THE USUAL

Usually, in California, a start-up or growing company will utilize Section 25102(f) to raise seed money privately. This is followed by a SCOR or Reg. A offering, keeping the integration rules in mind.

As an alternative, if the entrepreneurs know a number of accredited investors or are seeking VC financing, Rule 506 works well, and it avoids the blue sky issue (other than state fees and a Reg. D filing). Also, 506 avoids the integration problem of a possible six-month wait.

The next stage is either a Reg. A (public up to $5 million) or an SB-2; the latter results in the issuer becoming a reporting company (10K's, 10Q's, etc.).

The question of establishing markets for the stock deserves a separate primer. Suffice it to say there is much misunderstanding regarding market makers, what they do, when, and why. Responsible liquidity does not happen overnight unless there is an investment banker (underwriter) managing the effort.

## 11. SALES—"AGENTS" (CALIFORNIA)

A question frequently asked is: Who can sell our offering?

If Private: Officers and directors can all sell as long as they are not compensated in relation to the sales of securities. Third parties may sell only if they are not compensated.

If Public: Unless a licensed broker dealer, an officer or director may sell if not separately compensated for the sale. If separate compensation (officer or director) or third-party "agent," must have a $10,000 bond or post assets with the Commissioner of Corporations. An "agent" is described in Section 25003 of the Corporations Code; the bond requirement is in Section 25216 (Rules Section 260.216.15).

# Appendix B

# Preparing an Investor-Oriented Business Plan

## INTRODUCTION TO THE BUSINESS PLAN

This question-and-answer format is designed to guide you in the development of your business plan.

The probing questions will assist you in collecting the information you will need to make informed business planning decisions. This is a comprehensive workbook and, as such, explores all aspects of different types of businesses. Answer the questions appropriate to your company or venture. As you proceed, the questions will stimulate your thinking about your business, providing you with new insights into the planning process.

Remember that the business plan is not only a compilation of answers to a series of questions but a written reflection on the conclusions that you draw from going through the questioning, research, analysis, and answering process.

## WHAT DOES YOUR BUSINESS PLAN NEED TO CONTAIN?

The process outlined here is based on more than 12 years of experience, more than 200 major planning-related assignments for start-ups, small businesses, and large companies, on interviews with investors and lenders, and on review of hundreds of successful and unsuccessful business plans. We advise you to include the following sections in your business plan:

## CREATING A BUSINESS PLAN

I. Executive summary
II. Mission or charter
III. Description of the business
IV. Ownership structure and equity
V. Description of product/service
VI. The market
VII. Description of industry and trends
VIII. Marketing strategy
IX. Marketing plan
X. Sales plan
XI. Operations, research and development strategies, and plans
XII. Management, organization, personnel, and information systems
XIII. Objectives and milestones
XIV. Financial projections
XV. Supporting documents

### I. EXECUTIVE SUMMARY

Your objectives in this section are to create a readable, credible, brief overview of your business plan. A second, equally important, objective is to demonstrate appreciation of investor or lender needs. From a funding acquisition perspective, the executive summary may be the most important tool for introducing your offering to lenders and investors. A final objective of the executive summary is to motivate and entice the reader to review the document in its entirety.

Although mentioned first and placed at the front of your plan or under separate cover, the executive summary is best written last, since it serves as a concise overview of the business plan and highlights the key points from every section of your completed plan. In a few precise, clear sentences, the executive summary crystallizes the hours of labor you have spent in researching and writing each section.

Your objective in writing the executive summary is to get the reader's attention and to stimulate his or her interest.

### II. MISSION OR CHARTER

The mission statement says, in a few words, a graphic, or an image, what your business should be about. The statement defines the thrust of your business.

Exercise in preparation for writing your mission statement:

What do you want to accomplish from your business? Think about why you are in business.

What is important to you about your business? What excites you about it?

Explain how the short-term and long-term personal goals of the owner(s) harmonize with the business requirements and objectives.

List the benefits to the community—for example, retaining or creating jobs, building rehabilitation, meeting the community's needs, increasing the community's tax base.

## III.  DESCRIPTION OF THE BUSINESS

Your objectives in this section are to display your knowledge of your business and to provide the historical background leading up to your current situation and request for funding.

Describe the historical development of your business.

Describe the general nature of the business that you are in:

_____  Manufacturing
_____  Retail
_____  Services
_____  Wholesale

How do you generate revenues and make a profit?

What is unique about your business?

Is the company's development stage in start-up or is it a continuing business?

List the major expenses in your business.

Work into your description of the business the following information: Name of the business. Year founded. Name of founder. Location of the business. Number of employees. Features of the area (accessibility to customers). Description of facilities (size, zoning, age, and condition). Lease. Legal form of organization. Major equipment involved in your business. If current business is different from past business or firm is considering expansion, explain. Briefly summarize any future plans—both short range and long range—for expansion or relocation.

## IV.  OWNERSHIP STRUCTURE AND EQUITY

What legal form does this ownership take?

_____ Sole proprietorship

_____ Partnership

_____ Corporation (date, state of incorporation, type)

Explain any significant ownership changes that have occurred, subsidiaries, and degree of ownership, if applicable.

List the names of principal owners and roles they played in the firm's foundation.

Give the percentage of interest of principal owners or managers in the business. Present sources of funds.

Give the expected sources of future funds.

List the principal shareholders and note the stock that each principal holds.

Disclose the borrowings of the business.

If you are a start-up, be sure to consider the following:

How will ownership/equity be distributed?

Briefly give the background on the founders, active investors, key employees, directors, and consultants.


If the business is a corporation, give the classes of stock, shares authorized, shares issued and outstanding.


If the business is a partnership, give the respective partners' interests.


## V. DESCRIPTION OF PRODUCT/SERVICE

The key to writing about your product or service is to focus on its benefits and how you will meet a need. Include printed materials that provide detailed descriptions of features and how a service works in the Supporting Documents section, for example, drawings, photos, brochures, and services flowcharts, patents, trademarks, engineering studies, or proprietary features. Whenever possible, provide factual documentation supporting your belief that the market will buy your product, for example, sales performance, letters of commitment to purchase, or purchase orders.

Some questions to prepare you for writing the product/service description section are:

What problem does your product or service solve?


What results can customers expect? Are they visible? Valuable? Measurable?


What does your product do or your service deliver to the customer?


Is the product or service in a developmental stage?


How was the product developed?


If you purchase the products that your company sells, describe materials and supply sources, availability, and product cost. Also describe your purchasing department.

Are you dependent on one supplier for materials? If overseas sources or vendors are subject to shortages, what is your backup?

What makes your product/service different? How is your solution different from or better than the solution offered by competitors?

How complex is your product/service to use? Is training needed to use it?

What risks, if any, are inherent in its use?

Are there government regulations relevant to the use of your product or service?

Will customers need to change the way they do things in order to use it?

What is the cost of and profit on each product/service line and the break-even point?

How will funding affect product/service lines?

Describe your research on future products.

## VI. THE MARKET

Who are your customers? (It is essential to your success and credibility with the readers of your plan that you demonstrate knowledge of who your customers are or will be.)

The following questions will help you begin an evaluation and profile of your target markets: What is the geographic scope of your market: local, regional, national, or international? Current versus potential customers?

What are your targeted markets? Are they individuals or other businesses? How many potential customers are there in each target market segment?

What is the size of your market? What are the trends in your market?

Give a general description of your customers. Use demographics when possible to describe the following: age, gender, income. If your customers are companies, are they merchandisers? Service organizations? Manufacturers? Original equipment manufacturers (OEMs)? Government? Contractors? Industrial distributors? Etc.

What is the average purchase amount of your product(s)/service(s)?

How do you know that potential customers need your product or service? What evidence do you have of customer acceptance?

Is the target market aware of its need for the product/service? Explain.

How many competitors are there in your target market? Give name, location, and size. Who are the emerging competitors?

What is your competitors' market share distribution? Is there a single competitor or multiple competitors? Who are the most powerful competitors and who are your future competitors?

What percentage of the total market do you think that you can currently capture as customers? In one, two, three, or five years? How did you determine this figure?

What impact will funding or lack of funding have on these projections? What is the time frame?

What could prevent you from achieving your goals? Is the market aware of you? What is your image in the marketplace?

What is the major advantage of your company over the competition? What is your competitive edge, for example, barriers to competition or entry, stable customer base or proprietary technology? What are the strengths and weaknesses of competitors? (Barriers to entry include: patents, high start-up costs, substantial expertise required, and market saturation.)

Why do customers buy your product/service over your competitors'? Is it price? Quality? How will you exploit this advantage?

Who is involved in the decision to buy your product/service?

How do you—or will you—find out what your customers want?

_____ Customer surveys
_____ Outside market research
_____ Secondary research
_____ Trade association data
_____ Focus groups
_____ Suppliers/Distributors
_____ Trade literature
_____ Published market data
_____ Inquiries by prospects
_____ Pre-sales
_____ Orders

What do customers expect regarding customer service?

Is demand for the product/service changing? Explain.

How did you determine your price, by cost-plus-margin or market price?

How do your competitors price?

Will your price give the competitors some advantage? Explain.

Will the market pay your price? How do you know?

## VII.  DESCRIPTION OF INDUSTRY AND TRENDS

In this section you will describe both the industry of which your business is a part and significant current or emerging trends.

The trends you need to examine could be economic, regulatory, sociological, and technological trends that have, or may have, implications for your business's growth and/or survival. Any trend with a probability of occurring and having a positive or negative impact on any aspect of the business is to be considered and described in this section.

The forces considered at this stage in the writing of the plan are those that are out of your control but can significantly have an impact on your business. (This section may be difficult for some people because the task concerns thinking through hypothetical scenarios and developing possible alternative responses to events that have not occurred and for which there may be no precedent. This is, however, the time to consider these possibilities—not later, when an opportunity has been missed or when you find yourself in an adverse situation.)

What is the size of the industry? What are its growth trends? What is the maturity of the industry?

What is the competitive nature of the industry? Are there barriers to entry and growth?

What effect might emerging trends have? Do they represent opportunities or threats, for example, vulnerability to economic factors? What effect will seasonal factors have?

Describe the overall financial position and performance of your industry.

What are the economic trends that could have an impact on demand for your product and to which you need to adapt, for example, continued recession, worsening recession, more rapid recovery from recession than originally anticipated? Inflation? Labor costs?

What are the sociological changes to which you need to adapt, for example, changing demographics of the population?

Are there any trends in the customer market that could have an impact on sales projections, or in the labor market that could impact cost projections?

What are the new and emerging technological developments in your industry with implications for your growth or survival?

Are there any regulatory trends with implications for your business? What about new or impending legislation?

List your key assumptions about the economic, regulatory, sociological, and technological trends that may have an impact on the environment within which you operate or plan to operate or expand. Also consider supply and distribution factors and any other relevant financial considerations.

## VIII.  MARKETING STRATEGY

In this section you explain your marketing strategy. The first step in developing your strategy statement is to give thought to the driving force behind your long-term marketing goals.

### Driving Force: The Principal Behind Strategy

What is the driving force behind your business or dream? Are you driven by the products or services you offer? Do you have strong relationships with specific markets served?

Is your primary focus return/profit? Other?

Describe in detail the driving force behind your business.

## Defining Your Strategy

To begin the process of defining your strategy, answer the following questions:

What is the thrust or focus for future business development? What will be the scope of products/services that you will offer?

What is the future emphasis or priority and mix of products/services that fall within that scope?

What are the key capabilities required to make this vision happen (functional, human, and physical resources)?

What does the vision imply for growth and return expectations?

## Strengths and Limitations Assessment

What has made you successful?

What has held you back?

What are your company's strengths? What are you best at? What is your unique advantage? What value do you add?

What are your company's weaknesses?

What are some key assumptions about the competition?

## Strategic Issues Analysis

Based on your answers to all of the above questions, list the issues that you have identified that might affect your business's growth.

Now list your offensive strategy for leveraging your strengths into opportunities.

Now list issues you identified that will affect your business's survival. Where are you vulnerable?

Based on these survival issues, list defensive strategies to protect yourself from threats that result from your business's weaknesses.

Now build a strategy statement that incorporates the best mix of strategies appropriate to your situation.

## IX. MARKETING PLAN

To whom are you going to sell and how are you going to get them to buy? This section answers these important questions and displays to your audience that you know how to reach your customers. Show the reader your road map for successfully achieving sales projections. Your objective in this section is to be comprehensive, specific, and realistic.

The comprehensive Marketing Plan section will thoroughly explain the scope of your marketing activities quarter by quarter for the period encompassed by your business plan, including market research, positioning, pricing, collateral materials, marketing support systems, communications and distribution channels, merchandising, and sales.

The positioning paragraphs must cover your market research and competitive analysis and include answers to the following questions:

How many competitors are there?

Who are your major competitors?

Where are they located?

What products/services do they provide?

How profitable are they?

Differentiate your company from competitors among the following factors: market share, price, profits, quality, research and development, reputation, and sales and service.

How will you win customers away from competitors while building your own base clientele?

Given this data, how can you differentiate your appeal to potential customers and position product/service in your marketing communications?

Presentation on pricing considerations needs to include answers to the following questions:

What is your mark-up goal?

What is your cost per unit?

What is your selling price?

What is your pricing rationale and how does it compare with your competitors'?

Paragraphs about how you will communicate with your target markets need to answer these questions:

How will you reach prospects to communicate that you exist and have something to sell?

Where will you advertise: Print? Display? Electronic? Direct? Other?

What types of internal merchandising and visual displays do you plan?

What about your public relations: Press releases? Seminars? Speeches? Associations? Articles? Other?

Any promotions anticipated?

How will you implement referral development: Customers? Employees? Friends/family? Suppliers? Others?

What methods of distribution will you use? How will you get the product/ service to the customer? What will your distribution costs be? Will you use a direct sales force? Mail order? Are there other distribution channels you can access?

## X.  SALES PLAN

In this section you begin to build support for the sales projections. Your plan must satisfactorily resolve the basic sales issue of how to achieve the most cost-effective sales.

Respond to the following questions before you prepare your sales plan:

Will you employ salespeople?

If yes, how many?

How will salespeople be selected?

Based on realistic projections of sales per salesperson, how many sales-people will you need to achieve your sales goals?

What supervision and training will salespeople require?

What are the responsibilities of the salespeople? What commissions and incentives will you provide?

What type and number of sales support staff will be needed?

What will be your credit policy?

What are your sales forecasts? What have been the historical sales trends in your company or industry in the last three years?

How would funding affect sales forecasts?

What do you project to be the cost of sales?

What is the basis for your cost of sales projection?

What percentage of sales is cost of sales?

What do you estimate the total sales expenses to be per month? Per quarter? Per year?

How much does the business need to sell to break even?

What trends highlighted earlier could seriously change your projections?

How will you convert contacts into sales?

How will competitors respond to your sales tactics? What will be your response?

What percentage of sales do you expect returned?

If you are a larger organization, diagram the sales organization.

## XI.  OPERATIONS, RESEARCH AND DEVELOPMENT STRATEGIES, AND PLANS

### Service Firms

Describe the methods of providing services.

Provide an outline and schedule of all business activities.

Describe your hours and days of operation.

Include work flow diagrams if the service is complex.

What equipment and suppliers are needed? What is the relationship of price, delivery, credit, and quality?

Indicate how you will keep costs down.

### Manufacturing Companies

Describe the manufacturing plan, plant, and facility requirements.

How will products be physically produced, packaged, and delivered, including any special machinery that might be necessary?

What are your quality and cost control procedures?

Concisely describe your production strategies. Use these statements to answer the following questions:

What processes or technologies will be used to produce or deliver the product?

Describe your production schedule, equipment, and technology to be used.

What product costs are required in order to achieve sales goals, for example, variable labor requirements. Include wages and fringe benefits.

Describe quality control and productivity rates.

What is the manufacturing budget for the period covered by pro forma projections?

Indicate capacity utilization.

In order to meet growth goals, what is your future staffing? What are your supply and distribution requirements?

Are there any safety, health, or environmental concerns?

What is your future inventory storage and maintenance?

What are your future equipment and facilities requirements?

What impact would funding have on this plan?

Describe concisely your research and development strategy and plan. What are the research and development objectives within the time frame of the business plan? Have scheduled objectives been accomplished?

Are there any planned enhancements of current products?

Have results of past research and development activity justified investment?

What product development efforts are currently in process or planned? How appropriate are these in light of current marketplace developments?

Include a progress report on past and current research and development, for example, has it brought products to market in a timely manner?

Include a department budget for a time frame of the business plan.

Describe staffing, equipment, and facilities.

## XII.  MANAGEMENT, ORGANIZATION, PERSONNEL, AND INFORMATION SYSTEMS

In this section your objective is to show how the ability and track record of your company's management forms the key to its success. To do this you must objectively evaluate your management and board of directors (if appropriate) to determine the strength and capability of your business and to let the audience know the result of this evaluation.

Who is involved in the business? Include resumes for the founder, owner, key managers, and specially trained technical staff in the Supporting Documents section. These will include name, position, background information on performance, key accomplishments, history of positions held and length of time with the company, industry recognition, specialized skills, education, age, and community involvement.

How would you evaluate each of the key management and board personnel?

Describe the respective duties and qualifications of key employees, including years of experience in the assigned position.

How do key managers' skills complement the president's skills?

What roles do the key managers play in daily operations?

Who wrote the business plan? Did you use consultants or specialists? If so, list the consultants' names.

Are there any skills missing that are necessary for the firm's success?

What are the limitations of management?

List the names and addresses of all professional resources available to the business, including:

Accountant: _____

Insurance broker: _____

Attorney: _____

CPA: _____

Bankers: _____

Securities or investment banking firm (if appropriate): _____

Do you have written job descriptions for key management personnel? If yes, include a summary in this section. If no, write job descriptions.

Outline the succession plan in case of the loss of key personnel.

Explain remuneration for management. What is it about your remuneration plan that will attract and keep quality talent? Salaries? Benefits packages? Incentives? Promotion opportunities? Organization? Other?

If you are a corporation, who is on the board of directors?

Do you have an advisory board? If yes, what are the members' credentials?

Where is the location of the headquarters of the business?

Include a current organization chart for your business and anticipated organization chart if changes are imminent, or if you are a start-up.

Describe each division or department and its function and personnel.

Do any employees require special training, education, or experience?

Does the company provide any special training or educational programs?

Describe current staffing levels and the expected turnover in the business.

How competitive are the company's compensation and benefits programs?

Provide breakdowns on skill levels, hours worked, wage rates, whether unionized, and so on.

Describe recruitment strategy and major competitors for the local workforce. How successful have you been?

If you use independent contractors, explain. Show that you conform to IRS requirements.

Project personnel needs in order to accomplish business plan goals, e.g., management to be added.

Describe your compensation package including salary, insurance, advancement opportunities, and profit sharing.

Include personnel policies as a separate document available on request.

If unionized, describe your relationships with unions. When do contracts come up for negotiation, and are there any likely union drives?

### Management Information Systems

What method do you have for getting important information to help you manage your business?

What are your methods of record keeping?

What regular and timely reports do you generate that tell you how well you and the company are doing relative to the business plan objectives daily? Weekly? Monthly?

What computer hardware and applications are you using or going to obtain in order to generate these crucial reports?

## XIII.  OBJECTIVES AND MILESTONES

The purpose of this section is to get you to write down your goals for the business.

The following objectives-setting procedure has been used by hundreds of companies. It is brilliantly simple and will lead you to clear statements of objectives, and the important steps you must start taking now to achieve your dream tomorrow.

### Objectives

1. Clearly state where you want to be at the end of the period covered by this plan.

2. Identify the primary roadblocks to successfully achieving your vision.

3. Identify the internal strengths and resources needed to achieve success.

4. Identify internal weaknesses that must be overcome in order to achieve success, for example, facilities limitations, location relative to customers, and so on.

5. Put in priority the primary advantages and disadvantages identified above.

6. What external events or situations may impact your ability to achieve your objective, for example, legislation, regulation, economy, and so on?

7. If you are an existing company (not a start-up), what will be your ability to achieve goals without any changes, for example, sales, income, margins, working capital, liquidity, and so on?

8. What are the most serious challenges or problems you are currently facing? What benefit would be realized if these problems were solved?

9. Based upon the assessment provided in answering questions 1 through 8, list three to six objectives you want to achieve (long-term and short-term).

1. _____    4. _____
2. _____    5. _____
3. _____    6. _____

10. Now, for each objective, list the three most important tasks that *must* be accomplished in order to achieve the objective.

11. List any operational changes that must occur in order for these tasks to be accomplished.

12. What internal or external resources must be secured to accomplish these tasks?

13. What will each objective require in terms of personnel and costs?

14. List the risks associated with tasks to accomplish your objectives. What action can be taken to minimize or avoid these risks?

15. Which objectives and tasks leverage your strengths? Which are unaffected or limit the vulnerability caused by your weaknesses?

16. Are there any objectives or tasks that you lack the resources to accomplish?

17. Develop a chart that lists the following: the objectives you have chosen, the most important steps to accomplish for their realization, the dates for accomplishment, the milestone measures you will use to evaluate performance, who will be responsible, any status reports on your progress to communicate to all involved, contingency plans, for example, to agree with undercapitalization, promotion failures, quality issues, and so on.

## XIV. FINANCIAL PROJECTIONS

Financial management can be the determining factor in the survivability as well as the success of your business. It is important to make careful financial projections as a way of both planning and controlling the business. While accounting is essentially a record of historical performance of the business, financial projections, or the creation of pro forma financial statements and budgets, helps you to think through the financial implications of the decisions made during the preparation of your business plan.

In previous sections of the business plan, you have analyzed the market and set objectives. In this section you will put into financial terms the strategies detailed in the business plan. You document the past in financial terms (if applicable), take a forward look, and complete the final task in writing the business plan, that is, forecast likely conditions and project allocation of resources to support future operations.

### Will You Be Able to Reach Your Objectives?

Your projections are to be structured around the objectives developed by the management team during the planning process. The marketing, sales, and operations strategies and plans spell out the financial requirements. The industry and trends analyses imply specific assumptions about likely future conditions.

The key in preparing this section is to be realistic. Critically evaluate the potential for profitability of your venture. You have to believe in the accuracy and attainability of your projections and, equally important, convince others that the financial projections are realizable. If you have been in business, then you will have past financial data to guide your projections. If this is a start-up, you will need to be creative in seeking out comparative ventures, be detailed in capturing projected cost data, and be realistic in sales projections. Be reasonable. If your projections for market share, profit, growth rate, sales performance, and/or operating margins significantly deviate from industry standards, you will surely face an uphill battle building trust with funding resources.

Be prepared to defend both your projections and the assumptions behind the projections. Be consistent about assumptions. Start with all your key assumptions regarding wages, benefits, pricing, production costs, sales, volume, market projections, and inflation, and support them as clearly as possible. If you made an assumption in the operating budgets, be sure the pro forma statements reflect it. Document and footnote all assumptions on the pro forma statements.

*Interrelationships of Financial Projections*

We recommend that you include pro forma financial statements, cash budgets, and operating budgets. Begin by projecting separate sets of departmental budgets based on current *and* desired funding. Then develop cash flow, income projections, and, lastly, your pro forma balance sheet.

Also, consider developing the projections on a monthly basis for the first year, quarterly for years two and three, and annually for years four and five—if you forecast that far into the future. It is critical that you include footnotes describing significant assumptions used in preparing any financial statement projection. Worksheets to guide the preparation of your projections are included in this book.

Begin your financial projections with the operating budgets. These projections detail forecasted department revenue and expense patterns. For example, pro forma sales projections and pro forma departmental expense budgets can be consolidated into a forecasted operating budget for the sales department. The sales forecast projects when sales will occur, the volume of sales, and, thus, your gross revenue. (Refer to Worksheet #1 and Worksheet #2 for sample schedules.)

Next, develop cash budgets or cash flow statements using Worksheet #3. Cash flow statements are detailed projections of the cycle of turning sales into cash that, in turn, pays the cost of doing business and, you hope, returns a profit. The cash flow statement describes cash in and cash out and when. A cash flow analysis and projection will reflect your company's credit and collection policies, trade credit, and other financing activities, and purchase and disposal of fixed assets. This projection informs you when cash will be needed before a cash crisis occurs.

Last, prepare the pro forma financial statements, which include your assumptions about future performance and funding requirements, that is, income or profit and loss statement, and balance sheet. The pro forma income statement projects the company's revenues, expenses, and earnings over a specific period of time. When you subtract your expenses from your income, you will have your net profit or loss for the period. Use Worksheet #4 as a sample income statement to guide your projections. The balance sheet shows the assets and liabilities of the company on a given date. When you subtract liabilities from assets and owners' equity, the difference is the company's net worth. Worksheet #5 will guide your preparation of a pro forma balance sheet. Also, include historical income statements and balance sheets, if they are appropriate.

(If you are not familiar with the categories of expense and revenue listed on these financial statements, call INTERNATIONAL CAPITAL

RESOURCES, (415) 296-2519, for a free copy of "How to Read a Financial Report.")

Demonstrate that you understand break-even point. Describe the level of sales volume required to break even and candidly discuss the likelihood of earning at least that much. The break-even point is that level of sales that covers the fixed *and* variable costs of providing your product or service. You will need to know your fixed costs (rent, utilities, insurance, etc.), those that remain constant regardless of sales. You will also need to know your variable costs (cost of goods, sales commissions, etc.), those that will increase with sales. Explain why you are confident in meeting or exceeding the break-even point.

Comment on how you will adjust to situations differing from stated expectations.

If you are an existing business, include income statements, balance sheets, and cash flow statements for the last three years.

### What Are Your Financial Needs?

The purpose of these financial documents is to help you assess future performance and funding requirements. After completing the projections and statements mentioned above, you will be able to state (1) the amount of funds needed over the course of time covered by the business plan, (2) when funding will be needed, (3) the types of funding most appropriate—for example, debt or equity-based—and (4) what you are willing to give up to get the funding. In the case of a loan—for example, loan amount, collateral, interest rate, and repayment schedule—or, in the case of equity financing, state the percentage of the company to be given up, proposed return on investment, and the anticipated method for taking out the investor (buyback, public offer or sale). You also will be on firm ground when describing how the funding will be used and be able to prepare a uses of funds statement.

### Funds Sought and Exit Strategy

Indicate how much money you are seeking, how many investors you plan to have, how the funds raised will be used, and how investors or lenders will get their money out. *Attach a risk disclosure document that includes an evaluation of potential risks inherent in your enterprise; assess risks and describe steps to minimize risks.*

## XV. SUPPORTING DOCUMENTS

Once you have completed the main body of the business plan, consider the additional records that should be included pertaining to your business. These supporting documents are records that back up the statements and decisions in the body of the plan. Include resumes, financial statements, credit reports, copies of leases, contracts and letters of commitment to purchase, legal documents, maps of location, descriptive materials about your products or services, collateral sales and marketing materials, and any other miscellaneous documents best assembled with the plan.

## PRO FORMA SALES PROJECTION
### ABC COMPANY, INC. PRO FORMA SALES PROJECTIONS
#### FOR THE YEAR ENDED 20_

Product Line(s)
Product(s)

| YEAR | Jan | Feb | Mar | Apr | May | Jun | Jul | Aug | Sep | Oct | Nov | Dec |
|---|---|---|---|---|---|---|---|---|---|---|---|---|
| PRODUCT LINE A | | | | | | | | | | | | |
| 1. Product 1 | | | | | | | | | | | | |
| Shipments (Units) | | | | | | | | | | | | |
| × Avg Price/Unit | | | | | | | | | | | | |
| Gross Sales | | | | | | | | | | | | |
| 2. Product 2 | | | | | | | | | | | | |
| 3. Product 3 | | | | | | | | | | | | |
| n. Product N | | | | | | | | | | | | |
| PRODUCT LINE A GROSS SALES | | | | | | | | | | | | |
| PRODUCT LINE B | | | | | | | | | | | | |
| PRODUCT LINE C | | | | | | | | | | | | |
| PRODUCT LINE N | | | | | | | | | | | | |
| TOTAL GROSS SALES | | | | | | | | | | | | |

**WORKSHEET #2**

### QUARTERLY SALES BUDGET
### ABC CORPORATION QUARTERLY SALES BUDGET
### FOR THE YEAR ENDED 20__

| TOTAL | 1st Quarter | 2nd Quarter | 3rd Quarter | 4th Quarter |
|---|---|---|---|---|
| Basic data: | | | | |
| Unit sales (number of units): | | | | |
| Product A | | | | |
| Product B | | | | |
| Product C | | | | |
| Price level (per unit): | | | | |
| Product A | | | | |
| Product B | | | | |
| Product C | | | | |
| Number of salespersons: | | | | |
| Operating budget ($000): | | | | |
| Sales revenue | | | | |
| Less: returns, allowances | | | | |
| Net sales | | | | |
| Cost of goods sold | | | | |
| Margin before delivery | | | | |
| Delivery expense | | | | |
| Gross margin | | | | |
| Selling expense (controllable): | | | | |
| Salesperson's compensation | | | | |
| Travel and entertainment | | | | |
| Sales support costs | | | | |
| TOTAL SELLING EXPENSES | | | | |
| Gross contribution | | | | |
| Departmental period costs | | | | |
| Net contribution | | | | |
| Corporate support (transferred): | | | | |
| Staff support | | | | |
| Advertising | | | | |
| General overhead | | | | |
| TOTAL CORPORATE SUPPORT | | | | |
| Profit contribution (before taxes) | | | | |

## WORKSHEET #3

### PRO FORMA CASH FLOW STATEMENT
### ABC CORPORATION PRO FORMA CASH FLOW STATEMENT
### FOR THE YEAR ENDED 20__

| | 1st Quarter | 2nd Quarter | 3rd Quarter | 4th Quarter | YEAR | Assumption |
|---|---|---|---|---|---|---|
| Sources (uses) of cash | | | | | | |
| Net earnings (loss) | | | | | | |
| Depreciation and amortization | | | | | | |
| Cash provided by operations dividends | | | | | | |
| Cash provided by (used for) changes in: Accounts receivable | | | | | | |
| Inventory | | | | | | |
| Other current assets | | | | | | |
| Accounts payable | | | | | | |
| Income tax | | | | | | |
| Accrued compensation | | | | | | |
| Dividends payable | | | | | | |
| Other current liabilities | | | | | | |
| Other assets | | | | | | |
| Net cash provided by (used for) operating activity | | | | | | |
| Investment transactions | | | | | | |
| Furniture and equipment | | | | | | |
| Land | | | | | | |
| Building and improvement | | | | | | |
| Net cash from investment transactions | | | | | | |
| Financing transactions | | | | | | |
| Short-term debt | | | | | | |
| Long-term debt | | | | | | |
| Other noncurrent liabilities | | | | | | |
| Sale of common stock | | | | | | |
| Net cash from financing transactions | | | | | | |
| Net increase (decrease) in cash | | | | | | |
| Cash: Beginning of period | | | | | | |
| Cash: End of period | | | | | | |

## PRO FORMA INCOME STATEMENT
### ABC CORPORATION PRO FORMA INCOME STATEMENT

|  | Current Year | Year 1 | Year 2 | Year 3 | TOTAL | Assumptions |
|---|---|---|---|---|---|---|
| Net sales |  |  |  |  |  |  |
| Cost of sales (schedule will vary based on type of business) |  |  |  |  |  |  |
| Gross margin |  |  |  |  |  |  |
| Operating expenses |  |  |  |  |  |  |
| Depreciation and amortization |  |  |  |  |  |  |
| Selling, general, and administrative expenses |  |  |  |  |  |  |
| Operating income (loss) |  |  |  |  |  |  |
| Other income (expense) |  |  |  |  |  |  |
| Dividends and interest income |  |  |  |  |  |  |
| Interest expense |  |  |  |  |  |  |
| Earnings (before income taxes) |  |  |  |  |  |  |
| Income taxes |  |  |  |  |  |  |
| Net earnings |  |  |  |  |  |  |
| Common shares outstanding |  |  |  |  |  |  |
| Earning per common share |  |  |  |  |  |  |

**WORKSHEET #5**

## PRO FORMA BALANCE SHEET
## ABC CORPORATION PRO FORMA BALANCE SHEET AS OF _____
### PAGE 1 OF 2

|  | Current Year | Year 1 | Year 2 | Year 3 | TOTAL | Assumptions |
|---|---|---|---|---|---|---|
| ASSETS |  |  |  |  |  |  |
| Current assets: |  |  |  |  |  |  |
| Cash |  |  |  |  |  |  |
| Marketable securities |  |  |  |  |  |  |
| Accounts receivable |  |  |  |  |  |  |
| Inventories |  |  |  |  |  |  |
| Prepaid expenses |  |  |  |  |  |  |
| TOTAL CURRENT ASSETS |  |  |  |  |  |  |
| Property, Plant and Equipment |  |  |  |  |  |  |
| Land |  |  |  |  |  |  |
| Buildings |  |  |  |  |  |  |
| Machinery |  |  |  |  |  |  |
| Leasehold improvements |  |  |  |  |  |  |
| Furniture, fixtures, etc. |  |  |  |  |  |  |
| TOTAL PROPERTY, PLANT AND EQUIPMENT |  |  |  |  |  |  |
| Less accumulated depreciation |  |  |  |  |  |  |
| Net property, plant and equipment |  |  |  |  |  |  |
| Intangibles (goodwill, patents) less amortization |  |  |  |  |  |  |
| TOTAL ASSETS |  |  |  |  |  |  |

### PRO FORMA BALANCE SHEET
## ABC CORPORATION PRO FORMA BALANCE SHEET AS OF _____
### PAGE 2 OF 2

| | Current Year | Year 1 | Year 2 | Year 3 | TOTAL | Assumptions |
|---|---|---|---|---|---|---|
| LIABILITIES | | | | | | |
| Current liabilities: | | | | | | |
| Accounts payable | | | | | | |
| Notes payable | | | | | | |
| Accrued expenses | | | | | | |
| Income taxes payable | | | | | | |
| Dividends payable | | | | | | |
| Other liabilities | | | | | | |
| TOTAL CURRENT LIABILITIES | | | | | | |
| Long-term liabilities | | | | | | |
| Deferred income taxes | | | | | | |
| Securities payable (year) | | | | | | |
| Other long-term debt | | | | | | |
| TOTAL LIABILITIES | | | | | | |
| SHAREHOLDERS' EQUITY | | | | | | |
| Preferred stock | | | | | | |
| Common stock | | | | | | |
| Additional paid-in capital | | | | | | |
| Retained earnings | | | | | | |
| TOTAL SHAREHOLDERS' EQUITY | | | | | | |
| TOTAL LIABILITIES AND SHAREHOLDERS' EQUITY | | | | | | |

**WORKSHEET #6**

## SOURCES AND USES OF FUNDS

Complete the following form to describe how much money you are seeking and how you will use the funds raised. Be as specific as possible.

Number of funding rounds expected for full financing: _____

Total dollar amount being sought in this round: $ _____

Sources of funds

Equity financing:

Preferred stock: _____

Common stock: _____

Debt financing:

Mortgage loans: _____

Other long-term loans: _____

Short-term loans: _____

Convertible debt: _____

Investment from principals: _____

Uses of funds

Capital expenditures:

Purchase of property: _____

Leasehold improvements: _____

Purchase of equipment/furniture: _____

Other: _____

Working capital:

Purchase of inventory: _____

Staff expansion: _____

New product line introduction: _____

Additional marketing activities: _____

Other business expansion activities: _____

Other: _____

Debt retirement: _____

Cash reserve: _____

# Suggested Reading List

Alarid, William. *Money Sources for Small Business*. Santa Maria, CA: Puma Publishing Company, 1991.

Benjamin, Bob. "Analysing a Start-up's Potential." *Venture: The Journal of Entrepreneurship* 13, no. 11 (June 1998).

Benjamin, Gerald, and E. Sandles. "Angel Investors: Culling the Waters For Private Equity." *Journal of Private Equity* 1, no. 3 (Spring 1998).

Bergen, Helen. *Where the Money Is*. Alexandria, VA: Bio Guide Press, 1992.

Bibbens, Terry. "Capital Needs for Innovative Small Business and Entrepreneurship in the 21st Century." U.S. Government Small Business Administration Report, 1995.

———. "Of Angels and Patient Capital." *The Small Business Advocate* (March 1996): 15.

Broce, Thomas E. *Fundraising: The Guide to Raising Money from Private Sources*. Norman: University of Oklahoma Press, 1986.

Bygrave, William, and Jeffrey Timmons. *Venture Capital at the Crossroads*. Boston: Harvard Business School, 1992.

Carlsen, Clifford. "Investment Angels Answer Entrepreneurs' Prayers." *San Francisco Business Times*, Nov. 25, 1994.

Chandler, Linda. *Winning Strategies for Capital Formation*. New York: Irwin, 1995.

Chen, David. "Now in New York: Angels Who Rescue New Companies." *New York Times*, July 2, 1997.

Chimerine, Cushman, and Ross. *Handbook for Raising Capital*. Homewood, IL: Business One Irwin, 1987.

Daunt, Jacqueline. *Venture Capital: A Strategy for High Technology Companies*. Washington, D.C.: Fenwick & West, 1992.

Diener, Royce. *How to Finance a Growing Business: An Insider's Guide to Negotiating the Capital Markets*. Merritt, 1995.

Dingman Center for Entrepreneurship. *Alternatives to Venture Capital Financing*. University of Maryland, 1990.

"Dressing Your Company for Sale." *Growing Your Business* (January–February 1998): 5.

Evanson, David R. "Mega-Rich Investors: Where to Find 'Em." *Success* (July 1998): 54.

———. *Where to Go When the Bank Says No.* Princeton, NJ: Bloomberg Small Business, 1998.

Field, Drew. *Take Your Company Public.* New York: Simon and Schuster, 1991.

Fischer, Donald, ed. *Investing in Venture Capital.* Washington, D.C.: Institute of Chartered Financial Analysts, 1988.

Garner, Owen, and Conway. *The Ernst & Young Guide to Raising Capital.* New York: John Wiley & Sons, 1993.

Gibson, Gerhardt, and Charrier. *Texas Capital Network Survey: Critical Factors in Venture Funding.* Austin: University of Texas Press, 1994.

Gleba, David/VentureOne and American Entrepreneurs for Economic Growth. *Fourth Annual Economic Impact of Venture Capital Study.* Arlington, VA: National Venture Capital Association, 1992.

Harrison, Richard T. and Colin M. Mason. eds. *Informal Venture Capital.* New York: Prentice-Hall, 1996.

Henderson, James W. *Obtaining Venture Financing: A Guide for Entrepreneurs.* Boston: Lexington Books, 1988.

"Hitchhiker's Guide to Capital Resources." *Inc.* (February 1998): 74.

Howe, Fisher. *The Board Member's Guide to Fund Raising.* San Francisco: Jossey-Bass Publishers, 1991.

Hyatt, Joshua. "Smart Money." *Inc.* (May 1998): 115.

"Individual Investors Will Become a Major Source of New Venture Capital." *Los Angeles Venture* (June 1998): 1.

International Wealth Success. *Business Capital Sources.* Merrick, NY, 1994.

Lesko, Matthew. *Government Giveaways for Entrepreneurs II.* Information USA, 1994.

Linsey, Jennifer. *Entrepreneurs Guide to Capital.* Chicago: Probus Publishing, 1990.

Long, Mark. *Raising Capital in the New Economy.* San Diego: ProMotion Publishing, 1998.

———. *Unlimited Capital For the New Century Entrepreneur.* San Diego: ProMotion Publishing, 1998.

———. "Calling All Angels: How to Find Investors," *Your Company.* 1992.

Merrill and Sedgwick. *The New Venture Handbook.* New York: Amacom, 1993.

Miller, Eric, ed. *Attracting the Affluent: The First Guide to America's Changing Ultimate Market.* Naperville, IL: Financial Sourcebooks, 1991.

Muller, Joann. "Angels Willing to Help Start-Up Firms." *Boston Globe,* May 19, 1996, 76.

Nicholas, Ted. *43 Proven Ways to Raise Capital for Your Business: Where the Money Is and How to Get It.* Wilmington, DE: Enterprise Publishing, 1991.

Nichols, Judith. *Pinpointing Affluence.* Chicago: Precept Press, 1994.

O'Brien, Daniel. *Financing Sources Guide*. New York: Business Solutions Press, 1995.

Page, Heather. "Power Play." *Entrepreneur* (June 1997): 131.

Rappaport, Stephen. *The Affluent Investor*. New York: New York Institute of Finance, 1990.

"Results from the 1997 Coopers & Lybrand Money Tree Report." *Horizons: Newsletter of the Northwest Venture Group* (April 1998): 4.

Richardson, Clinton. *The Growth Company Guide to Investors, Deal Structure and Legal Strategies*. www.once.com

Richtel, Matthew. "Venture Capital Is Alive and Plentiful." *New York Times*, April 6, 1998.

Rubenstein, Frederick, and Mark Morgenstern. "Private Placements: What They Can Mean to Your Client." *Business Law Today* (November–December 1995): 27.

Schwindt, Richard. *Entrepreneurship, Small Business and Venture Capital*. Durham, NC: Enco River Press, 1990.

Shulman, J.P.A. *Venture Capital Financing: Agency Considerations and a New Taxonomy of Investment Philosophies*. University of Toronto, 1997.

Silver, A. David. *The Venture Capital Sourcebook*. Chicago: Probus Publishing Co., 1994.

Stanley, Thomas. *Marketing to the Affluent*. Homewood, IL: Business One Irwin, 1989.

———. *Networking with the Affluent and Their Advisors*. Homewood, IL: Business One Irwin, 1993.

Sullivan, Joanna. "New Firms Turn Angels." *Baltimore Business Journal*, February 23, 1996, 1.

"The State of Small Business." *Inc.,* May 1997, 11.

Tuller, Lawrence. *The Complete Book of Raising Capital*. New York: McGraw-Hill, 1994.

Wells, Edward O. *15 Steps to a Start-Up Investors Will Buy. Inc.* (March 1994): 72–80.

Wright, Susan. *Raising Money in Less Than 30 Days*. New York: Citadel Press/Carol Publishing Group, 1993.

Ziedonis, Arvids A. *Access to Capital for Small Technology-Based Business in California*. Berkeley: University of California Press, 1996.

# Index

AAII, 147
accumulators, 9
ACE-*Net*, 148, 225–28
acquisition/merger, defined, 71
AdVenture Capital Register, 148, 220
affluent, 6, 82–83
  career, 82
  low-end, 82
  retired, 82
  young, 82
allocation decision, 96–98
alternative funding sources. *See* funding
American Association of Individual Investors. *See* AAII
America's Business Funding Directory, 220
American Research and Development, 178
American Society of Appraisers, 194
Amit, Raphael, 79, 80
angel investment,
  size of, 85
angels, 5, 69, 78
angel investors, 7
  types. *See* investors
AOL, 86
Appel, Cass, 10, 11
Apple Computer, 237
Aristotle, xxi
Arnold, Matthew, 244

Arthur Andersen, xxii, 67
*Art of Negotiating, The,* 194
asset-based loans, 66

Bacon, Francis, 170
banks, 65
bartering, 64
Bay Area Venture Forum, 101
BBS. *See* electronic bulletin boards
Berkshire Hathaway, 7
Birch, David, xxiv
"black hole" service, 150
"blue sky", 32, 68, 70
"bridge", 231
Brodsky, Norman, 101
Buffett, Warren, xviii, 7, 98
Bureau of Labor Statistics, xxv
business owners, 82
business plan, 88–89, 267–299
*Business Trade & Technology Strategies Report,* 219

Cadle, John, 18, 19, 20, 95, 189, 190, 191, 194
California Capital Access Forum, 147
California Commissioner of Corporations, 48, 147
California Corporate Code, 30, 48
  25102(f), 147
  25102(n), 30, 48
*California Management Review,* 79

Calvino, Italo, 31
Capital Availability Program, 59
Capitalization strategy, 32
Capital Matchmaker, 220
capital source, 15, 16
Case, Daniel H. III, 178
cash management, 63
CDC, 64, 67
Census Bureau, xxi, 26
Center for Venture Research, xxii
Certified Development Companies.
    *See* CDC
Charles Schwab & Co., 60
Cienna Corporation, xxv
closing, 52–54
Commercial Finance Online, 220
commingling of funds, 238
common stock. *See* stock
Coopers & Lybrand, xxiii, 4, 33, 90
corporate investment, 62
Crick, Francis, 245
*Crossing the Chasm,* 66

Dara, Julian, 11
database,
    development, 44
    entry, 167–68
Da Vinci, Leonardo, 13
DealFlow, 220
dealflow, 242
*Death of a Salesman,* 198
debt,
    convertible, 13
    senior, 13, 14
    subordinate, 13, 14
Digital Equipment Corporation, 178
Digital Records Corporation, 10
dilution, 200
Direct Stock Market, 148
DNA molecules, 84
Donahue, Jim, 3
*Double Helix, The,* 245
DPO Central, 221
due diligence, 38–40
Dun and Bradstreet, xxii

early-stage financing, 17
Eastman, George, 178
EDIE-Online, 148, 221

electronic bulletin boards, 151
Employee Stock Ownership Plan.
    *See* ESOP
Enterprise Online, 221
entrepreneur, x–xiii
entrepreneurial associations, 148
Entrepreneur, 69
Entrepreneur Resources, 221
Environmental Capital Network, 221
equity, 27–28
ESOP, 66
Evenson, David, 69
Evers, William D., 67, 246
exempt offerings, 13, 63
exit strategies. *See* investments

factoring, 66
fair market value, 194
Federal Reserve of Consumer Finances,
    xxii, 26
Ferries, Jeff, 40, 204
Financehub, 148, 222
Financing Sources, 222
First Manhattan Consulting Group, 26
Flynn, David M., 68
*Forbes,* xiii, 4, 5
Forrester Research, xxii, 219
*Fortune,* xiii, 77
Foundation Study on Business Start
    Ups, xxi
franchising, 62
funding, alternative sources of
    directory of, 153–62
fund raiser, 22
funnel, 51

*Galante's Equity Guide,* 144
Garage.com, 148, 222
Gaston, Dr. Robert J., 10, 77
General Loan Program (SBA), 64
Giannini, A.P., 11
*G & W Premium Finance Gazette,* 7
Giant in the West, 11
Gloston, Lawrence, 79, 80
government financing, 63
Great Midwest Venture Capital, 146

Hambrecht & Quist Group, 178
hedging strategies, 182, 241

Henry II, 163
high-net-worth, 7
Home Depot, 7
Hudson Newsletter Directory, 150

ICR, xiv, xvi, xvii, xxvii, 5, 10, 30, 31, 32,
        39, 42, 44, 78, 85, 88, 90, 95, 100,
        101, 144, 149, 151, 164, 165, 169,
        183, 184, 189, 203, 235, 236
Idea Café, 148, 222
Inc., 26, 101
incubator-based financing, 66, 146
individual retirement account, 27
initial public offering. See IPO
Inside the Tornado, 66
Intel, 77
intermediary, xv–xvi. See also placement
        agent
Internal Revenue Service. See IRS
International Capital Resources.
        See ICR
international sources of capital, 65
investing,
    angel, 230
    direct venture, 86, 98–100,
investment opportunity profile. See IOP
investments,
    exit strategies, 188
    monitoring of, 187
investor market,
    high-net-worth, 81–83
investor networks, 152
investors, angel,
    criteria, 87, 90
    market, 7, 8, 9
    motivation, 93–95
    private, xiii–xv, xxiv, 7
    types of, 101
        barter, 126–29
        consortium, 120–22
        deep-pocket, 109–20
        family, 125–26
        manager, 92, 133–137
        partner, 123–25
        socially responsible, 129–31
        unaccredited private, 131–32
        value-added, 103–09
    unsophisticated, 147
IOP, 35, 42–44, 88

IPO, xxiii, xxiv, xxv, 3, 30, 60, 65, 69, 95,
        178, 188, 191, 194, 197, 198
IPO-Net, 148
IPO Reporter, The, 60
IRA. See individual retirement account
IRS, 8

Kelly, Raymond, 21
Kimberlin, Kevin, xxv

lease financing, 62
levels of involvement, 91–92
Levine, David, 60
licensing, 62
Lincoln, Abraham, ix
"liquidity event", 191
"living dead", 190–91
Los Angeles Venture Forum, 148

Mahcan, Jay, 202
management, 35
management buyout, 66
management team, 17, 36
manufacturing, 236
Marino Institute, 223
marketing, direct-response, 150
market size, 17
Martindale-Hubbell Law Directory, 45
Mason, C., 142
Mason, Harrison, 142
matching networks,
    computerized, 148
McDonald University, 62
MESBIC, 233
Miller, Arthur, 198
Minority Enterprise Small Business
        Investment Corporation. See
        MESBIC
MIT Venture Capital Network, 147,
        226
MoneyHunter, 148, 222
Money-Search, 148, 223
Montaigne, Michel de, 101
Moore, Geoffrey, 66
Morganthaler Ventures, 10
Muller, Eitar, 79, 80

National Federation of Independent
        Business. See NFIB

National Venture Capital Association.
  *See* NVCA
Nations Bank, 26
Nationwide Private Investors Network,
  235
negotiating, 194
Netpreneur Exchange, 222
networking, 29
newsletter, 149
*New York Times,* 66
NFIB, xxi
Nierenberg, Gerard I., 194
Northern California Venture Forum, 235
NVCA, xxii, 4, 75
NVST.com, 223

Office of Advocacy (SBA), xxi, 225
Omnibus Budget Reconciliation Act of
  1993, 59, 60, 61, 179

Pavey, Robert, 10
pipeline, 51
placement agent, 170–174. *See also* intermediary
*Pratt's Guide to Venture Capital,* 144, 146
precommittment, 42–44
preferred stock. *See* stock
Pre-IPO, xxvii, 233
"Primer on Securities Law Issues for
  Nonlawyers", 67, 246–266
*Private Equity Review,* 31, 151, 235, 243
Privatefinancing, 223
Private placement agent, 170, chapter 10
private placement investment, 13–30,
  63, 69
private placement investment,
  structure of, 186–87
private placement process, 33
PSI, 26
  1995 Affluent Market Consumer Survey, 82
public offering, 14

Queen Isabella, 178

raising capital, 38
R&D, 10, 13, 60, 63, 231
*Rand,* 9
*Red Herring,* xxii, 66

Regulation A, 225
Regulation D, 225
return on investment. *See* ROI
*Reviving the American Dream,* 4
risk, 15, 180, 192–94, 238, 240
Rivlin, Alice, 4
Robertson, Sandy, 60
Rock, Arthur, xxiii, 77, 88
Rockefeller, David, 95
Rockefeller, John D., 42
ROI, 183, 185, 186, 234, 239
route 128, xxiv
Ruby, Lucien, 240
"rules of civility", 23

Sand Hill Road, xxiv
*San Francisco Business Times,* 11, 60
*San Francisco Chronicle,* 60, 191
SBA, xiii, xxi, xxiii, xxv, 10, 59, 63, 65,
  180, 225, 233
  502 Local Development Company
  Program, 64
  504 Certified Development Company
  Program, 64
  7(a) General Loan Program, 64
SBIC, xxiii, 64, 225, 233
SCOR, 3, 14, 67, 68, 226
SCOR-Net, 148, 224
SDC, 48
Securities and Exchange Commission.
  *See* SEC
SEC, xii, 13, 31, 48, 68, 69, 70, 147, 228
securities data, 26
seed, 13, 71, 73, 231
self-finance, 67
selling,
  process of, 49–52
senior debt. *See* debt
Shoenberg, Matthew, 21, 22
Siebert, Don, 164, 165, 169
Sierra Designs, 10
"significant participation", 234
situational awareness, 21
*Six Memos for the Next Millennium,* 31
Small Business Administration. *See* SBA
Small Business Development Center, 10
*Small Business Economics,* 68
Small Business Guaranteed Credit
  Enhancement Act of 1993, 59

Small Business Investment Company.
See SBIC
Small Corporate Offering Registration.
See SCOR
*Sound Money Investor,* 151
Source Capital Network, 224
State Department of Corporations.
See SDC
stages of development, 33, 34, 71
startup, 13, 71, 231
stock, 13, 14
*Stock Deck Select,* 151
strategic alliances, 62
Strauss, Joseph, 11
subordinate debt. *See* debt
subscription warrant, 14
Sydran Food Services, 21
syndication bias, 183–84

tax strategies, 63
Thomas, Lewis, 59

University of California, Irvine, 10,
77
University of New Hampshire, 10,
Center for Venture Research,
225
U.S. Bureau of Census. *See* Census
Bureau

valuation,
and stage of development, 195
truisms in, 198

VanKirk's Venture Capital Directory,
144, 146
venture capital, 63, 75, 76
defined 230, 231
Venture Capital Network, MIT, 77
Venture Capital Online, 224
Venture Capital Resource Library, 224
Venture Economics, 179
VentureOne Corporation, xvi, xxiii, 30,
180
Venturescape, 224

Walgreen, Charles R., Jr., 178
Wall Street, xxiv
*Wall Street Journal,* xiii, 30, 184
W&W Investors, 21
warrants, 13
Washington, George, 23, 24, 40
Watson, James, 245
wealth,
established, 82
wealthy, 6, 81–83
Wells Fargo, xxi
Wetzel, William, Jr., 10, 77
White House Conference, 59, 225
Whittemore School of Business, 10
*Who's Who,* 45
Winthrop, John, Jr., 178
Wit Capital, 148, 224

Your Business, 148

Ziegfeld, Florenz, 3